**The Royal Court Theatre
1965–1972**

Theatre Production Studies

General Editor
John Russell Brown
Associate of the National Theatre of Great Britain
and
Professor of Theatre Arts, State University of New York
at Stony Brook

The Royal Court Theatre
1965–1972

Philip Roberts

Routledge & Kegan Paul
London and New York

69 88

First published in 1986 by
Routledge & Kegan Paul plc
11 New Fetter Lane, London EC4P 4EE

Published in the USA by
Routledge & Kegan Paul Inc.
in association with Methuen Inc.
29 West 35th Street, New York, NY 10001

Phototypeset in Linotron Plantin 10 on 12pt
by Input Typesetting Ltd, London
and printed in Great Britain
by The Thetford Press Ltd,
Thetford, Norfolk

Library of Congress Cataloging in Publication Data

Roberts, Philip, 1942–
The Royal Court Theatre, 1965–72.
(Theatre production studies)
Bibliography: p.
Includes index
1. Royal Court Theatre.   I. Title.   II. Series.
PN2596.L7R517   1986   792'.09421'2   86–3849

British Library CIP Data also available

ISBN 0–7100–9806–5

Contents

Plates

Acknowledgments

My primary obligation is to the Council of the English Stage Company, its Artistic Director, Max Stafford-Clark, and its then Literary Manager, Rob Ritchie, for allowing me access to the records of the company and to other archive material. Without the Council's generous permission, this book would not have been written. Equally, had it not been for the patience and help given by William Gaskill and Lindsay Anderson in both interviews and letters, I would have remained ignorant of certain important facts.

There is not enough space to indicate the particular and valuable contributions made by many people, especially those associated with the Court during these years and I do not value their help the less for having to list their names alphabetically. They are:

James Aubrey
J. E. Blacksell
Elaine Blond
Edward Bond
Howard Brenton
Pamela Brighton
John Russell Brown
Richard Butler
John Castle
Constance Chapman
Peter Childs
David Cregan
Keith Dewhurst
Anne Dyson
Bernard Gallagher
Peter Gill
Hayden Griffin
John Gunter
The Earl of Harewood

Malcolm Hay
Donald Howarth
Jane Howell
Nerys Hughes
Gordon Jackson
Anne Jenkins
Michael Kitchen
Brian Lawson
Oscar Lewenstein
Fulton Mackay
Rosemary McHale
Don McKillop
Joan Mills
Jim Norton
Louise Page
Judy Parfitt
Edward Peel
Greville Poke
Bettina Reeves

Neil Roberts	Peter Tegel
Peter Schofield	Peter Thomson
Jack Shepherd	Frank Williams
N. F. Simpson	Heathcote Williams
David Storey	Nicholas Wright

The Research Fund of the University of Sheffield aided financially in the preparation of this book, and the University granted me leave of absence to help in its writing.

Philip Roberts
August 1985

Introduction

It should not be supposed that attempting to define even recent theatrical history is anything other than an approximation to what actually happened. Yet, as another contributor to this series has accurately observed: 'Theatre historians too often neglect the hand-to-mouth instantaneousness of much theatrical decision-making.'[1] Quantifying the 'instantaneousness' is, to some extent, impossible. What prompted decisions or determined action is so frequently the product of mood, emotion, cumulative frustration or luck, that an attempt at recording it must be accompanied by a sense of the attendant dangers. For the most part, theatre companies adapt to the current situation, bend with prevailing conditions, occasionally stick out against the odds, but above all live with what they have as best as they are able. The process of making do sometimes produces occasional glories, which tend to be remembered and mask the often tedious nature of a particular struggle. What determines what is later described as a certain hallmark or style is, more often than not, how decisions are reached in a particular context. Very few companies begin, still less continue with, a pre-stated ideal, so proofed against varieties of cold that the ideal is undamaged. Most depend upon a conjunction of personalities placed, if they are fortunate, in a context which allows such a conjunction to work. A director not associated with the Royal Court, Michael Blakemore, offers a definition of policy which seems closer to the truth than an exclusively *post-hoc* analysis:[2]

> My previous experience suggested that the policy of a theatre is dictated less by statements of intent, no matter how complex or considered, than by those day-to-day crises that arrive on someone's desk at eleven in the morning demanding a solution by three in the afternoon. The policy of any theatre is most truly the accumulation of these daily decisions – decisions which reveal priorities, create precedents and eventually map out a discernible course. Alas, it is precisely in this area that no committee can possibly participate.

The truth of Blakemore's statement means that a reasonable account of the life of a company cannot content itself with an analysis of the plays performed. It cannot simply reflect the gloss. It must show the process by which the conditions evolve, which in turn lead to the productions. If ideals are evident, they are always under pressure and subject to what is feasible. The problem is to maintain, however precariously, the commitment, while ensuring the continuing existence of the theatre.

This book examines seven years in detail of the life of the English Stage Company. It does so by combining a reading of the minutes of the three company committees with the recollections of many people who worked at the Court between 1965 and 1972. The minutes reflect, as in any institution, the decisions taken, usually in a considered and frequently a bland way. By themselves, they would provide an inadequate account; unravelled and explicated by some of the members of those committees, they take on a rather different colour. The records are incomplete. It is said that at certain critical moments, the minutes were often rewritten and occasionally destroyed. Sporadically, no minutes were taken. Equally, the recollections of committee members may be affected by hindsight or simply by the view they took of the same set of facts. However, by adopting a process of recording rather than opting for one kind of view in this book, I hope that the nature of the decision-making may be more apparent.

The years dealt with here are the years governed by the successors of George Devine. As the company's first Artistic Director, he trained as a matter of policy those younger directors who succeeded him. Discussing their work contains a tribute to Devine of a kind of which he probably would have approved, since his commitment to the Court as a theatrical school was at least as strong as his many other beliefs. It should also be said that his successors inevitably faced one problem he did not have. For they had his legacy and they had to confront his achievements. They did not enjoy a comparable honeymoon because their work was subject to a constant comparative analysis. Some, like Gaskill, tended to repine at the burden, which was more frequently imposed from outside the Court. Others, such as Anderson and Page, were less concerned, since they stood more squarely with Devine's ideas. The two kinds of tradition which evolved after 1965, which had been implicit in Devine's years, occasioned arguments and confrontations which were often acrimonious. However, despite the conflicts of that period, the company and those running it were united on a sufficient number of levels so as to guarantee its existence. They all agreed about the importance of the work; about the fierceness with which it should be pursued; about the belief that theatre mattered. They all believed, often in an obsessive way, in the fight to establish and maintain what Devine called 'vital theatre'. That belief constantly came up against necessity, usually of a financial kind, and the belief intermittently goes underground, but it has persisted. It enabled one critic, writing on the occasion of the twenty-first birthday of the company, to describe the venture as 'the longest-running specialised production organisation, which . . . has no rival in the entire history of our theatre'.[3]

I have divided this book into narrative and production study. Four chapters tell the story of the theatrical seasons between 1965 and 1972. Four chapters deal respectively with Edward Bond's *Saved*, D. H. Lawrence's *The Daughter-in-Law*, David Storey's *The Changing Room*, and Howard Brenton's *Magnificence* (this last, though seen at the Court after Gaskill left, was commissioned by him). The choice is governed by a need to show something of the range of the Court's work, of its different kinds of commitment, and of its production values. Four plays can hardly stand adequately for the output of seven years, but they may indicate the diversity.

A final point. In the course of writing, I asked as many actors, writers, designers and directors as I could trace for their views about the Court. If it is true that 'instantaneousness' of decision-making is neglected by writers on theatre, it is equally true that theatre workers are often ignored. The response to my questions was generous. Since theatre is essentially the product of those who work to create it on stage, it seemed right to give prominence, wherever possible, to the views of the most important people involved. This book is dedicated to them.

1 · Prologue: William Gaskill's first season, October 1965 to March 1966

One of the central characteristics of the English Stage Company is that it has always known what it is doing but normally only as far as the next few productions. Whilst usually being very clear about the writers and plays it does not want to stage at the Royal Court, it is not always clear about what it does want to stage. This is sometimes termed pragmatism. What needs to be remembered is that in the early years of the company, perhaps the first ten, no one, not even George Devine, was sure what was going to happen, regarding matters such as finance, competition by other theatres, audience taste or the arrival of new plays of sufficient quality to underpin the Court's growing reputation as a different kind of theatre. George Devine's principal struggle during his tenure of office was somehow to keep the theatre open, prevent its decline into becoming a tryout venue for the West End and to make a space available for whatever emerged. At the same time, his scheme subsisted upon the idea of the Court as a school of theatre, a means of training and educating talented figures in all aspects of theatre, so as to provide a continuity. To proceed on such a broad front made near impossible demands on one figure, for it is the case that, then as now, the overall responsibility for the Royal Court rested with one man.

It follows that affirmations, reaffirmations and modifications of policy are a perennial feature of a theatre which steers a course between an overall view and *ad hoc* decisions. To go through the Court files in both Devine's and Gaskill's years is to find frequent statements of policy, sometimes flatly contradictory, occurring within a few months of each other. For the most part, such statements are not made public. Occasionally, however, they reach the press, usually because they are leaked from the Court. One such moment arrived in 1960, and, while angering a number of workers at the Court, provided a valuable opportunity for George Devine to take stock of the first four years of the company's life. Ronald Duncan, one of the founders of the English Stage Company, had become increasingly antagonistic both towards Devine and towards the

4

plays being favoured at the Court. On 1 March 1960 he submitted to the Council of the Court a document headed 'Notes on the Artistic Policy of the English Stage Company'. This document was answered by the Artistic committee on 27 April. The chairman, the Earl of Harewood, crystallized Duncan's attack into six main points, which were:

(a) That we have departed from the original aims and objects of the English Stage Company, as discussed in the preliminary leaflet.
(b) Artists are not impressed with our achievement.
(c) We have constantly produced plays of a social realist kind.
(d) We entirely ignore the language in which plays are written.
(e) Plays by competent established playwrights which do not conform to Mr Devine's ideas are dismissed.
(f) The Minute dated 5 May 1958, when the Council last debated artistic policy, has not been carried out. This Minute reads:
  (i) That the preliminary readers of manuscripts should be changed at frequent intervals to avoid any similarity of minds reading plays submitted.
  (ii) That established playwrights and writers should be approached with greater energy to write for the Royal Court Theatre.
  (iii) That every effort should be made to encourage writers of different points of view so as to widen the general artistic scope of the productions presented.
  (iv) That the Artistic Directors should get out to the provincial repertory companies to see new plays and performers.

Duncan's document added 'that the Artistic committee acted as a rubber stamp to the wishes of the Artistic Director'. To ensure that the matter was not ignored, he allowed the press to see his complaints and made himself available for interviews.

The Artistic committee (which at the April meeting consisted of Harewood, Peggy Ashcroft, Robin Fox, Oscar Lewenstein, John Osborne and Tony Richardson, as well as Devine himself; and had also in attendance, Lindsay Anderson, John Dexter and William Gaskill) answered Duncan point by point. It felt 'that the spirit of the original Aims and Objects had been carried out'. However, the committee was clearly sensible of the fact that the route taken by the company did differ in some ways from the one originally envisaged. To put it crudely, no one had foreseen Osborne and what followed. The company's route had been in this sense determined for it. Devine had been forced in the very early days to hedge his bets. Some of his scenarios had not endured, but it was not naïveté which, for example, had led him to think of persuading novelists to write for the theatre. It was part of a determined effort to reinvest theatre with intellectual seriousness and to link it strongly with other forms of art. The view from 1955 showed few dramatists of the kind that interested Devine, although in his careful way he was not above listing as allies writers whose work he did not endorse. In the original declaration ('Aims and Objects'), made while the English Stage Company was briefly based at the Kingsway Theatre (where it announced its existence on 7 July 1955), Devine did list the intentions which formed the basis of Duncan's accusations in 1960. This earlier document does state that 'The following artists are in sympathy with our aims, and the Company hopes to present their work: T. S. Eliot, Christopher Fry, Peter Ustinov, John Whiting, Ronald Duncan, Gabriel Marcel, Benjamin Britten, John Piper.' The names are those of established writers. None of them, with the exception of Duncan himself, ever featured at the Court. The reason is clear. Whatever the committee might say in response, the nature of the Court by 1960 was different from its theoretical base of 1955. In the committee's words, 'our activities have developed somewhat since the inception of the Company and new and important writers have turned up, whose names would now appear instead of, or in addition to, those names included in the original "Aims and Objects".' The blandness of the statement is awe-inspiring as is the comic 'or in addition to'. A list which had tagged on to the above names such as Osborne, Arden, Wesker, Simpson, Hastings, Jellicoe, Howarth and others, would truly have indicated a lack of direction in the theatre's affairs.

Nevertheless, the meeting did deal with the authors on the original 1955 list. Of T. S. Eliot, it was noted that he had written only one play since the Company was formed (*The Elder Statesman*), which had been performed elsewhere. A play by Christopher Fry (*Curtmantle*) had been considered 'but it was rejected by a majority of the committee'. A similar fate befell a Ustinov play (*The Empty Chair*). Whiting was 'unwilling' to write for the Company. A play by Marcel was not considered to be sufficiently important. Britten was too busy to respond to an invitation to write a pantomine for Christmas and Piper had not been approached. Dealing with this particular matter (which lay at the heart of Duncan's complaint), the committee then bluntly made its central point: 'The committee agreed that plays by competent playwrights have been rejected, as they do not conform to the policy of the Company.' Devine would have been unable to make such a clear statement at the beginning of the Company's life. By 1960, however, things were more certain. The Company's structure was now geared to, if not an absolute policy, a knowledge of what was unacceptable. In this regard, the English Stage Company stood up clearly in 1960. Thus the committee could say with some strength regarding its script readers that 'they are people who have some sympathy with the Policy which has been successfully evolved by the Company'. Its final statement was to define its function (and set a pattern for the years which followed). This was one of 'sifting the ideas the Artistic Director wants discussed . . . it positively supports the policy which has been pursued by the Artistic Director and it emphatically denies that it is a policy dictated against its inclinations'. Devine had by this stage, partly by placing on the committee figures sympathetic to his aims, established the autonomy of the Artistic Director, particularly as regards the choice of plays. However, the role of the Artistic committee as supporter and, on occasions, buffer for the Artistic Director, was and remained a crucial part of the Company structure. This was particularly the case for both Devine and, later, Gaskill. They were both fortunate in working with Lord Harewood as chairman, as will be seen later.

Duncan lost his battle and accurately reflected that 'My real difference with George Devine and his supporters on the Artistic committee of the English Stage Company was on what drama should be about. . . .'[1] Though he remained part of the Company until 1966, his role in the formation of the Court's work was effectively over. What he did usefully provoke, however, was a new 'Memorandum on Artistic Policy – Aims and Objects' which the Artistic committee received from George Devine on 13 May 1960 for consideration and onward transmission to the Council of the English Stage Company on 31 May. Devine's confidential Memorandum (which was rewritten and signed by Harewood before being transmitted to Council) is a statement of what has been achieved and what is necessary for further achievement. The original document noted that 'Since the foundation of the English Stage Company, and largely because of it, the theatrical scene has greatly changed. The position of the new dramatist has greatly improved and the balance between classical and modern theatre has been redressed.' The idea of a balance is significant in so far as it should be taken as an accurate reflection of Devine's priorities. The emphasis for Devine was not exclusively to do with new work but rather to produce the best work available and to define talent, which was to emerge via the Company's making opportunities for young writers to measure themselves against accepted (which means older) dramatists. The quotation above comes from the preamble, as does the assertion that:

> The English Stage Company still remains the only theatre with a consistent policy towards dramatists and modern theatre. This has only been achieved by sacrificing certain artistic principles and living a hand-to-mouth-existence. The new programme calls for a recognition of these facts and a vigorous activity to put right the deficiencies in our organisation which can no longer be borne if the Company is to continue being creative.

Behind Devine's views lies four years' exhausting experience, where he had seen a number of basic principles subsumed by the pressure of surviving. His vision of a permanent ensemble playing in 'true' repertory (that is, holding a number of plays in one season and playing them all at intervals) had provided the opening productions at the Court. It was replaced in September 1957 by the more orthodox limited-run system thereafter. The idea, however, persisted and William Gaskill was to try the same system of 'true' repertory in October 1965. It failed (financially) for similar reasons (see pp. 44–5). In Devine's submission, the concept remained, although it is now related to the potential of what was termed the 'Club', which was at that stage a room at the top of the building, held on a lease by Clement Freud, who used it as a private club. Devine looked forward to a time when the Company would acquire the room as a base for experimental work, where a permanent company would be envisaged and 'a simplified form of presentation'. It is noticeable, however, that in the document presented to Council none of the statements so far quoted finds expression in its original form. What was said in the Artistic committee was always subject to modification before it was scrutinized by either the Management committee (which oversaw the business administration of the Court) or the Council, the Court's ruling body. The Council submission, referring to new developments, suggested that 'Wherever possible . . . the Artistic Sub-Committee visualises the formation of semi-permanent companies, at least on a seasonal basis. It would like the emphasis on "permanent" companies to be maintained wherever possible in future.'

In 1960, Devine opted for expansion and a broadening of the Company's range. Whilst the main object remained to 'promote a consistently progressive policy towards the discovery and development of contemporary dramatists, especially the English dramatist', such an aim did not preclude 'the presentation of outstanding foreign works. . . . Nor does it preclude the classical revival provided that its presentation emphasises some special aspect in performance or style.' The mixture here is a happy one of idealism and careful strategy. Devine thought of the Court's range as a catholic one (he was particularly occupied with contemporary French theatre) but he was also well aware of the salvation offered by classical revivals. His production of *The Country Wife*, which had opened on 12 December 1956 and which transferred to the Adelphi Theatre after sixty performances at the Court, had rescued the Company from a potentially disastrous financial situation. Involved in broadening the scope of the Company was, as Devine argued, the creation of a provincial link, the acquisition of a larger theatre in addition to the Court and the establishment of a studio. As to the first, Devine considered such a link to hold advantages for both the Court and the repertory theatres in the scheme. It would, for example, provide more outlets for dramatists, as well as developing 'extra-metropolitan talent in all fields'. The idea, which had at root something of Devine's ideas for reinvigorating theatre on a national scale, foundered quite quickly on the twin rocks of insufficient finance and a suspicion from provincial repertory companies that they were being used to try out productions aimed at London.[2] For the second proposal, the acquisition of a larger theatre appears throughout the continued life of the Company, always with negative results, either because the finance was not available or because the idea of removing the Company, if only in part, from Sloane Square, always met opposition from those who felt that whatever it was that characterized the Company would be lost in such a venture.[3] Interestingly, although it does not appear in the Council document, Devine had another reason for wanting a larger theatre. In a discussion on 'Vital Theatre' in 1959, he insisted that 'each period had got its own special kind of vitality'. He instances the theatre of Brecht, Lorca, the Abbey, Dublin and Granville-Barker, arguing that 'They were theatres of the right sort in the right place, at the right time.' This idea of the appropriate kind of theatre for its time leads him in the discussion (and it is strangely pessimistic for Devine) to assert that 'the theatre as a place for the discussion of ideas is finished. Radio and television have entirely replaced it.' Out of this emerges the idea of 'musical theatre' which finds its way into the 1960 Memorandum. Thus in 1959 he says: 'My own thought is that the use of music, song and dance in the so-called straight theatre is the direction in which we must go. Society today needs to be taken out of itself, not driven into itself.'[4] Behind this opinion looms the omnipresent difficulty (which has never receded) of a regular audience for the Court's work. By June 1960 Devine was saying publicly:[5]

I deliberately set out to create a disturbing, exciting form of theatre.
I want to appeal to a vast, new, untouched audience. They are the
LP record public, the serious jazz public. They think of the London
theatre, as a weird, tiara world. To appeal to them I will broaden
my technique, use music and dancing and try to find a large theatre.

None of this, though argued by Devine, ever left the Artistic committee's room. What it does show, however, is that Devine (and his successors) constantly looked for how his theatre could relate to what was happening outside its doors.

The third area of development envisaged by Devine was to do with the training and teaching of dramatists, actors, directors, designers and musicians. The Council document calls for a studio. Devine labels it 'an obvious and necessary adjunct to our work. . . . The movement created at the Royal Court cannot possibly develop without the means to widen the horizon and dramatic experience of all those who participate.' Devine understood, as did his successor, that without the means of training as a

sine qua non of the theatre's work, there could be no long-term development. A nursery in all aspects of theatre was essential. At the time of
writing his Memorandum, Devine had begun his process of teaching at
the Court. In residence by this time were Lindsay Anderson, John Bird,
John Dexter, William Gaskill and Anthony Page, as well as Tony Richardson and Devine himself. Anderson, Dexter and Gaskill made up a trio
of Associate Directors; Page and Bird were Assistant Directors. Most of
these figures established themselves by directing what became known as
'Sunday night' productions. These were of plays which were thought to
show some ability but not yet ready for the main bill. They were worked
up to dress-rehearsal standard and given on the main stage for the English
Stage Society on a Sunday evening, with a minimum of set and decor.
Actors were paid two guineas for their appearance. These shows, which
went on for one or two performances, provided opportunities for both
writers and directors. They began in May 1957 and proved an enduring
contribution to the life of the Court for over a decade. In addition to the
Sunday night productions, and as part of the teaching at the Court, a
Writers' Group had begun in 1958. It continued until 1960. Devine had
noted that a characteristic of 'vital' theatres was that they all had a
dramatist or a group of dramatists attached to them[6] and out of this
emerged such a group. It evolved from a discussion group, chaired by
Devine, into an improvisation group via Gaskill and Keith Johnstone,
then running the script department.[7] Amongst the writers who attended
the weekly classes were Bond, Arden, Wesker, Jellicoe and Soyinka. The
demand for a studio in 1960 was in effect a demand for a central base
where all these activities could be co-ordinated. The encouragement of
directors and of actors had begun. As yet, there was little room except
intermittently for the systematic rearing of all kinds of theatre workers.
A studio might provide the opportunity. In 1960 it remained a strong
idea.

What cannot be emphasized too strongly is that these early years of the
Court were experimental in every sense. No one at the theatre would
confidently predict its continuing existence. Devine wrote early in 1961:
'I feel that the first statement of the Court has now been made, and all
sorts of people are looking to me and saying, "What are we going to do
next?" It's terribly difficult to know for sure because there are so many
things to do, so many fields which are quite unexplored.'[8] Amongst the
possibilities for Devine were the total renovation of the Court's interior
to 'create a playhouse with a very different feeling', a bigger theatre,
proper contact with schools and the theatrical education of the young,
and 'the need for sheer *education*, of authors and actors and directors and
audiences'. It is in this article that he cites the celebrated phrase (originally
coined by Tony Richardson) of '*the right to fail*'. What is important is to

see Devine at this stage of the Company's life debating its future. On the sixth birthday of the Company, he wrote an account of what had been done so far. Characteristically, he is more occupied with what it is to do in the near future. After rather pugnaciously compiling lists of productions done since 1956, Devine offered some analysis of the work. Between early 1956 and April 1962, ninety-five productions had been put on (sixty-two in the main bill, thirty-three on Sunday nights). Of these, sixty-four were plays by new writers, twenty-three by known or foreign writers, and eight were 'Classical revivals'. Of the sixty-two main bill productions, twelve covered their running expenses at the Royal Court (eight by means of transferring to the West End). Of the remaining fifty, all of which lost money, one half lost more than £3,000. What is truly remarkable about the figures is not that most of the shows lost money but that the Company survived the loss, and projected an overall surplus of £6,250 at the end of the sixth year. In his commentary, Devine sardonically offered reasons as to why the English Stage Company was still in business:[9]

> In order to survive we have been forced to participate in the
> commercial jungle, subject to the normal commercial risks. A 'bad
> press' and down we go. Apart from about a thousand people there is
> no regular public to support us through thick and thin. To pay our
> way we have to achieve 'rave notices'. It is this kind of climate which
> drives people like Joan Littlewood out of the theatre. And as a fairly
> respectable group, led by two Oxford intellectuals, we have fared
> better at the 'hand-outs' than she ever did. She had a permanent
> company, but it was split up in the West End earning money to keep
> the new company going in the East End, which in turn, etc.

At the end of his comments, Devine sounds the note of defiance which echoes through the history of the Court: 'I suppose in our minds we know that to be accepted completely by the middle, to be smiled upon by the top, is the first sweet kiss of death. So we carry on, flirting with death in order to live.'

The benefit of not only Devine's years at the Court but a lifetime's activity in English theatre[10] is to be found in an unpublished 'Open Letter to the Brazilian Theatre', which Devine wrote at the conclusion of a four week tour of Brazil in November and December 1963, as a guest of the British Council. In it, there is a kind of *credo* in evidence, and, as is frequently the case when writing of one subject, another is easily discernible, for Devine suggests that the Brazilians

> have a unique opportunity to learn from other people's mistakes, and
> although there is a theory that art thrives better if it has to fight for
> itself, I believe that it thrives best if conditions are created in which
> it can develop. I realise also that the economic problems attendant on

such plans are difficult to solve but I never have believed that lack of money was the *primary* reason for not achieving things if the will was there.

Amongst other things, Devine proposed a theatre organizer for the whole of the country, the establishment of theatre schools, the creation of provincial theatre centres using as a model the French system, a National Theatre Company, a biannual theatre festival (and every three years a South American festival), the training of administrators and the encouragement of new writers. At the end of his essay, Devine, perhaps mindful of his own theatre says:

It finally comes down to this. Some people of vision and passion and sound sense have got to pool their resources and sink their own individuality to some extent in order to produce the conditions for a civilized theatre system in any country. . . . And after the job is done you can all split up again and spit at each other, like all good theatre people.

Few of the ideas advocated by Devine to the Brazilians were feasible in England and throughout the piece the nearest analogy used by Devine is that of the French theatre system. However, one of his central obsessions did come about in 1963, when the Royal Court Theatre Studio began to operate. As ever, the opportunity when presented was quickly taken up. Jocelyn Herbert, who even by this time was becoming one of the most influential designers of the day, discovered that the Jeannetta Cochrane Theatre, built by the Central School of Arts and Crafts (of which she was a trustee) was unused during the day. After two experimental terms, a three-year grant was given by the Gulbenkian Foundation at a rate of £2,500 per year. William Gaskill was appointed director for the first year. In August 1964, the first of two reports on the Studio was circulated internally at the Court (the second, by Gaskill and others, reported on the period from August 1964 to September 1965, when the Studio entered its last term). The Studio was founded, in the words of the first report, to provide 'advanced training courses in all aspects of theatre'. It would be open to the whole profession but be directly associated with the Court. There was no other such theatre studio existing in England. The Studio's bias was to be towards improvised theatre, 'based on the precedent of the Commedia dell'Arte'. During its first phase, Gaskill had become an Associate Director of the National Theatre, as had John Dexter. Thus two of the original Associate Directors appointed by Devine went to help Olivier in the founding of the National Theatre. One consequence was that the Studio, with Gaskill at its head, linked both theatres and, for a time, National Theatre actors attended the classes until the pressures of playing in a repertory system forced them to drop out. What Gaskill and Keith Johnstone (his assistant) found was that they could not assume any basic training amongst the actors who arrived at class and there were proposals to initiate movement classes and, later on, voice classes. The work done at the Studio included mime classes by Claude Chagrin; Devine worked on 'Comedians' tricks'; Johnstone took the narrative class; and Gaskill taught sessions on epic theatre and the use of the half-mask. Later, there were demonstrations of 'Comic Text' and 'Serious Text', improvisation, movement, and narrative and epic theatre. Peter Gill, then an actor, and Desmond O'Donovan, a Court assistant, played a part. Gill, who was seriously interested in design, gave a series of art classes 'for those who wish to attend'. However, the classes faltered whenever Gaskill or Johnstone were engaged on productions, since the cornerstone of studio work was the improvisation classes which they taught. By March 1964 the National Theatre actors had virtually ceased to attend and 'For practical purposes the link with the National Theatre was severed.' The work continued and other teachers included Yat Malmgren, co-director of the London Drama Centre, Doreen Cannon, an American actress, who taught 'Method' acting and Marc Wilkinson, the composer. Out of the classes came a specialized Actors' Group and a reconstituted Playwrights' Group for, as Johnstone remarks in the first report: 'The methods Gaskill and I use at the Theatre Studio originated in our work with this group.' Johnstone envisaged a collaboration eventually between these two groups.[11]

It will be obvious from this account that the Studio was both innovatory, exhausting and problematic. It flourished uniquely, gave serious attention to all aspects of theatre and fulfilled a need. At the end of fourteen terms, some 250 actors had attended. But the demands upon the personnel involved were considerable. The grant was for only three years and the real difficulty was to do with trying to make such work feed into the mainstream theatre activity. It was Gaskill's intention to make the Studio central when he became Artistic Director (see p. 17) but it never quite succeeded. What the Studio did reveal in one area also proved almost impossible to manage and was indicative of how large a gap had previously existed in theatrical affairs. That area was to do with education.

In one sense, the education of the young, a favourite theme of Devine's, contained within itself the basis of the Company's future. It was inextricably linked with the development of an audience faithful to the Court's work which in turn would go some way towards relieving commercial pressure and consequently allow freedom for experiment and development. Without a regular audience, the Court lived a hand to mouth existence. The Arts Council was well aware of the problems. In the early 1960s, it noted that:[12]

The company's fortunes at the Royal Court are as variable as they always have been; after six years as the outstanding contributor to the contemporary theatre in Europe, there is no reliable audience to ensure a reasonable amount of financial stability.

Devine hardly needed telling, even in the sympathetic tones of the Arts Council, for what he clearly understood was that if it was true that the Court had hosted great changes in the kind of plays available to the public, it was equally true that the public had not yet accustomed itself to the change. He found time early in 1963 to be interviewed by two schoolchildren and blamed theatre generally for the current state of affairs:[13]

> I'm convinced that the general attitude of the theatre towards its
> public is really completely out of date . . . to change people's
> approach and attitude to theatre is a terribly difficult thing because
> where do you start? I think the only place you can start really is
> when people are young enough not to have their ideas set and formed
> about what theatre is and what it ought to be. . . . It is a question
> of educating the audience.

Devine was attempting to combat ignorance about the possibilities of theatre as education. He echoes Raymond Williams's concern that 'we have not yet done nearly enough to bring drama and theatre into the schools. . . . The social economy of art can never be based on the law of supply and demand. We do not base education on the cash-nexus, but on a valuation of learning and of ultimate human needs. . . .'[14] The ignorance extended to critics. W. A. Darlington had suggested in 1962 that the poor financial figures for the Court 'prove that the kind of new play generally put on at the Royal Court has little appeal to the general theatre-going public'.[15]

What was actually the case as far as a young audience was concerned emerged via the work of the Studio. In its first report, Johnstone writes of how, in order to extend the abilities of actors producing improvisations, after a disastrous 'public show' at the Court, he decided to take his actors to colleges, schools and youth clubs to give demonstration classes. These classes, he notes, 'were ostensibly to show the method used in our training, but our true purpose was to learn how to work with an audience'. The reaction was enthusiastic. Johnstone and Gaskill were invited to a conference of Drama Advisers, inspectors from the Ministry of Education visited the Studio and proposals were made to take demonstration classes to training colleges. Johnstone then argues that, since 'our future audiences depend to a great extent on the work in the schools', the Court should help as much as possible. It did. Between September 1964 and July 1965, Studio actors worked at five London training colleges and visited Winchester, Dartington Hall and Rolle College, Devon, Oxford, Hatfield, Bath, Cambridge and Henley-on-Thames. After overcoming initial suspicion from educationalists, the number of requests for visits increased. This brief experiment is one of the unsung successes of the Court's work, but it fell away shortly after Gaskill became Artistic Director for a number of reasons, not the least of which were finance and manpower (see p. 25). If the actual means of developing an audience described above was not specifically continued, the idea remained and subsequently emerged in a different form.

Towards the end of 1963, Devine began to think about a successor. He told the Management committee on 20 November that working without help over the previous year had placed a great strain on his health. Devine put forward the name of William Gaskill, who would be available at the end of the summer of 1964 and who would 'free him from the day to day burden . . .'. Devine was clear at this stage that Gaskill should take over from him. According to Lord Harewood, 'Bill was a chosen son of George . . .',[16] but for the moment, he remained at the National Theatre and declined the Court's offer, as did Michael Elliott and Tony Richardson. At its meeting of 17 January 1964, the Management committee considered a suggestion from the Artistic committee that Anthony Page be appointed Artistic Director and Lindsay Anderson Associate Artistic Director for one year from September 1964. According to Richard Findlater, Page and Anderson announced that new plays would be presented 'only if they are deemed to be suitable for production and not solely because they happen to be new',[17] a theme they were to take up once more when they renewed their association with the Royal Court in 1969 (see p. 123). Anderson resigned before the new season opened and Page remained. In November 1964, Devine announced his retirement, which did not become public until January 1965. On the occasion of the annual luncheon for critics given by Neville Blond as chairman (and, as always, paid for by him), Devine summed up his years as Artistic Director. There had been 145 productions at the Court and eighty-seven 'Sunday nights'. Of this total, 126 were plays by contemporary English writers.[18] Gaskill himself has described the occasion. The announcement[19]

> was greeted politely but with no sense of the importance of the occasion. But Lindsay, whose feeling for the occasion has always been remarkable, leapt to his feet and made an impassioned speech about George. The critics sang *For he's a jolly good fellow*. I was very moved by Lindsay's speech, and although I had turned down the chance of taking over the Court the previous year I realized that the continuity of George's work was more important than working at the National Theatre, and I told George I would do it. Olivier sent a telegram: 'The Lord gave and the Lord has taken away.'

Ironically, Anderson's speech, though instrumental in Gaskill's return to the Court, also occasioned Anderson's exclusion for a number of years from the Company's affairs. Gaskill's determination to run the theatre his way meant that there was no place for many former colleagues. Gaskill's decision to return also allowed the Company to breathe again, for it had been considering alternatives since Devine's intention of resigning had been known late in 1964. At one point, the Artistic committee, though ruling out the idea of winding up the whole venture, had considered letting the theatre for long periods to the National Theatre and Royal Shakespeare Company.[20] However, when Gaskill changed his mind and submitted an application, Lord Harewood reported to the Council on 29 January 1965 that a number of applications had been received, including one from Gaskill, who indicated his willingness to serve for three years. Because of his growing reputation as a director and his former association with the company, the Artistic committee had not investigated the other applications any further. The Council unanimously agreed Gaskill's appointment as Artistic Director.[21] Gaskill's appointment began officially in July 1965, when his National Theatre contract expired, but in the early months of 1965 he was already planning a programme and making new appointments. In April, he reviewed the current theatrical scene in a paper prepared for the Management committee. While he saw 'every reason to continue the basic policy of the Court (the development of new writers, directors and designers)', he also thought that 'organisational changes are necessary and will be reflected in the work. We cannot afford to ignore certain major changes that have happened in the theatre since 1956. . . .' Gaskill then highlights three of these changes:

1 The emergence of the two large-scale permanent companies – The National Theatre and the Royal Shakespeare, playing in repertoire modern as well as classical plays.

2 The decline of the West End Theatre as a home for straight plays.

3 The death of weekly rep. and the growth of two or three weekly rep. companies and the raising of the standard of plays (though not necessarily of the performance) in the provinces.

The overall pattern, Gaskill noted, 'is of a non-commercial increasingly subsidized theatre. What is the function of the Court in this framework?' Gaskill accurately identifies the differences in important areas between where the Company now stood and its position in 1956. Devine did not have either the advantages or the particular problems facing the new Artistic Director.

He answered his own question under five headings. The Court's role would primarily be 'To maintain itself as a theatre where risks can be taken in a way that the larger companies cannot afford.' To do this, Gaskill reverted to the initial proposal of Devine's which argued for a permanent company playing in repertoire. Such a theatre would play:

only contemporary work – whether revivals or new plays, with a small nucleus of actors under short term contract – either six months or a year and playing in true rep. This is the only structure in which one can nurse failures, support them with successes and give new writers the right conditions for their work to be seen. It will also remove the endless panic about the next production and spread the load over a much longer period. I don't want the Court to become institutionalized, but I think it should have continuity of work to ensure the growth and development of all working in it.

Further, Gaskill wished to bring the Studio into the main theatre 'and relate its activities more closely to the work seen on the stage by having classes for the Company and experimental projects running parallel with the main bill. We should also try and develop its educational work which is increasingly successful.' He made two more proposals. One was to use the repertory system to build a more regular audience, so as to establish the Court as a theatre 'with a consistent policy, not only artistic but managerial'. With a season planned in advance, it became possible to sell season tickets and subscription schemes. The second raised the possibility of links with provincial theatre and of regular tours.

What is striking about this manifesto is not that it is novel (for most of it had been in Devine's mind when he began) but that Gaskill believed the time was right to try again, moreover with an exclusive diet of contemporary work. In this, he was clearly influenced by two key experiences. One was that of watching the performances of the first visit by the Berliner Ensemble in 1956; the other was his attempts to analyse that experience via his work at the Royal Shakespeare Company and the National Theatre. He was not alone in the first, for it is the case that a whole generation of theatre artists was profoundly affected by the staging and production values of the Berliner, if not necessarily by what was being said.[22] They were also not a little envious at the work conditions of the Berliner, in terms of the rehearsal time allowed to the Ensemble as opposed to the usual few weeks available even to a major English company. Gaskill said in 1965 that the Berliner's production of *Mother Courage* 'is for many of us working in the theatre the most important single production we have ever seen – the most influential'[23] and his list of productions between 1957 and 1965 (see note 21) attests to the radical effect upon him of that experience. At the Royal Shakespeare Company and particularly at the National Theatre (where he and John Dexter were recruited by Olivier as the next best alternative to Devine himself), Gaskill attempted to bring to bear on his work, especially in rehearsal, his understanding of the Berliner's achievement. A crucial time came in working on his production of *The Caucasian Chalk Circle* in 1962 where[24]

I suddenly had the experience of something which may have been

obvious to some people for a long time, but which I *experienced*:
that what one is dealing with in directing a play by Brecht is not just
the play, nor just an artistic expression of oneself or the actors, but an
attempt to waken the lives of all the people involved, and through
them, society itself. . . . I found it opened up so many questions
that it really threw me at rehearsal. I suddenly felt that everything I
had done before had to be questioned.

Out of this episode came another important revelation for Gaskill. He
discovered a capacity for teaching, a fact which had repercussions for his
work at the Court:[25]

I suppose what I have learned most significantly is that I am by nature
a teacher. That is, I teach well. And in the first fortnight of
rehearsals, I taught rather than directed. The danger here is that one
tends to want a kind of ideal state in which one has endless time.
And because I discovered this, to me, essential thing that one must
use a Socratic method in rehearsal . . . then one has failed if one
cannot carry it out to the very end. . . . This does not necessarily
mean that I am going to direct in this way from now on, because
the time factor is essential, and therefore in certain circumstances
authority and discipline are required. . . . I think one must find a
way of combining the faculties of teaching and directing.

In part, these discoveries surfaced when Gaskill was at the National
Theatre. Though he said 'two of the happiest working years of my life
were spent with Larry'[26], it is also true that Gaskill left when he saw that
the National was to develop in a way inimical to his kind of work.[27] The
second invitation to join the Court came at an opportune time.

Gaskill was not naïve in his opening proposals for the Court as regards
an ensemble playing in repertoire. He had seen it fail (with Devine) and
turn into something else (at the National). Some of his colleagues at the
Court were dubious. Greville Poke, a member of the original Council,
and the longest serving member of the Company felt 'Very suspicious . . .
but a feeling that if you've got a new Artistic Director he should be given
his head. We pointed out what happened when George tried a similar
scheme, but Bill wanted to have a go and . . . our attitude was, O.K.,
good luck to you and we'll see how it works. And it didn't.'[28] Lord
Harewood is more explicit: 'George tried it and we had to give it up,
because we wanted to be able to transfer. Simple as that. . . . You have
to bend with the wind on these things . . . in a way, Bill was going
back to something before that and that also offended Neville's business
instincts. . . .'[29] Gaskill was to offend Neville Blond's business instincts
often over the next four years and frequently clashed with the Company's
chairman. Oscar Lewenstein, generally a supporter of experimental work

at the Court, similarly thought the system could not hope to work either in Devine's or Gaskill's time:[30]

> because I believe that running a theatre, which was primarily devoted to productions of new plays, and trying to run in rep., both without large funds, was an impossibility. First of all, we wanted to do a wide selection of plays, so that you'd have needed a very, very broad company to encompass those plays . . . always there would be a struggle between casting the play as well as possible and the use of a small permanent company that we would inevitably have. On the other hand, directors always wanted to have permanent companies . . . but I think most permanent companies . . . are used by theatres with a classical basis, or a basis in one or two playwrights . . . something where the style of play isn't tremendously varied. Our style of play was constantly varied and by not having a permanent company we were able to cast the plays exceptionally well . . .

However, the idea of a permanent company playing in repertoire was seen by many as the only solution for the production of new work, especially when such work genuinely broke new ground and might possibly therefore need a nursing period until the audience grasped the terms of reference. By May 1958, *Encore*, while reviewing the great difficulty of true repertory, nevertheless maintained that a permanent company was really possible and that the alternative of separately conceived and executed productions would be 'governed by the law of the commercial theatre'.[31] One of the strongest features of the Court under Gaskill after the first season was a modification of the permanent company idea into the concept of a nucleus of actors coming together for a series of productions. As Gaskill says:[32]

> Starting with an extreme statement, that you are going to have a permanent company, does mean that you bring together a group of people who work with enormous intensity. When it broke up, it had already created a pool of actors who were used over a number of years . . . and that did give the Court an identity. If we hadn't done that it wouldn't have happened and I think that's one way the Court has renewed itself over the years.

The 'pool of actors' was in one way an accidental spin-off from the central idea, for Gaskill was very clear about the real aim:[33]

> it was a very straightforward attempt to take the Court back to its initial policy . . . when I was working there as an assistant we felt there were two kinds of Royal Court . . . the Royal Court . . . which used the same group of actors, which had tremendous loyalty to particular writers and their relationship with directors, and there was an alternative Royal Court which was always looking towards the West

End and the stars, and I think that dichotomy was in the Court from
the very beginning. . . . George always stood for . . . the kind of
Michel Saint-Denis tradition of the ensemble and the workshops and
the school, the whole training, the development of style. . . . Tony
Richardson's influence was, do everything which was immediate . . .
of the moment, possibly involving stars, certainly involving commercial
exploitation, certainly looking towards films, Broadway, which he of
course amazingly achieved in a very short space of time, and without
which probably the Court wouldn't have survived. . . . Of course, if
you just look at the whole period, in fact you'll see the Court's
pattern repeating itself . . . mainly due to economic necessity . . . it's
very difficult to create an ensemble, except for the work of particular
writers, so that we created ensembles for Edward Bond and Arnold
Wesker and D. H. Lawrence. Much of the Court's best work was
in those groups . . .

In the same interview, Gaskill states that he already faced the possibility
of its not working but 'if you're going to do it, then the important thing
is to start as strongly as you possibly can. If you are going to be eroded
by compromise, then let it happen, but it's really important to start with
the clearest principles you can.' It is important to note that his proposals
were supported to the hilt by George Devine.[34]

Early in 1965, Gaskill began to form his new team. He engaged Iain
Cuthbertson, then director of productions and general manager at the
Citizens' Theatre, Glasgow, for twelve months at a weekly salary of £40
(plus £5 expenses). In May, he asked that Keith Johnstone be appointed
as the other Associate Director at a weekly salary of £30. Cuthbertson's
specific brief was the organization of the seasons, while Johnstone would
continue to run the Studio and the script department. These were very
deliberate appointments. Cuthbertson knew the repertory and provincial
theatre world better than most people at the Court, while Johnstone
represented the actuality of bringing studio work into the mainstream of
the Court's activities. Looking back on it, Gaskill 'didn't think it had
worked out with Iain at all. . . . I'd seen a pantomime he'd done at
Glasgow which I liked very much. I thought there'd be something robust
and un-Royal Court like about him but in fact he was rather overawed,
I think, by the set up. You can't just inject another element into the
Court.'[35] Equally, Johnstone, who was, 'as John Arden called him the
unpaid conscience of the Court', was not able in the event to centralize
the studio work, through no fault of his own. It was partly a lack of
finance. It was, more crucially, that the work in the Studio irresistibly
went in a different direction for 'it tends to evolve a certain kind of work,
a style, often a writerless style. In fact the only product of the Studio was
the Theatre Machine, which was a group which essentially worked

without a writer. . . .'[36] A little later, Jane Howell became an Assistant Director at the Court, with particular responsibility for schools work.[37] She was to become one of the most important figures during this period. Another crucial figure was Helen Montagu who replaced Doreen Dixon as General Manager, when Dixon went to Chichester late in 1965. Helen Montagu by then was Casting Director to George Devine. An Australian actress, she arrived at the Court Studio on the first day and 'did an extraordinary improvisation [but] had done very little professional work. We got to like her very much . . . and Peter Gill suggested she would be a good person to take over the casting. So she did.'[38] When Montagu moved from Casting, she was replaced by Corinne Rodriguez. Peter Gill was of course already at the Court and currently in the publicity department. He was a close friend of Gaskill's (and was eventually thought of as Gaskill's natural successor). He had worked as Gaskill's assistant on the York Mystery plays, in 1963.[39] In the field of design, Gaskill decided to hold a competition. He asked the Management committee on 20 May to allow £25 to each of four young designers for them to prepare a project for the new season. They were Christopher Morley, John Gunter, Ariane Gastambide and Brenda Briant. The project consisted of designing models of *Serjeant Musgrave's Dance*, *The Knack* and *The Pope's Wedding*, which could co-exist in the theatre at the same time during the repertory season. Peter Gill was responsible for the competition because of his interest in design. The designers were given four-and-a-half weeks to handle three plays. *The Pope's Wedding* proved particularly difficult for Gunter which he 'funked totally, because I just didn't understand it . . . the whole bloody thing . . . it was a whole new teaching process when I went to the Court. . . . We were all learning at the same time.'[40] Nevertheless, Gunter was engaged as Resident Designer (followed briefly by Christopher Morley) and had the task of designing the first three productions of the new season.

By the end of July 1965, Gaskill had four plays definitely in mind for the new season. Three were by established 'house writers', Ann Jellicoe, N. F. Simpson and John Arden. The fourth was by a writer associated with the Court since 1958 but, to date, with one Sunday night production to his credit.[41] Edward Bond's *Saved* was to turn into the sensation of the season. Gaskill estimated that casting all three plays together would need about eighteen players, possibly less, 'so that some artists would be given "run of the play" contracts' only. In the event, he engaged a company of twenty-one actors. These were Jean Boht, John Bull, Richard Butler, Timothy Carlton, John Castle, Frances Cuka, Iain Cuthbertson, Avril Elgar, Barbara Ferris, Lucy Fleming, Alison Frazer, Bernard Gallagher, Nerys Hughes, Kika Markham, Gwen Nelson, Ronald Pickup, Tony Selby, Sebastian Shaw, William Stewart, Dennis Waterman and

Frank Williams. They came in diverse ways and with diverse experience. Bernard Gallagher, who has worked at the Court as much as anyone, emerged from[42]

> five years in weekly rep. and two in repertoire at the Victoria, Stoke. My function at this stage was a minor one: Walking Gentleman in *Shelley*, understudy to Richard Butler in *Saved*, a character role in *The Cresta Run* . . . the personnel were intriguing and wildly diverse. The cast ranged from distinguished elders like Sebastian Shaw and Gwen Nelson – whose approach to the work was as fresh and adventurous as anybody's – to young actors, then unknown, who soon emerged as extraordinary talents, such as . . . Jack Shepherd . . .

Shepherd got in at this stage by sheer determination:[43]

> I wrote a kind and honest letter to Bill Gaskill. . . . I suppose a romantic and rather desperate letter, saying can I work for the Royal Court because it does plays that are about . . . and it worked. I got an interview and I got the lowest of all the jobs at the theatre which was understudying what emerged to be 16 parts in the first season of plays.

Frank Williams arrived to play in both *Shelley* and *The Cresta Run*, but since Celia Johnson 'who was to play Lilian in *The Cresta Run* was only going to be in that production, I was withdrawn from *Shelley* in order that I could rehearse the Lilian/Leonard scenes. . . . Celia Johnson withdrew . . . during the early stages of rehearsal and the part was in fact played by Avril Elgar.'[44] Richard Butler had been in *A Collier's Friday Night* in August 1965. The Sunday night production was repeated the following week, where Gaskill saw his work. He was not therefore auditioned and was persuaded, albeit reluctantly, to play more old men: Harry in *Saved* and Walsh in *Serjeant Musgrave's Dance*, as well as understudying Sebastian Shaw in *Shelley*.[45] And Nerys Hughes arrived via a good deal of repertory and a television play, 'Diary of a Young Man', directed by Ken Loach: 'I was terribly small fry and very excited. . . . I wasn't at a stage where I could pick and choose'.[46]

With Arts Council approval of his plans (though with reservations that the season was under budgeted), Gaskill planned to open with *Saved*. The estimated loss for the six months season was £37,906, based on a box-office of 50 per cent of capacity. The season would be divided into three eight-week booking periods and, as Gaskill said to members of the English Stage Society, there would be a chance to see three world premières in a very short space of time. *Saved*, however, was already coming under fire from the Lord Chamberlain, without whose licence the play could not be publicly performed. By 9 August Gaskill was informing the Management committee that the author would not agree to the Chamberlain's demand for cuts in the script. The only solution was to adopt, very reluctantly, a device used sparingly by the Court, that of turning the theatre into a club for the production. Devine had always resisted totally the implications of a club production, though he had been forced into it when Osborne's *A Patriot for Me* (June 1965) had been savaged by the Chamberlain.[47] With the agreement of the Arts Council, the Court once again became a club and *Saved* was put down the bill to third place (as was *Look Back in Anger* in 1956 for different reasons). Despite this, Gaskill had sufficient confidence in the long term to outline on 1 September his policy for 1966–7 and beyond. It would be 'the continuation and development of the policy for the repertory season opening in October 1965'. In an internal, draft document, presented to the Management committee of 27 August 1965, Gaskill spoke of 'a five year plan for the Royal Court by April of next year'.[48] In addition to this, Gaskill wanted finance for two Assistant Directors 'to continue the work of the Royal Court in developing young directors', provision for an audience builder, a permanent company of some twenty-five actors and a reduction of productions from twelve to ten, with equal costs for all productions. He concluded by hoping for a box-office increase in takings from 55 per cent to 60 per cent for 1966–7. Gaskill's policy statement also referred to the possibility of moving to a larger theatre. M. V. Linklater, representing the Arts Council, warned of the danger involved in moving. It could involve the loss of the intimate ethos of the Court. At the same time, Linklater suggested that the costs of the Studio be excluded from the budget, with Gaskill objecting for obvious reasons. It was decided, cautiously, that the document be revised to exclude the notion of a five-year plan, 'but indicating the development for '66–'67 being dependent on the experience gained during the '65–'66 season'. There should be a further policy statement in six months' time.

Gaskill's first season, after a week of previews for the English Stage Society, opened on 18 October 1965, with Ann Jellicoe's *Shelley*. As with Devine's opening season, *Shelley* and the following two productions were served by the same permanent setting, both as a matter of economy but also as a statement of intent via the decor. After its nineteen performances, the box-office produced figures of 28.1 per cent of financial capacity (the budget was set at 55 per cent overall). Critically, it was almost universally disliked. *Theatre World's* reaction was unfortunately typical. The production 'is the first by the new triumvirate management who have succeeded George Devine at the Court. They have a difficult task ahead if the Court is to regain its old high standards.'[49] On 27 October, N. F. Simpson's *The Cresta Run* began its nineteen performances and returned a box-office of 26.5 per cent.[50] Again, the play was not liked. Two of the actors in it felt slightly differently. Frank Williams thinks 'It was assumed that it would be the box office success of the opening plays, and that *Saved* would be the least popular. As it turned out, the reverse was true;[51] and Bernard Gallagher felt that the play 'though great fun to work on actually came out looking rather silly (and I fear I made little of my part)'.[52] The third play to be shown, beginning 3 November, was Bond's *Saved*. Though it played to only 36.7 per cent for its twenty-four performances, it did rebuild the shaky image of the Court in a quite spectacular way and placed the theatre once more in the centre of controversy (see chapter 2).[53] However, reviewing the results of the first booking period (Management committee, 3 December), Gaskill knew that it was 'very disappointing'. Nonetheless, at this stage, the theatre was totally in support of its Artistic Director. Alfred Esdaile in the same meeting said 'he was not at all dismayed as the theatre always had its ups and downs', and the committee agreed 'that *Saved* had restored our reputation as an experimental theatre'. The Arts Council, though, needed to be informed that the estimates would have to be increased: 'We had learnt from experience.' Gaskill's obvious problem, or one of them, was to do with the demands of playing in repertoire. For example, on 9 November, there was a discussion as to whether *The Cresta Run* could be improved. The Management committee was informed that many improvements had been made since the opening night, that it was virtually impossible to re-rehearse a play during a repertoire season and that it was too costly to make changes in scenery which might make for a smoother performance. As well as thinking ahead to the programme to mark the tenth anniversary of the Company, Gaskill had to run the theatre 'which means that I spend a great deal of time artistically directing the box-office, the cleaners, the programme-sellers and so on. . . .'[54] On 9 December Gaskill's first revival of a modern play, *Serjeant Musgrave's Dance*, opened for an eventual total of forty-five performances. It had first been seen in October 1959, directed by Lindsay Anderson, and had, by and large, received a critical drubbing and been taken off. Now Gaskill declared his allegiances and some of the critical response was more encouraging. In the first series, of thirty-two performances, the play reached 49 per cent of capacity but Gaskill would not allow it to continue as a long run. He therefore scheduled six performances of both *Shelley* and *The Cresta Run*, because it was important that the repertoire system 'should be adhered to' (Management committee, 9 November 1965). The remaining thirteen performances of *Serjeant Musgrave's Dance* achieved 34.8 per cent.[55] On 12 December, the first Sunday night performance of the season offered the Actors' Studio with a programme called 'Experiment' and the Christmas show opened on 20 December. The show was called *Clowning*. Directed by Johnstone and using studio work, it ran for fifteen afternoon performances. The box office receipts dropped to 9.7 per cent. It actually replaced a proposed show by Johnstone and David Cregan, which was left out because of cost, and, since it consisted principally of improvisation, a script as such could not go to the Lord Chamberlain. Eventually, an outline was sent, the show was described as a 'lecture demonstration', and it was allowed.

Council met on 9 December to be told by the company accountant, Frank Evans, that the season up to 4 December had realized only 31 per cent of capacity and that a revised budget was necessary. The season had, however, begun with an overall cash balance of some £35,000. Evans also reported that by the end of 1965, the Company would be entirely free of all mortgage and loan liabilities. What is significant about the meeting is that the Council, despite 'certain misgivings . . .', accepted Gaskill's policy in full. Though it was not always so welcoming, particularly later on, it is the case that the Council here was prepared to back Gaskill's attempt to follow the policy through. It even swallowed his request that Council members should not attend first nights.[56] If he was allowed his way on this, in another area he was unable to perpetuate one of his central strands of policy. The Studio effectively ceased its operations at the end of 1965 mainly because of the demands of the repertoire system. Put simply, there was too much to carry:[57]

> The amount of activity we did in those first months was amazing. . . .
> In my first season, we used to meet the audience every night, after
> every show. We used to take it in turns. . . . At the same time we
> were giving classes while we were rehearsing, so people were
> snatched from classes to rehearsals and vice versa.

In his 'Memorandum on the Studio' which went up to September 1965, Gaskill clearly regarded the work done there as central to the activity and development of the Company. When it ceased, a fundamental ideal of Devine's also ceased.

1966 opened with the prosecution of the theatre by the Lord Chamberlain for presenting an unlicensed play (*Saved*). The matter was to rumble on for several months and, ironically, was to unite the Company in the first of its major battles during this period against theatre censorship (see chapter 2). Here it is sufficient to notice that the reaction of the Management committee meeting of 14 January was to insist that the play be kept on. In addition, on 13 January, Middleton's play, *A Chaste Maid in Cheapside*, in an adaptation by Edward Bond, opened for twenty-five performances. It played to mixed reviews and 39.7 per cent capacity. During its run, George Devine died. Six days before his death, the Management committee had proposed a benefit night for him in a large theatre. Lindsay Anderson summed up simply and accurately: 'He was unique in his time.'[58] The Company continued and, four days before George Devine died, presented a Sunday night double bill by David Cregan, a writer much liked by Devine. The plays were *Transcending* and

The Dancers.[59] Though officially described as being directed by Jane Howell, the final stages of *Transcending* were supervised by Gaskill himself. It is a recurring feature of the Court's work that young directors, as well as writers, were scrutinized in their development and, on occasions such as this, rescued. *Transcending* transferred to the main bill, together with a play by Keith Johnstone, *The Performing Giant*, on 3 March. Prior to that, Ann Jellicoe's *The Knack* was revived on 17 February. None of them did well at the box-office, even though the reviews for both Jellicoe and Cregan were reasonably good.

By this stage, the finances of the Company were causing real concern. Though Gaskill had told the Artistic committee on 8 February that the average weekly box-office was more even and argued that an audience was gradually being established, he also voiced his concern that the new play policy did not have the advantage of a company presenting classical works. On the other hand, a lack of adventurousness in the choice of plays might result in a smaller grant from the Arts Council. What it did result in was a sharp reaction from the Arts Council. At the Management committee of 23 March, the figures showed an overall loss for the six months of £48,000. The original cash surplus of £35,000 had been absorbed and, with a supplementary grant from the Arts Council of £9,000, the Company still entered the next financial year with a £4,000 overdraft. The Arts Council remarked at the meeting that it was the committee's job to ensure that the Artistic Director produced a programme which kept the Company solvent.

Two main reasons contributed to the acute financial difficulties of the system. First, the cost of playing in repertoire and the consequences, had been severely underestimated, as had production costs. Second, this could have been borne, had the Company had one great success and Gaskill at the end of the financial year reviewed the current situation, without immediately giving in to discernible pressure to abandon the repertoire system (see chapter 3). Paradoxically, he had kept faith with the writers nursed at the Court, but the new plays from such writers on offer for the first season proved unpopular. Reflecting on this later, Gaskill felt there was always a potential problem:[60]

> particularly when you commission plays or if you have a kind of
> obligation . . . it may be that none of them or perhaps most of them
> are not good enough . . . and you've got this commitment to them,
> because they're writers you like, admire . . . N. F. Simpson [and]
> Ann Jellicoe . . . were the writers I was closest to, because of the
> early days, and so they were writers that I very much wanted to
> include in the first season, together with John Arden and Arnold
> Wesker . . . you're doing a play by a writer that you like just because
> he's a writer that you like, not necessarily because you like the

particular play and I think that can be risky. You can take loyalties so far, but you mustn't overstretch.

Even the, by now, clichéd notion of 'the right to fail' must not involve the complete failure of the theatre.

If one aspect of the Court looked gloomy in March 1966, there were happier perspectives. The Company at the end of March finally acquired the club space at the top of the building and, with Jocelyn Herbert supervising the designs, was to be converted for use by members of the English Stage Society. If the Studio as such had gone, another potential studio was emerging. And there were the achievements of the first season, which are not diminished by the financial state of play. The actor, Bernard Gallagher, gives the best account of being there during that time of any available:[61]

the atmosphere was unquestionably exciting. It was an optimistic time and you felt you were in on something special. . . . The stage and theatre staff too were a bit special and the atmosphere in the place somehow engendered the feeling of a large, complicated but essentially like-minded family, all going somewhere interesting together. George Devine still breathed over it. . . . I suppose the fairest thing to say about the actors there is that they offered a comprehensive cross-section of theatre practice at the time, from the most conventional to the most experimental, tempered by a general willingness to try things one hadn't ever done before (I imagine we were all chosen not merely for ability but for a suspected readiness to have a go). Thus we worked on movement with Yat [Malmgren]: 'You are *all over* the place', an alarming experience to some of us steady rep. hands, a walkover to the Drama Centre alumni. We did mask work with Bill Gaskill; clowning/fantasy experiments with Keith Johnstone; an attempt at some kind of Brechtian approach to *Serjeant Musgrave's Dance*, for which some of us had to learn clog dancing. . . . The multiplicity of influences on us was by turns stimulating and confusing and at one stage I fell into something like despair when I felt unable to cope with the demands being made on me . . . it was a disturbing, salutary and in the long run very productive experience . . .

. . . when I joined the company we were all offered a year's contract and the hope of another year after it . . . this proved impossible, but we were told we would all be used as much as possible over the following year and indeed we were. . . . This moral tone [of the choice of plays] was extended to the style of presentation, which was characterized by an almost chaste simplicity and economy and an odd sort of gentleness of expression. It was embodied in the cleanness of the lighting, the plainness of the costumes and the spare settings. . . .

For me at any rate it was a revelation to experience theatre in which any image, and hence any imaginary event, was presentable on an ordinary proscenium stage . . . it *wasn't* all wonderful. How could it be, with so many ambitious people of energy and talent together in a small space and when the initial euphoria had worn away? We had our fair share of late-night recriminations, weeping at parties and strong silence in rehearsals. There were times when treachery and ingratitude lurked in the wings . . . as in all triumvirates people got landed with the routine work and either left or were shunted into a siding. No common enterprise, from Shakespeare's Globe to the Berliner Ensemble, has ever held together in its original form . . .

. . . overall my memory is of good times: of a small, manageable, friendly stage within spitting distance of the audience; a warm, close house you could take in at a glance (though you had to remember the strange acoustic dead spot under the circle overhang); shabby but hospitable dressing rooms never far from the acting area; little warrens of corridors and poky offices with people reading scripts over cups of tea; a front-of-house staff who were on your side, however vile they might be to the public trying to get seats for one of the sellouts; a backstage crew who seemed to live there and were as interested in the plays we were doing as we were. . . . I am sure I was not the only one to find it a watershed in my working life.

And a then comparatively unknown Nerys Hughes recalls the production of *Saved*. She saw it several times and 'I remember being very proud of being part of the Company. . . . I remember feeling special being part of it all.'[62]

2 · Edward Bond's *Saved*

Late in 1984 the Court revived *Saved* in repertory with Bond's earlier play, *The Pope's Wedding*. The tone of the reviews ranged from the respectful to the adulatory. Twenty years after the play was written, it was judged to offer 'an experience no serious playgoer should deny himself' and to be 'a brilliant and pioneering play – a masterpiece of modern drama'.[1] The reviews of the first production for the members of the English Stage Society, which opened on 3 November 1965, were for the most part intensely hostile and extravagant in their condemnation. They contained phrases such as: 'this revolting and distasteful play'; 'a concocted opportunity for vicarious beastliness'; 'patently designed with no purpose above mere titillation'.[2] Defenders of the play were few.[3]

The play which caused such a stir was commissioned by George Devine as a consequence of the successful Sunday night showing of *The Pope's Wedding*. It was delivered to the Court on 18 September 1964, and an option on it was taken out. It was originally thought of as another Sunday night play, to be directed by Keith Johnstone. However, by April 1965, no production was proposed and the option had lapsed. Doreen Dixon, the Court's General Manager, wrote to Bond on 5 April to apologize for the delay and to say that 'It appears that Keith has read it once, and it was passed to Anthony Page, where it has remained since. . . . It is now going to Bill Gaskill to see if he wants to renew the option.' On 22 April, Dixon wrote again to say that Gaskill proposed to option either *The Pope's Wedding* or *Saved* 'with a view to production in his new season. As soon as he has had an opportunity of reading *Saved*, I will be in touch with you again.' No decision could be taken until Gaskill had read the play. Once he had, he acted very quickly: 'I remember reading it straight through and being absolutely convinced that it should be done and that I should direct it myself. I had some doubts about the extremes of violence but I knew the play had to be done.'[4] Up to that point, Johnstone was going to do the play 'but Bill got very high on it so I swapped it for the new N.F. Simpson play'.[5] Bond received a new contract for *Saved* on 30 April.

Gaskill's reading of the play caused him to consult George Devine, who, on 28 April, sent the new Artistic Director a memo concerning the possible reactions of the Lord Chamberlain:[6]

1 The intrinsic violence will automatically disturb the reader.

2 I have marked with pencil all the things I could spot that are likely to meet with objections. I may have missed some. It should be checked.

3 My advice is to cut out all the words we *know* will not be passed – such as bugger, arse, Christ etc. *before* submission. To have them in creates immediate hostility. The problem is to *get the play on with a licence*: not to alter the L.C. I presume.

4 I suggest that Charles Wood's technique is a good one. Swallow pride and reinvent, even one's own swear words and phrases. Re-write scenes, if necessary, to retain intrinsic rhythms etc. rather than arguing over words or phrases which he will never yield on.

5 Cut out stage directions which suggest sexual situations. I have bracketed these.

6 I think you might get away with the stockings scene if you present it carefully, as I have indicated. Often things are *said*, which don't always need to be *said* – except in free circumstances which you don't have.

7 As for the baby, I don't think the scatological bits will get through under any circumstances. Worse kinds of violence may well be passed but references to shit and piss will never pass in my opinion.

8 I suggest E.B. works on all this – show it to me again if you like . . .

9 The passages I've marked with a *squiggle* are dubious – finally it's give and take, but the shorter the list of dubious passages and *obvious* disallowances (piss, bugger etc.) the better chances you have.

P.S. a few less bloodies would help – esp. Act II.

Devine spoke accurately and with a good deal of experience, but the play was sent as it stood to the Lord Chamberlain's office on 24 June. It was returned on 30 July with a demand for over thirty cuts, as well as most of scenes six and nine. Bond would not cut his play, the Chamberlain was unresponsive to a visit to his office by Gaskill and Iain Cuthbertson on 3 August, and Gaskill reported the state of play to his Management committee on 9 August. Gaskill proposed that the Court be turned into a club in order to get *Saved* on. At Alfred Esdaile's suggestion, the committee agreed to open with the two plays which had a licence and then include *Saved* in the repertory season. There were misgivings about the extent to which the public might be confused by the inevitable mixture of public and private performances, but clearly neither Gaskill nor Bond was prepared to compromise further. As it already stood, *Saved* would be restricted to members of the English Stage Society, a situation at the Court which no one liked. Equally, though, no one believed that, having submitted thus far, there would be further repercussions.

The stage on which *Saved* was played was essentially as George Devine had made it. The original stage of 1888, complete with a grave trap and two star traps, was modified thus: the house curtain was removed and the proscenium borders were taken up, so that the proscenium was opened to its fullest height of 17′ 9¾″. By building out over the orchestra pit and making the original stage-level boxes into entrances, 9ft was added to the depth of the stage, making an overall depth of 18ft. The width of the stage amounted to 21′ 4″. There were a number of important consequences of these modifications. Taking up the borders made the lighting grid visible to the audience, then a novelty in English theatres. Jocelyn Herbert, who was both involved and influential in this early process, saw the advantages: 'Out of this grew the luxury of designing a lighting grid to suit each play, i.e. the grid to echo the contours of the set, which made it possible to light an acting area leaving darkness all round, thus creating a surround out of light.'[7] In addition, the height itself could be used. A designer influenced by Herbert's work, Hayden Griffin, noted that 'the secret at the Court (which I think Jocelyn discovered first) is that if you want space, you can't go very far backwards or sideways. But you can go upwards.'[8] The addition to the depth of the stage had two effects. It brought the overall proportions closer to that of a square, and it brought the actor into a more intimate relationship with the audience. Working in the space posed a real challenge for designers. Griffin regards his time at the Court as one where he learnt the most:[9]

> No designer who has worked there is ever likely to forget it . . . the fact that the Court is such a difficult stage – and yet such a beautifully proportioned one – means that anyone who has worked there knows how to use a space. . . . The extraordinary thing is that I've seen bigger landscapes on the tiny Court stage than anywhere else. Think of Bond's *Lear*, or the Gaskill *Macbeth*: the space seemed vast.

Gaskill echoes this: 'The wonderful thing about the Court is that it looks big enough to be an epic stage, just. If it was smaller it wouldn't be possible and if it were bigger it wouldn't be economically viable.'[10] The intimacy of actor and audience created by building out over the pit defied the assumptions created by the proscenium arch. Jack Shepherd, who was involved in the early years of Gaskill's time, felt that 'The buildup of atmosphere in the building can be, if things are going well, extraordinarily powerful. I can remember watching *In Celebration* . . . the atmosphere was terrifying and probably would have been lost elsewhere.'[11] The intensity which can be generated at the Court for the designer William Dudley means that 'you can state a poetic idea . . . more easily than at any other theatre I've known. It's such a lyrical stage. . . .'[12] And Bond himself once characterized it as 'a sort of in-between thing because, although it's a proscenium stage, it is wonderfully intimate'.[13] The intimacy seems vital as a distinguishing feature of the physical layout of the Court's stage. It compensated for a number of severe disadvantages. The sight lines at the sides of the auditorium were poor (designers refer to actors having to work in a diamond-shaped, or cone, area on the stage); the wing space is limited and the scene dock inadequate.

Much of what with hindsight is described as Royal Court style proceeds, therefore, from the nature of the building itself. Jocelyn Herbert's response to those who commiserate with her at having to work in such a small theatre and on such a small stage is to suggest that 'the answer you give depends on whether you are interested in designing plays or spectacles'.[14] Contained in her reply is the expression both of her own and Devine's conviction, which in turn was endorsed by Devine's successors:[15]

> George Devine wanted to get away from swamping the stage with decorative and naturalistic scenery; to let in light and air; to take the stage away from the director and designer and restore it to the actor and the text. This meant leaving space around the actors, and that meant the minimum of scenery and props, i.e. only those that served the actors and play: nothing that was for decorative purposes only, unless the text, or the style of the play, demanded it. So everything on the stage had to be even more carefully designed and made, as they would be so exposed on a comparatively bare stage, not supported by the trappings of a naturalistic set. . . . There was also the growing conviction that the bare stage was a very beautiful space and, as with a bare canvas, the moment you put one subject on it – even just a chair – all sorts of things happened. The actor could immediately use the space in so many different ways . . .

That Edward Bond had absorbed the basic approach described above is evident at the beginning of his career. His first performed play, *The Pope's Wedding*, contains an initial general account of what the stage should look like:[16]

> In these sixteen scenes the stage is dark and bare to the wings and back. Places are indicated by a few objects and these objects are described in the text. The objects are very real, but there must be no attempt to create the illusion of a 'real scene'. In the later scenes

the stage may be lighter and Scene Fifteen may be played in bright light.

For *Saved*, his demand is that 'The stage is as bare as possible – sometimes completely bare.'[17] Of the thirteen scenes, six are set in a living-room, two in a bedroom, three in a park and one each in a cell and a café. The living-room set consisted of three flats. The two side flats, together with the front of the stage 'make a triangle that slopes to a door back centre'. Gaskill recalls his first impressions of this setting:[18]

> He's very extraordinary. . . . I remember vividly when he described the first scene. . . . I didn't know what he meant when he said it's like a bowling alley. I'd never seen a piece of scenery like that before . . . and then he was very precise about all the details . . . and the colours. He was absolutely specific . . . it had a kind of enclosing feeling.

Placed within these flats was the furniture: a table and two chairs, a sofa, a television set, and an armchair. Bond's placing of the furniture was adhered to as precisely as the sightlines would allow, but their effect within the set was a strange one. John Gunter, the play's set and costume designer, found that the objects placed within the flats 'didn't relate to the triangle at all. That was the weird thing about it'.[19] Rather than the furniture and the setting offering a unified statement, the overall sense was of objects sitting in a space, which in turn enclosed those objects by means of the flats. The bedroom scenes repeated the pattern of the living-room. The same door flat was used and the furniture changed to a bed and a chair. The three park scenes took place on a bare stage, apart from scene two, which contained a rowing boat. A scene in a prison cell was done very simply via a flown-in-flat with a door in and Gaskill eventually was unhappy about this solution:[20]

> There is a problem about the cell scene, in that it's a very unexpected scene after the baby-killing, which could well be the end of the first half . . . so that it's quite difficult to establish it immediately as a prison, and I didn't think that was very good in the first production.

Finally, the café scene contained a roughly painted flat, three tables and chairs. In other words, as described in the text. As Gunter remembers, the rule was to do with what was essential. As he put it: 'It's only when Edward says what about the plastic flowers and one said that maybe we should . . . and Bill said absolutely not needed . . . all we really needed was the tables and chairs and they should be specific tables and chairs.'[21]

The object of such care is a play set in the South London area. The play opens with Pam, who is twenty-three, bringing back the twenty-one year old Len to her parents' house. She's picked him up for casual sex, but what looks as if it is about to be a scene where they have sex becomes a comic scene about not having sex. For Len is immediately shown as nervous and insecure, taking any opportunity to delay that presents itself. Pam's father, Harry, an old man of sixty-eight, interrupts the scene twice by putting his head round the door and leaving without saying anything. He is preparing to go on night-shift, and Len's alarm at someone else being in the house enables him to avoid what he is ostensibly there for. Instead, Len tells dirty jokes and creates the sound effects for Harry's benefit of an orgy. The scene closes with Harry leaving and Pam initiating the lovemaking. By the second scene, Pam and Len, now a lodger, are in a rowing boat in the local park and talking of marriage, but the gap between the two figures is already apparent and created primarily by Len's characteristic and important curiosity. He cannot help asking questions, even when Pam is clearly becoming riled by what she regards as his nosiness. The scene modulates from a cosy intimacy to begin with to Len's worming out of Pam that her parents lost a son in the war, who was blown up by a bomb in a park, and that her parents have not spoken to each other for years. The threadbare lives of the parents are established in scene two, as is Pam's unhappiness about them, and Len's determination not to end up in the same way. As they return the boat, Pam and Len encounter Fred, who is the same age as Len, and in charge of the boats. Fred's wit and crude jokes about Pam close the scene. Scene three stays in the park and introduces a group of young men, whose ages range from eighteen to twenty-five. Barry, Mike and Colin are having their dinner break. Pete is wearing a suit to attend the funeral of a child killed in a road accident in which he was involved. It is treated casually and brutally as a daring exploit and what this part of the scene demonstrates is both the high energy and the boredom of the group as a whole. The competition between them is fierce. Pete with his pipe sees himself as steadier, more mature than the others, while Barry constantly tries to impress the others. Len enters the scene and is recognized by Colin as having gone to the same school. Hilariously, Len's statement that he is about to be married is related by the group to Mary, Harry's wife, who enters with the shopping. The men feed off the confusion as Len and Mary exit until the dinner break ends.

Up to the end of scene three, the picture presented has been one of boredom, frustration, bottled up energy and laughter. This last quality went unremarked by most reviewers of the 1965 production, but it is an essential feature of the context of what happens later. The optimism claimed for the play by Bond resides not simply in the minimal gestures of reconstruction and judgment by Len of the others later in the play; it exists very strongly in both the situations and the characters. Len's desperate attempts in the opening scene to hide his alarm are recognizable on an ordinary realistic level. Pam and Len's near hysteria as they tell dirty jokes to each other prevent the scene's becoming predictable. The gang's seizing upon moments and extracting the maximum laughter from them makes much of scene three broadly comic. Yet Bond establishes these very carefully as moments, incidents, caught at one time, used, and then dropped. The pattern of the lives of his characters is thereby brilliantly conveyed. It implies the lack of a real life, of a consistency and of any kind of commitment. The play's physical context underpins this approach. If the living-room set encloses its furniture and the figures who exist there, the boat on a bare stage conveys the isolation of the two figures which sit there and the bare stage setting for the park simply conveys emptiness. By avoiding a style which would call for a formal narrative progression, the play is thereby able to show moments, extracts from an implied narrative. Isolated in this manner, the objects (including the actors) on the stage form their own commentary. They make, as William Dudley notes (see p. 32) 'a poetic idea'. What follows from this is that the audience is invited to observe and examine, rather than to suppose that the line of the play is available from an immersion in the psychology of the characters. As Bond puts it:[22]

> Of course the plays require the psychological integrity of the characters, but I have no difficulty in creating this and it's only when that's done that my . . . major work really begins. What you have to dramatize is the commentary and to show not the structures which the characters impose but those which define them: the characters' freedom is only possible when they themselves understand those structures sufficiently enough to change or control them.

Saved dispassionately examines the inability of all but one of its characters to understand the structures which define them. From the fourth scene, some of the comedy begins to drop away. Pam now has a child, which she insists is Fred's, and her animosity to Len is vented throughout. Her attempts to get him to leave the house produce only the response that Len will stay because of the child. As Mary goes about the business of cooking, and Harry sits, partly asleep, Pam gets ready for Fred's arrival, and the child begins to cry. It will cry for most of the scene. The main response is to turn up the volume of the television set. It is a terrifying scene and carefully judged to force the audience to put its horrified responses to the rage of the child against the indifference of the characters on stage. None of them cares sufficiently to do anything about the baby. It is an annoyance but no one will admit responsibility. Even Len says only 'It'll cry itself t'sleep.' Harry refuses to become involved. Mary relies on aspirins. Pam resents the child as a burden and when Fred arrives she puts the baby in her mother's room. Pam is beginning in this scene to show a real depression as the scope of her life becomes even more narrow.

The scene had begun with Harry sitting in the dark. After Pam and Mary have left, Harry surprisingly talks to Len a little and the scene ends once more with Harry in darkness.

Scene five is a summary and one not originally envisaged. It 'was added after the play was written, and is really unnecessary – nothing happens that isn't made plain somewhere else. But somehow I felt that before the killing it was necessary to sum things up for the audience.'[23] Fred has lost interest in Pam, who lies upstairs in Len's room, pathetically waiting for Fred to turn up. Len, as ever, tries to help her, treats her as a sulky child, making her take her medicine, and straightening the bedclothes. It all imposes itself on Pam as a series of oppressions, particularly when Len brings her child in to try to make her acknowledge it. Pam only comes out of her depression on hearing that Fred might drop round. He doesn't and in the sixth scene Pam takes the child to him in the park. Before Pam's arrival with the pram, Len talks to Fred, who is fishing (out over the front stalls). It is here that Len's persistent curiosity is most apparent, as he tries to understand why Pam is obsessed with Fred. As he had irritated Pam previously, so now he annoys Fred with a stream of questions. Mike enters. He's also been fishing and he and Fred decide on a Saturday night out. What wrecks the plans is Pam's arrival with the baby, who has been drugged with aspirin. Pam's pleading turns to anger and she storms off the stage, leaving the pram. The night out is spoilt. The rest of the group drift in, all ready for the evening. Gradually the pram attracts attention. The scene is most carefully paced. What happens evolves out of waiting, larking about. The destruction of the child is triggered not by animosity against the baby but by Pete who 'touches' Barry, and all the pent-up energy begins to find its outlet with the child. Fred remains aloof from the initial activity. As Gaskill said:[24]

> You get that wonderful, extraordinary perspective of Fred being
> downstage, just lying there, doing nothing, just half sitting with legs
> stretched out, and the whole of the other scene is behind him . . .
> like a film director would see it. That he must have seen in his mind
> as he wrote it . . .

As the pace mounts, so does the abuse of the child until it is destroyed. But the focus is always on the group rather than the child. Gaskill points out the effect upon the scene of the silent child:[25]

> The killing of a child in a pram when it doesn't cry – it can make no
> statement about the pain it feels – has already a kind of abstract,
> symbolic quality about it, although one tries to do it as naturalistically
> as possible but there is something very strange about it because you
> know there's only a dummy. You are watching a kind of ritualised
> action. What you're really watching is the boys.

Nevertheless, the scene demands great care in production. As the park bell goes for closing time, the youths initially do not react, but continue to assault the baby. Maintaining the credibility of this moment is a delicate matter. Gaskill recalls Keith Johnstone once saying that 'it wasn't quite convincing that they went on after the bell in the park sounds, that the instinct of self-preservation would be stronger than the instinct to hurt the child and it's things like that where the actual direction seems quite tricky, because you have to convince the audience that they are a group of real boys, that it isn't just a ritualised murder. . . . I used to spend a long time working at it.'[26] Bond says of his text that the youths are in one way possessed and defines it as 'atavistic fury' (Author's Note). They come into a kind of collective animal state and go off making a noise like that of a swarm of bees. After a while, Pam finally returns, collects the pram and leaves. That she doesn't notice what has happened speaks volumes for the degree of attention she actually pays to her child.

Where such a scene would conventionally provide an ending to part one, Bond then adds the brief scene seven. Fred has been arrested and is waiting in a prison cell, probably to be remanded. The scene is a vital one for Bond's purposes. It confronts the audience's desire for revenge but places Fred in a context where his indignant assertion that 'The bloody police don't do their job', although designed to conceal his guilt from Pam, identifies him as both a murderer and also a victim who cannot comprehend. A figure who can say 'It was only a kid' demands of an audience that it both judge Fred and Fred's situation. A society which allows Fred eventually to emerge from prison as a glamorous figure to his friends may need to look to itself, rather than suppose that Fred is an aberration. It also needs to judge Len, for it is in this scene that Len reveals that he watched the killing. He is in effect as guilty. Len's inaction is important. An easier course would have been to remove Len entirely, but the text insists on involving him as spectator. It enables Len, who spends most of the play as an outsider, to arrive later at a judgment of Fred and of his situation in the house, but crucially the judgment is minimal. Len learns and begins to articulate what he has learnt. It is very little. It is also more than anyone else in the play.

Apart from one scene (scene ten) which sets Fred's release from prison in a café, the rest of the play returns to the house. Scenes eight, nine and eleven follow the growing pressure on the family. Pam is preparing for Fred's release the following week. Harry and Mary in their own ways are trying to establish contact with Len. Harry in scene eight talks to Len, but only when they are alone together. As soon as anyone else enters, Harry reverts to silence and his ironing. Similarly, Mary, as before, treats Len as if he had replaced the son she lost in the war. Throughout the domestic scenes up to scene eleven, she alternately scolds and cossets him. Each of the parents attempts to enlist Len in aiding the bankruptcy of their lives, while Len for Pam is the same continual irritant as before. Her nervousness at the imminent release of Fred finds its outlet in scene eight in a furious row between her and Len over Pam's missing *Radio Times*. By scene nine, Bond begins to gather together the underlying references to the model of Oedipus. Using the belief that '*Oedipus Rex* isn't a play about family trouble but about the disorders in a society',[27] Bond builds a formal underlying pattern which identifies elements of Oedipus, Laius and Jocasta in Len, Harry and Mary. In scene nine, Mary is alone with Len and she is preparing to go to the cinema. The underlying comic eroticism of the scene, as the two of them discuss sex, with Mary dressing in front of Len, becomes more explicit when Len repairs the stocking Mary is wearing. The dialogue is skilfully permeated with innuendo and Harry witnesses the scene. Len fails to persuade Mary to stay in and the scene ends with his beginning to masturbate. If Mary's relationship with Harry is over, she still feels enough to suggest another one with Len. Where an obvious course would have been to show immediately the consequences of Harry's seeing the incident, Bond instead switches to a café for scene ten. Pam and Len wait for Fred's arrival. To the rest of the group, Fred's new status is assured. The group closes ranks to protect its leader as Pam tries desperately to reclaim him. Len, as always, watches and, as always, tries to get from Fred an account of what it felt like to kill the baby. By the end of the scene, Pam is rejected and Len tries to give her his judgment of Fred as a consolation: 'They ain' done 'im no good. 'Es gone back like a kid. Yer well out a it.' Len's view of Fred is important, as is his pity for Pam and his refusal to desert her.

The Oedipal strands to the play reach a climax in scene eleven. After years of silence, Harry and Mary quarrel violently over the scene Harry saw earlier. The row should traditionally involve Len destroying his 'father', Harry, and sleeping with his 'mother', Mary. But Len breaks the cycle by controlling the fight as Mary hits Harry with a teapot. Oedipus is rejected, as Pam, Cassandra-like, cries with despair. Bond had noted in his first draft that Pam 'repeats over and over again her prophecy of future calamity'.

Bond explains the importance of the Oedipus story in his 'Author's Note' to the published edition. If Len begins as 'Oedipus', a stranger in the house, and subsequently becomes embroiled in the events within the house, and if, thus far, Bond allows the parallels to stand, the refusal to re-enact Sophocles's conclusion to his play turns *Saved* 'into what is formally a comedy'. The significance of using and then discarding the Greek model is that it indicates alternatives to despair. That Len does not understand but does act to prevent disaster indicates crucially for Bond the capacity of individuals to take control, however briefly, of their own lives.

As the quarrel subsides, Pam cries pathetically: 'No 'ome. No friends. Baby dead. Gone. Fred gone' and even Len appears to give up. In scene twelve, in Len's room, he is packing, when Harry, with his head bandaged, and dressed in white combinations and pale socks, comes to ask Len to stay in the house. Harry speaks for his family's needs in vaguely recognizing Len as necessary for survival. For the only time in the play, Harry talks of himself and of his experiences during the war. He offers statements about himself with an intimacy which has the effect of persuading Len to stay, if indeed he ever intended to go. Thus the family, silently in the last scene, accepts Len's presence, as he mends a chair broken in the row between Harry and Mary. It is totally silent apart from one line by Len: 'Fetch me 'ammer', and the noise involved in repairing the chair. The family sits in a social stalemate. The minimal gesture of optimism resides in what Len is doing, but on a larger scale the fact that Len is still there, now fitted for and accepting the role which he has been evolving throughout the play adds strength to Bond's original assertion in his 'Author's Note' that the play is 'almost irresponsibly optimistic'.[28]

Gaskill's direction of *Saved* in 1965 was centred upon precision and accuracy. He described it as 'a very pure work in every way . . . a sense of everything being fixed physically in space' and thought that the speaking of the text is 'almost the first essential':[29]

> It's got to sound right. . . . I suppose you could describe the style as a kind of pared-down naturalism; the actual placing of everyone on the stage sculpturally is very important, and the actors have to have a kind of awareness of the economy of themselves, without that becoming in any sense a stylization. It was a laconic style that should feel very natural, but should look simplified. . . . When you have a thing which is extremely accurately written, the text has to be extremely precisely played even in the moments of extreme violence. And the orchestration has to be exactly right. And in working like that, what comes out is bound to be very controlled . . .

Richard Butler, who played Harry, remembers that rehearsals only rarely included any improvisation: 'We never had soul-searching group-therapy sessions . . . which can be pretty bloody tedious actually',[30] and Jane Howell as Assistant Director watched Gaskill directing and commented:[31]

> I couldn't understand it. I wondered when he was going to start directing the play. . . . He rarely puts pressure on an actor when he's happy with the casting . . . it was an explicit thing at the Court that you were there at the service of the text and you weren't there to show off . . . you could start using your brain instead of thinking your soul was important. The emotion followed. . . .

Thus the demands of the play and the prime belief as to the supremacy of the text came together from this production.

Nevertheless, the pressure on a production forced out of the public arena mounted steadily. Butler felt that the Company became 'more and more nervous as rehearsals progressed':[32]

> I remember the first night very well. Bill was white at the gills and we were all a bit edgy, more so than on an ordinary first night and I remember him saying to us, 'Look, don't get upset if people protest from the front, if people walk out, be prepared for that', he said, almost visibly shaking, and in the event nothing like that happened. The audience were a very civilised lot . . . there was one walkout and that was a critic's wife. It was a nailbiting time.

However, one member of the audience on 3 November saw it differently:[33]

> I've always felt the stories of the opening of Ibsen's *Ghosts* and the first performance of Stravinsky's *The Rite of Spring* to be exaggerated romance justified by theatrical licence. That night at the Royal Court I came to believe in their veracity. There *was* verbal interruption and abuse in the course of the play, and there *was* the odd physical punch-up in the foyers at the interval and afterwards. The cause was in particular the scene in which the baby was stoned to death . . .

Most of the attention given to the play did focus upon the baby-stoning scene. The attention made the play almost instantly notorious, and the Court held a teach-in on 14 November, chaired by Kenneth Tynan, where prominent people and public alike aired their views. During the teach-in, Gaskill directed the quarrel between Harry and Mary (scene eleven) in two ways, in an attempt to show that his production style was based upon restraint, wherever possible, so as to enable his audience to watch the events with a degree of detachment. As one critic noted, 'the greater economy of gesture and emphasis in the second run-through was far more effective than the first'.[34] The controversy began to subside, but revived quickly when on 13 December, Detective Chief Inspector Rees visited the Court and questioned Gaskill under caution, as well as Iain Cuthbertson. On 5 January 1966, summonses were served on Gaskill as Artistic Director, Greville Poke as Company Secretary and Alfred Esdaile as the licensee to appear at Great Marlborough Street Magistrates Court on 13 January. The charge was that of presenting an unlicensed play contrary to section fifteen of the Theatres Act of 1843. In fact, the Court asked for and got a postponement, since 13 January was the opening night of *A Chaste Maid in Cheapside*. It did not prevent the Court holding a meeting with its counsel, John Gower, on 13 January, to try to determine what was behind the charge. Clearly there was confusion, since club performances up to this time had not been prosecuted. Counsel's view of the matter, as recorded in the transcript, was unequivocal:

I think he [the censor] is gunning for the Royal Court as an avant-garde theatre. There are pressure groups watching the plays and presenting complaints in a concrete form and forcing him to take action. It is an attack on the Royal Court and not on club theatres in general.

What was less clear was the real nature of the charge. It appeared that, since 'a whole lot of policemen . . . got in' without producing membership cards of the English Stage Society, the charge would say that there was no real difference between club and public performances. In other words, the censor might be acting to secure the distinction between the two, even though the charge was one of presenting an unlicensed play. Counsel advised against pleading guilty, since such a plea would generate adverse publicity, prohibit the right to test evidence in cross examination and might result in the theatre's licence being revoked. Equally, what could happen would depend on the magistrate. Even though the charge did not include one of obscenity, counsel's view was that 'we may get a magistrate who becomes personally involved . . . and may say that this theatre has made itself a vehicle for presenting dirty, unlicensed plays disliked by the Lord Chamberlain and therefore he might find it his duty to close it up'. Gower further urged that the theatre find 'people with as much standing in the community as possible to speak for the play'. Joe Hodg-kinson for the Arts Council spoke for the theatre in arguing that 'We all want to know what is behind it and the only way to find out is to plead not guilty on the grounds it was the Society who presented the play and not the Company.'

Saved was thus in the ironical position of being denied a public audience on the one hand and now being prosecuted on the grounds that the public had seen it. At the first hearing on 14 February before the magistrate, Leo Gradwell, Oliver Nugent for the Director of Public Prosecutions, alleged that members of the public had seen the play without being required to furnish proof that they were members of the Society. Two such members were Ronald Hill, assistant secretary to the Lord Chamberlain's office, and Detective Sergeant Robert Potter. The former, answering questions by John Gower, defending, asserted that 'Warning shots were fired across their [the Society's] bows on two previous occasions.' The prosecution demanded that *Saved* be taken off immediately. Gower said that their case was that the club was a bona fide one and, since the performances were therefore lawful, they would continue. The hearing was adjourned until 7 March. What had emerged from the hearing was that the proceedings were not a test case to establish the legal position of theatre clubs. The summons, had that been the case, would have been brought under section fourteen of the Theatres Act which enabled the Chamberlain to forbid the presentation of any stage play 'anywhere in

Great Britain'. Section fifteen, on the other hand, provided penalties for anyone who acted in or presented a stage play for hire without a licence. The crucial phrase is 'for hire'.

The second hearing of the case took place on 7 March. Leo Gradwell rejected a defence claim that there was no case to answer, whereupon Gower called Laurence Olivier, Lord Harewood and Norman Collins, all of whom, but especially Olivier, spoke in eloquent praise and defence of the Court. Olivier, in particular, testified to the importance of the Court as a breeding ground for the whole English theatre. Like the others, he asserted that the regulations governing a club production were strictly enforced. Nevertheless, at the final hearing on 1 April at Marylebone Road Court, the danger and ludicrousness of the affair emerged. Leo Gradwell ruled that performances of *Saved* had contravened the Theatres Act. The defendants were all conditionally discharged for a year and the Company was ordered to pay fifty guineas costs. John Gower pointed up the dilemma which the case had brought about. The prosecution was saying that if the presentation had been by a genuine theatre club then no offence had been committed. Gower was arguing exactly the same point but that the English Stage Society was a genuine theatre club. The magistrate, observed Gower, was saying that both prosecution and defence were wrong. The magistrate was reported as saying: 'I am not saying a word. I am sitting on the rock of the statute and inviting you as Perseus to come and rescue me.'[35] Though the picture is comic, the potential consequences were not. Publicly, Gaskill's reaction was to talk of an appeal against the ruling and to feel that 'this decision is a serious blow to the theatre, which will be all the poorer for it. It means that the few brilliant but controversial plays will not be performed without censorship.'[36] Some, however, felt that the case would strengthen the arguments for abolishing the system of licensing plays. Kenneth Tynan felt that 'Now . . . the full extent of the Lord Chamberlain's powers have been shown, it will be the more difficult to make excuses for them.'[37] Privately, the Court was determined to continue with the battle. The Artistic committee meeting on 19 April heard that, if it wished, the English Stage Society could, once the year's conditional discharge was up, present an unlicensed play and, if it were to be prosecuted, the case would have to be retried. By a curious turn of events, within the year, Bond's *Early Morning* was delivered to the Court (early in 1967) and the battle against the censor surfaced again (see chapter 3). The pre-censorship of the theatre, a growing issue in Devine's time, became one of the central battles of the mid-1960s. At that centre was the Court. Greville Poke testifies that 'the whole atmosphere of everybody fighting together for what they believed in cemented friendships, cemented beliefs. It was a very remarkable period. . . .'[38] It is also sadly remarkable that by the end of the decade, *Saved* had been given forty-five separate professional productions in twelve countries. Thirty-three of these productions happened before the British public was allowed to see the play for the first time in February 1969.[39]

The first production of *Saved* was overshadowed by the prosecution it engendered. A play which in many respects was a perfect practical example of Devine's theories about stage usage (see above, p. 32), which fulfilled the convictions to do with the spareness and economy of stage and actors, the eschewing of naturalistic trappings and irrelevant decoration, and the concentration only upon what was absolutely necessary to demonstrate the nature of the text, was, because of its subject matter, hounded by the press and by the law. Yet the play set a style and an approach which was to hallmark much of the best work done at the Court during this period. Devine had argued for the restoration of the stage to the actor and to the text, away from the intrusions of the director and the designer. It was a belief shared by his successor and most of the directors who subsequently worked at the Court. With *Saved*, Gaskill made an opening and definitive statement.

3 · From April 1966 to March 1968

On 31 March, Gaskill reviewed the Company's position, as agreed with the Management committee in August 1965. In a policy statement for 1966 to 1967, he accepted that the repertory season had not done well at the box-office (though it should be noted that 47 per cent of seats had been sold and that the difference between the financial capacity figure of 32 per cent and the seats sold reflected not simply seat price reductions but also an increase in the number of students buying the cheaper seats)[1] but argued that 'So far the increase in costs has not been enormous.' He was clearly under pressure to take measures to redeem the box-office position and warned that 'if we are to continue in repertory and import leading actors from time to time and increase the lavishness of productions the costs – particularly of actors and production costs – will mount steeply'. Part of the reason for suggesting that increased costs would result from importing leading actors and increasing the lavishness of productions was an attempt to hang on to a large increase in grant from the Arts Council. The grant rose to some £85,000 for 1966–7 and Gaskill in a subsequent Management committee meeting (28 June), which discussed the policy statement insisted on stating why the grant increase, originally given for a continuing repertory policy, should remain even though the Court was modifying the repertory system. Thus, if the Court subsequently did achieve a measure of commercial success, the grant money might be available for other kinds of work.

Gaskill clung to the idea of repertory playing for as long as he could. He accepted that, unless there was an unlikely surge in box-office takings, the policy should be one of reverting to straight runs from the end of July 1966. It could not be done before July because of actors' contracts. Should the takings increase before July 'I think we should consider a more limited form of repertory, i.e. two plays a week rather than three for shorter seasons of three to four months, with gaps between for straight runs and therefore possible transfers.' It is not difficult to gloss this as an attempt to maintain the essential life of the repertory system, while at

44

the same time deliberately employing 'prop' productions to bring in the money. As Gaskill said in the same document, 'I think it is very important that the continuity of the work and the excitement, which has been generated in an admittedly small audience, which springs from the repertory system, should not be given up without a struggle.' He had organized the budgets, however, to meet a policy of straight runs from July 'for the time being'. A further nod in the direction of economy was the proposed reduction of the artistic administration to an Artistic Director, an Associate Director, two Assistant Directors, a Literary Manager and a Casting Director. At the same time, it had proved, against his hopes, very difficult to integrate studio work into the work of the Company, but Gaskill asked for permanent contracts for six young actors both to understudy, play small parts and be developed as a studio group within the Company.

This change in policy was not at this stage made public. The company celebrated its tenth birthday in April by giving a press reception on 5 April to announce the establishing of the George Devine Award. John Osborne gave details of the fund. It was hoped to raise about £20,000, which would enable annual awards of £1,000 to be made to a promising playwright, director or designer. Such recipients would be welcomed as working visitors at the Berliner Ensemble, the Théâtre de France, the National and the Royal Shakespeare Company.[2] At the reception, which was a week after the Company had been found guilty in the *Saved* trial (see chapter 2), Neville Blond reviewed briefly the first ten years of the Company's life, noting that he and George Devine 'had our fights of course'. Gaskill was clearly conscious of the Company's current public image: 'There are no doubts that the English Stage Company will still be here in another ten years time', and he added that by its nature as an experimental theatre it was bound to go through bad periods. The Royal Court was perhaps the only subsidized theatre anywhere which criticized the establishment in a serious way.[3] The Company marked the birthday with a production, opening 11 April, of Granville-Barker's *The Voysey Inheritance*. During the opening week, there were free lunchtime performances of Keith Johnstone's *Clowning*. The story of the Company in brochure form would be on sale. The lights in Sloane Square would be switched on. And 'There has been mention of a brass band', added Gaskill.[4] On the same occasion, Blond voiced the perennial worry of the Company: 'We are trying to put on a show but we are not being successful, let's face it. And we are not being successful because the vehicles we have to ride on are not good enough. We would welcome any young man with good plays to offer.'[5]

The Voysey Inheritance ran in repertory for fifty-five performances, alongside some performances of *Serjeant Musgrave's Dance* and a new

Wesker play, *Their Very Own and Golden City*, which opened on 19 May for twenty-six performances. It is the case that Gaskill happily saw Barker's play produced, since he had always thought Barker underrated. Not quite the same feelings held true for the Wesker play and in one way Gaskill was still satisfying the Court's household gods. He was in fact persuaded by Edward Bond to put the Wesker on 'because of the largeness of the idealistic theme'.[6] The box-office from these plays (41.2 per cent and 40.1 per cent) was probably instrumental in finally eroding the possiblity of continuing in repertory for the foreseeable future. At the same time, and most ironically, the first transfer under Gaskill's regime came from a Sunday night production of Christopher Hampton's *When Did You Last See My Mother?* Hampton's first play had been performed by the Oxford University Dramatic Society on 24 February. It played at the Court on 5 and 19 June. On 4 July, it opened at the Comedy Theatre for a three-week run.[7] A Heathcote Williams play, *The Local Stigmatic*, first seen on Sunday 27 March, was given another performance on 26 June.[8] Both writers were to become an important part of the Court's subsequent work.

The general atmosphere at the Court at this point in 1966 was uneasy in the sense that there was pressure to end the repertory system and a dearth of good new plays. At an Artistic committee meeting of 19 April, it was reported that Bond, Cregan, Frank Hilton and Heathcote Williams had been commissioned and it was hoped that these would produce plays for the 1966–7 season. For the moment, however, the immediate future programme would consist mainly of revivals. At the same time, there were plans to use the club space for presenting new plays, or scenes from plays 'in primitive conditions'. The possibilities for productions ranged from Charles Wood's *Dingo*, to *Loot* by Joe Orton, to Nicol Williamson's version of *Lulu*, to a new version of Brecht's *Mann ist Mann* (it took until March 1971 to clear a production with the Brecht estate). *The Widowing of Mrs. Holroyd* was a possible choice for another Lawrence play at the Court. Osborne had said he would have a play ready by the summer which could be included. Other possibilities included *A Provincial Life* which was being adapted by Peter Gill. On a more definite note, it was reported that Sir Alec Guinness would like to return to the Court, 'but only if he could play in repertory'. Guinness was interested in a documentary on the trial of Charles I, and might play in *Three Sisters* or *The Madras House*. What this demonstrates emphatically is that, far from the ideal of five-year plans, or even one-year plans, a Company such as this at certain stages could only list possibles and probables. At the same time, stringent financial savings had to be made. The Management committee on 22 April considered the role and value of the Literary Manager and whether the job could be combined with that of an Assistant Director.

The same amalgamation was suggested for Company Manager and House Manager. An assistant Wardrobe Mistress was dispensed with. And a report was called for as to whether the store was still necessary once the Company went out of repertory. Even the use of the telephones was to be monitored. It was at this meeting that Keith Johnstone asked for it to be minuted that 'he and Iain Cuthbertson would not be continuing at the Royal Court in the future'. The Management committee was clearly determined in the future to keep a very tight grip on the Company's finances, partly because of the attitude of the Arts Council. The Arts Council in turn, now the recipient of an increase of nearly two million pounds for the year 1966–7, was anxious that its clients did not exceed their subsidy, and requested that companies would undertake to stay within budgetary limits. In this, the Arts Council had the support of the Court's chairman, who, throughout the months to follow, kept a very careful eye on the Company's affairs (Management committee, 28 April 1966). On the one hand, the Court needed to proceed very cautiously; on the other, there was proof of its reputation in the form of invitations to Zurich, Venice, Berlin and Prague. At the same meeting on 28 April, one more link with the past was severed, as Neville Blond announced the resignation of Ronald Duncan from the Council. As before (see chapter 1) Duncan made no secret of his disillusion with the way the Court had developed and told the press that as with Devine, now with Gaskill, 'any work not in accord with their political views' was excluded from the Company. Gaskill rebutted this, perhaps with a weary irony:[9]

We're often accused now of having too diffuse a policy, lacking a strong social or artistic theory. One of the main problems is knowing just what audience we're going for. *The Voysey Inheritance* has pulled in the West Enders, but the younger audience which will take a risk on a new play is still very small, though devoted. We have to try to strike a balance between popular but not obvious revivals and the right new plays when they appear.

By this stage, the straight run policy, to be initiated with Iain Cuthbertson's version of *Ubu Roi*, which would be the first professional English production, consisted of eight plays for the season. They would take an average of six weeks per show. However, by 20 May, Gaskill had decided that such a policy carried real dangers and he announced to a no doubt startled Management committee that, instead, there should be four major productions of masterpieces, which would run for eight weeks each and four shows, ideally new plays, which would run for four weeks each. Some insight into Gaskill's thinking is contained in a letter to Lord Harewood, written after the 20 May meeting but on the same day. It shows Gaskill's awareness of the probable annoyance of the Management committee, and his using Harewood, as chairman of the Artistic

committee, in the way Devine used to. If George Harewood agreed with
Gaskill's ideas, there would be a much better chance of those ideas being
accepted, since Harewood and Neville Blond were close friends. In the
letter, Gaskill says that he probably upset the committee that morning
'by projecting a very radical change of policy'. His concern about a season
of eight, long running productions is partly derived from the figures for
The Voysey Inheritance: 'If a play like *Voysey* does not ring the bell we are
in real trouble.' Reflecting on the six months past, he told Harewood that
there is 'a dearth of new plays and my attempts to revitalise the situation
by putting on the plays of our own writers in which I did not always
have an absolute confidence show predictable results in critical reaction
and box office take'. The central part of the letter identifies a certain lack
of commitment on occasions:

> Perhaps most important of all I feel that all of us, in the attempt to
> recapture the early tradition of the Court, sometimes do things for
> which we do not have an intense enthusiasm. When we say to
> ourselves what would we really like to do we always say jokingly,
> *King Lear*, *Three Sisters* and *Galileo* and I have come to the conclusion
> that it would be better not to joke and to do seriously those things
> which most stir one's blood. It is certainly impossible to say of any
> show under the present system that it would automatically fill the
> theatre for eight weeks without an international star.

Obviously, in proposing to take this line, Gaskill is only too aware of the
inevitable comparison with the two major subsidized companies:

> Our failure with classics, particularly Shakespeare, in the past has
> been largely due to having an *ad hoc* company assembled for the
> show and rehearsals for only a month. Now that the National and the
> Royal Shakespeare both have a much longer rehearsal period and
> have set a very high standard, I think that if we are going to compete
> on that level we have to create similar conditions.

Gaskill's idea of four plus four is similar to Devine's strategy earlier in
the Court's life but the key element is one of advance planning, and the
model resembles more the season of 1965 planned by Anthony Page and
that at the Queen's Theatre in 1964:

> The main advantage of all this is that one can plan a firm programme
> for a year ahead in the knowledge that the plays themselves are sure
> masterpieces and will always command a public, thus giving us time
> to set in motion a series of Sunday nights and the reorganization of
> the script department and the search for new writers. . . . I do feel a
> real enthusiasm for the idea.

Tactically what Gaskill was doing was priming Lord Harewood, for the
Management committee's response was to ask for a joint meeting with
the Artistic committee to discuss the change of policy. At the joint

meeting, Gaskill outlined his most recent thoughts, which were essentially contained in his letter to Harewood on 20 May. He is remarkably forthright about the repertory system in saying that 'With the exception of *Saved* the ability of repertory to nurse an unsuccessful play has not been proved. Conversely, a successful play such as *The Voysey Inheritance* seems to have been damaged by being taken out of the bill soon after its opening.' The central admission concerns flexibility: 'much of the excitement at the Court in the past has come from a certain flexibility in being able to put on new plays at short notice and this I feel has been lost during the repertory system . . . the Court under George Devine was essentially an empirical theatre exploiting talent as it appeared and I think it would be foolish after nine months to make a large new policy statement about the Court's future'. Neither committee had known what Gaskill was to say on 20 May. The Management committee was clearly rather wary of the proposals. Neville Blond's immediate and proper response was to ask if a play such as *Three Sisters* would transfer. Gaskill had to reply that if Alec Guinness were to be in it, it would not, since Guinness would not have the time. Hodgkinson, for the Arts Council, felt the Company might be to some extent moving away 'from the individualistic line' of the English Stage Company. There were, too, doubts as to whether four new good plays could be found. Gaskill countered with the argument that a lot of work would be done with the Sunday night productions.

The proposals were accepted, though with misgivings, but it is the case that for the next three years there was no deficit. Gaskill went ahead and reorganized his staff for the new season. In a letter to Neville Blond (7 June), he indicated his wish to replace Cuthbertson and Johnstone with Desmond O'Donovan as Associate Director. O'Donovan had been one of Devine's assistants, had directed *Spring Awakening* at the Court, Peter Gill's play, *The Sleepers' Den*, and the revival of *The Knack* under Gaskill. He was currently working at the National. Gaskill was clearly conscious that, unlike Devine, he had not yet got the nucleus of trainee directors, of which he was a product. The time when Devine had a number of assistants 'was certainly one of the healthier times in our ten years'. He therefore suggests, apart from himself, Jane Howell, 'who is a splendid director', and who would supervise the script department, O'Donovan as Associate and two assistants.

While Gaskill was implementing these changes, the Company in its traditional way, having accepted Gaskill's ideas, then closed ranks to present a united front. When the Management committee met on 20 June, Linklater for the Arts Council wanted to know what the difference now would be between the Court, the National and the Royal Shakespeare and the rest of the committee rose to the challenge. The Court provided the competition for the Royal Shakespeare, as that theatre did for the

National. The Court's function as the major risk taker on new work remained. Neville Blond pointed out that the National owed its existence to staff and actors trained at the Court. When Linklater referred to the change in Court policy, he was told that the policy consisted of reverting to an earlier one, of having four 'prop' productions during the year.

At the same time, the formation of the future programme was not yet absolutely clear, and had changed considerably from 19 April when the Artistic committee last met. At its next meeting, on 21 June, the committee was told that *Dingo* had been heavily cut by the Lord Chamberlain 'and had lost most of its flavour'; *Loot* could not find a director; *Mann ist Mann* would be a long time in the translating; an earlier idea of *The Madras House* with Guinness was dropped because it was too soon after *The Voysey Inheritance*; and *Lulu* might be planned for the Aldwych by Peter Hall. Remaining from the original list was a Lawrence play, which could be 'fitted in to the programme at any time'. By June, the programme consisted of *Three Men for Colverton*, the commissioned work by David Cregan, *The Tutor* (a Brecht adaptation of a play by Lenz), Gozzi's *The King Stag* for Christmas (with which Devine had opened the Young Vic in 1947), the new Osborne play or, as an alternative, Nicol Williamson in *King Lear*, Bond's new play for March 1967 and *Three Sisters*, 'with Sir Alec Guinness, if he wanted to return to the Court . . .'. The question of what Guinness would do was still open. He wanted, as reported in the meeting, to work in the autumn on a comedy. Gaskill had suggested to him Jonson's *The Silent Woman* but Guinness was not interested. Guinness wanted to do *A Trip to Scarborough* but Gaskill did not like the idea and suggested a Farquhar play. No one at this stage is anywhere near raising the idea of *Macbeth*, which is what finally came about. The programme was agreed, with the exception of *King Lear*, which was held over for a year. In fact, the only survivors from this list were the Cregan play, a Lawrence play and *Three Sisters*. The others either did not materialize at all or appeared rather later and it demonstrates vividly the day-to-day problems of constructing any programme, let alone a balanced one. Unsurprisingly, the Council at its 5 July meeting, presented with the new policy, agreed only with reservations. J. E. Blacksell 'asked what our artistic policy was now', to be told by Gaskill that the basic policy had not changed. Peggy Ashcroft pointed out that the Court had lost its monopoly of new plays, given the existence of the National and the Royal Shakespeare and there were clear concerns about the production of classics at the Court. Gaskill, in a statement which was shortly to have quite considerable repercussions, argued that the Court's version of classics would be distinctive: 'He wanted to present Shakespeare, for example, differently to the National and Aldwych but did not think there had ever been such a thing as a Royal Court style.' Twelve days later, at a Management committee meeting, Gaskill announced a production of *Macbeth* with Guinness and Simone Signoret, to open in mid-October. Helen Montagu was to seek permission from the Ministry of Labour and Equity for Signoret to work at the Royal Court.

The first two main bill productions under the changed policy were *Ubu Roi* (21 July) and *Three Men for Colverton* (21 September). In between, the theatre was let to the National Youth Theatre for productions of *Bartholomew Fair* and David Halliwell's *Little Malcolm and His Struggle against the Eunuchs*. One Sunday night double bill appeared. Orton's *The Ruffian on the Stair* was accompanied by Howard Brenton's *It's My Criminal*.[10] Though both of the main bill productions were well received critically, they neither of them did well at the box-office. The first managed 38.3 per cent, the second 27.1 per cent. David Cregan's play was one Gaskill was doubtful about and perhaps fell into the category of commissioned work which wasn't quite up to par. As Cregan himself said:[11]

> When it came to *Three Men for Colverton*, he distrusted the play to begin with, and it was only because Desmond O'Donovan liked it . . . that it got done. But I remember when it really was very near going on, he said, 'I'd love to get my hands on it', and years later said that it was the one play from that time he would like to do again. Yet it didn't quite satisfy his rigorous questioning, back at the beginning.

Gaskill's next production was *Macbeth*. At the end of July, it was announced, together with the policy changes for the season. If anything, the casting of Simone Signoret attracted more attention than that of Guinness. She had never played Shakespeare or appeared on an English stage or played a stage part anywhere in English. She was, however, an accomplished film actress, and never under any illusions about what she was taking on, when Guinness invited her to play Lady Macbeth. In July, immediately after she had accepted the role, her instinctive worry was to do with the play's language: 'My only fear now is how I speak the words. My aim must be to ensure that people in the theatre do not laugh because they feel I am torturing the language. . . .'[12] Guinness himself had attempted the part only once, at Sheffield, when he was twenty-three, and that was because the actor playing the part had dropped out and Guinness had to learn the part in four days.[13] He had, as has been seen, from April of 1966 been discussing possible productions with Gaskill. The penultimate suggestion had been *The Tempest*, before both of them settled on *Macbeth*. Guinness was also involved in bringing in Gordon Jackson to play Banquo. As Jackson says: Gaskill 'had never seen me in anything. It was Alec Guinness who suggested me . . . (I'd just worked in a Scottish film with Alec – *Tunes of Glory*)'.[14] Another actor new to the Court was Maurice Roëves, Glasgow trained, at this stage completing work on Joseph Strick's film of *Ulysses*, in which he played Stephen Dedalus. His account of his engagement is that he arrived to audition for the part of Malcolm,[15]

> a role that I was not interested in. However, I did the audition and
> when it was over I asked Bill if I could be considered for the role
> of Macduff. He wanted me to do another audition speech for this role
> and it just happened that I had one prepared, naturally! I did the
> 'Balls of the Medici' speech from *Luther*. This seemed to impress and
> I did get the role although the offer included the clause that I
> understudy Sir Alec. I had never done understudy work before. In
> fact I had just turned down the job of understudying Albert Finney
> in the National's production of *Armstrong's Last Goodnight*, but
> somehow this time I knew that I would go on . . .

He did just that after the production had run for a little over four weeks, together with Susan Engel, who played Lady Macduff and understudied Signoret.[16]

Rehearsals proper had begun on 13 September and, though it is usual to find complaints about the shortness of rehearsal time in the English theatre, the five weeks were barely sufficient for the task in hand. Gaskill had said that playing Shakespeare at the Court would have to be different from those productions at the National or Aldwych, but his approach to *Macbeth* was not, as critical reaction subsequently suggested, the product of perversity or bloody-mindedness. It was actually entirely within the logic and priorities of the Court tradition. An insistence on the primacy of the text, the role of actors one of serving the text, a refusal to employ light as an independent agent and a rejection of any elaboration of set, costume, props or business, were all elements which the Court had subscribed to at its inception. Devine's early notes of 1955 had stated, and sometimes implied, most of the basis of a production such as *Macbeth* (including the idea of playing in full light and acting darkness).[17] It is true to say that nothing quite like this production had been seen in the English theatre. In a sandpaper box with one entrance at the back, a bare stage and continuous white light, the actors performed the text with hardly any furniture and only those props which could be brought on and off by the person concerned. The design by Christopher Morley later became the model for design work at the Royal Shakespeare Company[18] and for most of the actors who have spoken about it, the experience was an extraordinary and demanding one. Gordon Jackson's view is not untypical:[19]

> My favourite part of any production as an actor is the rehearsal period,
> before getting cluttered up with furniture, props, curtains, lighting
> and scene-changes. With Gaskill's *Macbeth*, all of these things were

eliminated, which to my mind, made it absolutely rivetting. Working
with Gaskill on *Macbeth* – and Orson Welles on *Moby Dick* – were
the two most exciting theatrical experiences of my life.

Maurice Roëves felt 'that you were working under a microscope. The
slightest movement revealed itself as did the abrasions if you fell and
scraped along the sandpaper walls or floor! But the excitement of working
in such a set made up for the loss of the odd bit of skin.'[20] And Guinness
himself echoed Olivier's reasons for working at the Court:[21]

> The work I've been doing lately has been lazy work. It hasn't
> demanded things which might be above me . . . in this production,
> where there's scarcely any set and the lights are blazing most of the
> time, everything is stripped down bare. You, the actor, are absolutely
> on your own. You cannot flick your little finger without it seeming
> as significant as a pistol shot. You can't be protected by lots of lush
> scenery. . . . None of us did this play for money or reputation or
> anything like that. . . . We did it for the gamble, for the
> excitement. . . . I have this feeling that this production may be seen
> some time in the future as being something quite germinal to a new
> approach to Shakespeare.

Though it is untrue to say that the entire Company thought of the
production in this way, it is remarkable how many of the actors involved
recognized it as a significant moment, as did a number of young designers
who were subsequently to come to prominence.

Not so the critics. The production was greeted with almost total
hostility. Signoret's performance was regarded as incompetent and unin-
telligible. The set was dismissed. Gaskill was simply in contempt of the
play and its audience. Guinness was treated on the whole respectfully.
Gordon Jackson, Maurice Roëves and Susan Engel emerged with credit.
Sample headlines includes phrases such as 'Treble trouble on the bubble'
(*Daily Mirror*, 20 October); 'Thank goodness it's Shakespeare's shortest
play' (*Evening Standard*, 21 October); 'Why no passion, Simone?' (*Sun*,
21 October); 'Blasted and Threadbare' (*Sunday Telegraph*, 23 October).
Some reviewers attacked the production on the grounds that *Macbeth*
originally was played for the most part 'in grim gloom or shadowy darkness' (Milton Shulman for the *Evening Standard*). What enraged Gaskill
was the apparent lack of readiness of many critics to try to understand
both what the production was attempting and the production's place in
the Court's work. Gaskill's response was not to do with the box-office,
for the production was sold out. Rather, it brought to a head the
simmering hostility of the Court to what was regarded as the incompetence
of most theatre critics.[22] In the wake of the row over *Saved*, Gaskill
had instanced the critics and the Lord Chamberlain as 'two persistent
irritations'.[23] Desmond O'Donovan had responded to criticisms of his

production of *Three Men for Colverton* in September by writing to most
London reviewers to suggest that they should not be allowed inside a
serious theatre. Gaskill now went on to the attack. Five days after the
production opened, Gaskill wrote to the editors of most of the major
periodicals and newspapers. He also wrote individual letters to the
reviewers. The first letter, sent without being cleared by the Court's
Management committee, read:[24]

Our production of *Macbeth* has produced a predictable crop of cheap
journalism from the so-called critics of the national dailies. I am
writing personally to all the critics, including yours, but the situation
between the serious theatres and the newspapers has been deteriorating
to such an extent recently that I feel I must write to you about this
problem.

I have always thought that no-one could doubt the seriousness of
the intentions of the Royal Court Theatre, however critical they
might be of some of its work. Our programme is planned in
consultation with an artistic committee and with the full approval
of the Arts Council.

Our record in the last ten years is such that the British theatre is
now considered the best in the world. We are given a reasonable subsidy
by the Arts Council to carry on this work but our financial position
is constantly endangered by the flippancy of theatre critics. I do not
consider the work of a serious theatre to be a subject for sensational
news items, which is all most critical notices amount to.

The concept of the First Night with all that it entails – notices
hurriedly written to catch a deadline, the need of a critic to make
journalistic capital out of his notice – is destructive of serious work.
It is notorious that the Broadway theatre, where the stress on the
First Night and the subsequent notices is even greater, has failed to
produce any new writing talent and that the commercial pressure on
managements has strangled creative enterprise.

The present vitality of the British theatre springs directly from the
work of George Devine and his associates at this theatre – a work
which I am proud to carry on. It would be sad if this vitality were
threatened by a situation increasingly similar to the American one.

In the circumstances, we are seriously considering whether we
should invite your critic to future performances. This would be a
grave step for any theatre to take but we feel the present level of
criticism is so low as almost to warrant it.

The only other solution would be to give critics the opportunity to
reflect a little before writing their reviews and staggering their visits
over several days, to avoid the appalling mass of them on a First
Night.

I realise that this will reduce the newsworthiness of their reports.
I personally could not be more happy but you as an editor might feel
differently. I would welcome your comments . . .

Many of the editors replied to Gaskill's letter with varying degrees of
surprise and annoyance, although the Arts Editor of the *Financial Times*
thanked Gaskill 'for the excellent article you wrote for us'. None of them
would countenance the proposal of staggering the visits of theatre critics.
The reviewers themselves were prompt to reply. Herbert Kretzmer (*Daily
Express*) said he 'did not enjoy writing my *Macbeth* notice any more than
I enjoyed the production' and ended with the assertion that 'I don't have
to justify myself to you.' B. A. Young (*Financial Times*) took the long
view: 'I now have in my folder letters from Lindsay Anderson, Edward
Bond, Ann Jellicoe, Desmond O'Donovan and yourself, which I hope to
sell at Sotheby's one day. The disease must be contagious.' Milton
Shulman wrote in the *Evening Standard* for 27 October that the Court's
record under Gaskill was 'dismal . . . and the public has indicated its
agreement with the critics by staying away. . . . Instead of whining against
the critics, Mr. William Gaskill should take a hard, objective look at what
he has done, and is doing, to the Royal Court. In any other field of
activity it would be clear what the responsible course of action would be.'
David Nathan of the *Sun* contented himself with the thought that 'Letters
from disgruntled Directors of the Royal Court are becoming as crude and
as boring as their productions.' On 30 October, Gaskill cut short a holiday
in Tunisia to appear on television's 'The Look of the Week' with
Shulman, Hobson and Wesker. Gaskill freely admitted that his letters had
been written when he was angry but that the main criticisms remained. By
this stage, Gaskill was under pressure, at least publicly, to modify his
position. Thus he argued that the suggestion of a ban in his letter was
'an expression of feeling rather than intent'[25] and the Council and Management committee were becoming seriously worried. Greville Poke had
written to Gaskill on 27 October (Neville Blond was in America) to protest
at not being consulted. As a former newspaper man, he was absolutely
against any proposal of a ban (an issue which was again to involve Poke
in 1969; see chapter 5). And Alfred Esdaile, who, as the company vice-
chairman, was in charge in Neville Blond's absence, permitted himself to
appear in various newspapers as saying he would call for Gaskill's resignation but 'Before doing anything I will discuss the matter with other
members of the committee.' He also criticized the production of
Macbeth.[26] Gaskill rejected the call for his resignation and said (probably
through gritted teeth): 'Mr. Esdaile is just making trouble. I do not think
he has a personal motive. He is a very warm-hearted but impulsive man.'[27]
Two critics who supported Gaskill, in private letters to him, over Esdaile's
statements were Irving Wardle of *The Times*: 'I'm very sorry you were

stabbed in the back by Mr. Esdaile, and I hope you win'; and Alan Brien of the *Sunday Telegraph* thought it 'intolerable, however, that anyone should suggest that you be removed from your position for speaking your mind. I assume there is no actual danger of the committee taking such a step but just in case I have written to Mr. Esdaile explaining that I for one would regard this as a retrograde and stupid step.'

Once Neville Blond returned, the Management committee met on 2 November and issued a press statement to waiting reporters. The statement carried a denial by Esdaile that he had called for Gaskill's resignation and a strong declaration by the committee that the question of resignation was only discussed because of press allegations. Gaskill expressed his regret that his letter appeared to suggest a ban on critics but had the committee's sympathy about certain notices of the production. The press would continue to be invited but the committee 'is far from satisfied with the present circumstances in which criticism of plays at the theatre are made'. According to the *Guardian* report of the meeting (3 November), Esdaile left without speaking and his criticisms of *Macbeth* were said by Neville Blond to be 'unwarranted'. *The Times* for 3 November did consider there to be a case for critics taking seriously the possibility of staggered notices. There the matter rested, but uneasily. The relations between the Company and the reviewers did not improve and the notion of banning critics was never far from the surface. Equally, the tight and unreserved support of the theatre's administrators for the Artistic Director began to dissolve gradually. As Gaskill himself put it:[28]

> I had tremendous backing, particularly in the early days, because of course the *Saved* thing happened almost immediately, and I had tremendous support from the Council on that, amazingly so. . . . It started to be eroded over the years by a succession of crises, the crisis over *Macbeth* and the critics, and the crisis over *Early Morning* . . . and gradually Neville started to turn against me, but to begin with . . . I couldn't have had more support.

Part of the difficulty referred to here involves two figures with equally strong beliefs, but sometimes different priorities. As Greville Poke puts it:[29]

> When we started to lose money . . . whether it was George or whether it was Bill, Neville used to beef on like anything about the losses on the financial side and in a way he was quite right to do so. His job as chairman was to keep the artistic boys, as he always called them, within the narrow path of the budget . . .

Blond already entertained worries about his Artistic Director, as a consequence of the losses on the repertory system. His Artistic Director, however, was not easily shifted from his position:[30]

> It was a matter of principle. George had had many years previous

experience of dealing with awkward personalities and George had a way of getting his own way. Bill wasn't that kind at all. He took up a point of view as a matter of principle and he stuck to it and it did lead to quite considerable animosity between himself and the chairman as a result . . .

And Lord Harewood, as so often in these early years, was the person who attempted to mediate. He was trusted by Blond and by Gaskill who was 'less interested in telling the committee than George was and there were one or two occasions when we had to smooth ruffled feathers between Bill and Neville Blond. . . . I tried to make it a little easier for Bill. I don't know if I succeeded.'[31] Perhaps the last word on it should go to Signoret:[32]

Now you can say I'm happily going back to my speciality: a good camera, 80 people round who do the work for you; and good lighting and good lines which you can dub in if you're not clear enough. And a good director and good make-up. And it's so easy. But I wouldn't regret having been in this tunnel all these few weeks. Because I think I'm going to get out of it stronger and richer. Except moneywise. It's a funny, happy company: they're all young and trying to do something . . .

The programme for the rest of the season, as before, was still being formulated, though Peter Gill's version of *A Provincial Life* appeared as a Sunday night performance on 30 October. A play by Wole Soyinka (one of the members of the original Writers' Group), *The Lion and the Jewel*, was scheduled for 8 December (it in fact opened on 12 December, because of the illness of the director, Desmond O'Donovan, who replaced Athol Fugard, when Fugard was unable to do it).[33] Gaskill told the Artistic committee on 11 November that Soyinka's play would be followed by Gill's production of *The Soldier's Fortune*.[34] Thereafter, *Three Sisters* would open in February (it eventually appeared as the opening production of the 1967–8 season). Bond's new play could be ready early in 1967. *Lulu* was still possible; the new Osborne was thought of as opening next season.

Soyinka's play at Christmas played to just under 50 per cent, while the Otway play achieved 52.3 per cent. Gaskill was congratulated at the December Council for reducing an operating deficit as at 1 October of £7,496 to £989 by December. The principal reason for this was, of course, *Macbeth*, which had achieved figures only surpassed by *The Entertainer* (1957) and *Rhinoceros* (1960). Box-office receipts for *Macbeth* were not bettered subsequently until 1977.

After *The Soldier's Fortune*, and instead of *Three Sisters*, there was a revival of *Roots*. It was put on as part of a developing schools project. Gaskill explained to the Artistic committee on 11 November that he had, while *Three Men for Colverton* was running, talked to sixty teachers at the suggestion of the Greater London Council and the Inner London Education Authority. As a consequence, at short notice, schools had been informed of the two-week extension to *Macbeth* and there had been a very good response to an offer of party bookings at reduced rates. Jane Howell then outlined a schools project. It would consist of performing a set play each morning during the last fortnight of each main bill production. The schoolchildren would then spend the afternoon in discussion and practical work in the club. Thereafter the older ones would discuss and then see the main bill show. The committee's reaction was a nervous one. Some members felt that it might divert energy from the search for new plays, but Gaskill felt that the assistants needed to do more concrete production work. At the December Council, Gaskill announced the results of a questionnaire sent to all Inner London schools and that *Roots* had been chosen to inaugurate the scheme. At the same time, there would be a student card which would enable them to see an evening performance for five shillings. *Roots* played for eighteen evenings at 63.5 per cent and for six matinées at 82.7 per cent. On most counts, it was a great success. On one count, the Company became very concerned. While everyone agreed with the idea as important, there was considerable anxiety at any suggestion of diffusing Company energy from its central purpose. Obviously, the question was begged, increasingly, about the central purpose. Thus Lord Harewood at an Artistic committee for 7 February 1967 submitted a letter for consideration. On seeing *Roots* at the head of a list of future productions, Harewood commented that he 'would hate the company to reach a position whereby its main energies were going into the programme for schools'. In his letter, Harewood said that, though both the schools programme and Gaskill's ideas for a studio were 'highly desirable', they were not the main reason for the Company's existence. The committee was split on these issues. Oscar Lewenstein felt that the studio could further the Company's work, but that the schools programme must not interfere with the Company's main work. Jocelyn Herbert felt that no one man could manage all of these tasks. Peggy Ashcroft thought that studio actors should be entirely separate from the Company. Gaskill insisted on the importance of the studio both for the theatre and for his own development, but agreed to rethink it. The main impression from this is that there was not a great enthusiasm for the schools work, both practically and financially. That it did develop, albeit peripherally for a while, is to do with Gaskill's tenacity, Jane Howell's work and, later, the energy invested by Pam Brighton, as Howell's assistant.[35]

As the future programme continued to form and re-form – *Three Sisters* did not have opening dates, the Living Theatre would be contacted,

Bond's play was only in draft form and 'it would almost certainly be banned' – Peter Gill presented D. H. Lawrence's *The Daughter-in-Law* in the main bill on 16 March, and initiated what was to be one of the greatest critical successes of Gaskill's time as Artistic Director. Nearly two years after directing *A Collier's Friday Night* as a Sunday night production, Gill embarked upon work which was to make his reputation (see chapter 4).[36]

At the end of the financial year 1966–7, the Company accounts showed a surplus of £4,099. Gaskill stated the obvious at the Council meeting of June 1967: 'there was a definite relationship between the programme of revivals, which had been higher than usual, and the improvement in the figures. Our reputation had not been lessened by this, but he did not want to envisage another year doing quite so many.' Partly at the urging of the Arts Council, which was unhappy at the number of revivals, when the grant was primarily for the development of new work, but mainly because Gaskill wished it, a programme of four new plays was launched, each with a proposed two-week run and a very low budget of £1,604 each. It will be recalled that, during the repertory season, the Arts Council sharply insisted that the Company stayed within budget. Now it complained at the measures taken to achieve that. For once, however, the Arts Council and the Artistic Director agreed. In another area, Gaskill found a way of encouraging his assistants to become involved in production, if not via the schools scheme and the studio proper. The club had opened upstairs on 15 February 1967. Initially, it was equipped for members of the English Stage Society during the evenings, but was used for Company rehearsals during the day. It became an obvious venue for productions of an experimental nature and as such marks the real beginning of what two years later was to become the Theatre Upstairs. In April, two performances were given, with National Theatre actors of a Japanese play, *Love's Suicides in the Women's Temple* by Chikamatsu. Subsequently in 1967, the club hosted the Don Rendell–Ian Carr Quintet and pop groups every Saturday. A fire caused its closure after 1 July, together with lack of funds, but the idea of its use was to surface again, when the club re-opened in the following March.

The new financial year opened with Edward Bond's translation of *Three Sisters*, with Avril Elgar, Glenda Jackson and Marianne Faithfull in the leading parts. It was alleged that the casting of Faithfull was set up, that mock-auditions had been held, and that the basic reason was as a publicity gimmick. In fact, the part had originally been offered to another actress, and only to Marianne Faithfull, when the original casting was refused.[37] The production was generally liked and played to 75.2 per cent. Gaskill then began the group of four low-budget shows, which were a double-bill by Joe Orton, James Casey's *A View to the Common* (which had appeared as a Sunday night on 2 April), David Storey's *The Restoration of Arnold Middleton*, and Donald Howarth's *Ogodiveleftthegason*. Even as Gaskill had proposed this programme to the June Council, he had been worried that standards might drop, particularly in production, by rushing these plays on. Complaints were duly made by some critics.[38] The financial returns, with one exception, were poor. The exception was David Storey's play, which had gone through several versions since the first in 1958. It had been considered by both Granada and the B.B.C.; four repertory companies turned it down; Lindsay Anderson had read it while on location for the film of Storey's novel, *This Sporting Life*, and had three times proposed a Royal Court production, twice with Richard Harris and once with Nicol Williamson. The plans came to nothing until Gordon McDougall of the Traverse, Edinburgh, put on the latest version in 1966. Robert Kidd from the Court saw the Edinburgh production and 'he was more enthusiastic than anyone had been'.[39] At the Court, the play achieved close to 60 per cent, was extended for a third week and provided the first main bill transfer of Gaskill's regime, when it opened at the Criterion on 31 August, where it ran for fifty-eight performances. The transfer caused some discussion in the Artistic committee for 17 July: 'It was finally agreed that although it might bring the theatre more prestige if it were kept at the Court, we owed it to the author to make as much money for him as possible and encourage him to write more plays.' Storey was, as it turned out, a major find for the Court and, in financial terms, was as significant to the Company's fortunes as Osborne had been in Devine's time. Jack Shepherd, the actor who had fought his way into Gaskill's first company, won the *Variety* award for best new actor and the *Plays and Players* award for most promising actor.[40] Storey himself won the *Evening Standard* award for most promising playwright.

As a result of the success of Storey's play, Donald Howarth's play ran for only one of its scheduled two weeks, opening 24 July. Howarth, who was an amateur in Shipley with Gaskill and Richardson says that his play[41]

> was put on because of the enthusiasm of Desmond O'Donovan, who with other assistants thought there weren't enough new plays being done. The play didn't work, my fault, and Bill was encouraging. I remember he and Helen Montagu acted scenes after rehearsal when everyone had gone in an attempt to try and make them work – a lively demonstration and funny. The play was too loose though. Nothing could be done.

The work with schools during this period, against a background of worry by the Management and Artistic committees, flourished intermittently. Gaskill had invited Wandsworth school to the Court and on 23 April, the school had given two performances of *Billy Liar*. In July, another Sunday night production had consisted of a double bill. The boys of Dulwich College had played *Dance of the Teletape*, written and directed by the fourteen-year-old Charles Hayward. On the same bill was Ann Jellicoe's *The Rising Generation*, a play, written between *The Sport of My Mad Mother* and *The Knack*, for the Girl Guides, who promptly turned it down.[42] It was also during this time at the Court that the student card scheme was extended to university students. The suggestion by Greville Poke, was a great success. More than 3,000 students had seen *Three Sisters*.

One of the decisions taken at this time was a cause of regret on Gaskill's part. He decided to close down the workshops which had up to then been an integral part of the Court's policy, and to use the money saved (estimated at between £5,000 and £6,000 a year) for other purposes, including the restarting of the Studio. He later felt that the action[43]

> was a great loss. There were very strong economic reasons why they
> had to go . . . but it is marvellous having a group of people working
> from the beginning as a team of carpenters, painters . . . they used
> to make all the scenery and some of the costumes. We had wonderful
> scene painters. For George it was a very central part of the work, that
> everything should be made by people who actually belonged to the
> theatre . . . that changed the nature of the theatre.

By July, Gaskill had developed what appeared to be a firm programme for the immediate future. The Company had been invited to go to the Florence festival in November with *Twelfth Night*, but Gaskill remained indifferent to the idea. It was also the case that the British Council, which had set the idea in motion, was unwilling to provide any finance. In the Artistic committee for 17 July, Gaskill argued that 'since the financial position was very stable we should not consider any major classical revival for some time, but should have a very full programme of new and modern plays'. Amongst these would be two plays by Charles Wood, *Fill the Stage with Happy Hours* and *Dingo*, *The Dragon* by Schwartz for Christmas, Tabori's *The Nigger Lovers*, and Isaac Babel's *Marya* to mark the fiftieth anniversary of the Russian revolution. January would see the première of *Early Morning*, February a Lawrence trilogy and April the new Cregan play. In addition, the Company had been invited to Prague. It was also at this meeting that Gaskill asked for the co-option of writers and it was agreed that four should be invited. The meeting also considered a letter from Lord Harewood on the subject of Gaskill himself, who had clearly suggested that he was on the point of resignation. Harewood reviewed the work to date:

> I hope very much that you will not make any decision at the moment
> about leaving. It seems to me that we have got through some pretty
> trying weather and come out triumphantly on the other side. Myself,

I think that *Saved* was one of the best things we have ever done at the Court and I am also inclined to think that the recent David Storey play comes into the same category. Each of them seems to be a sort of classic of the 1960s, both as regards writing and playing, and absolutely worthy to join *Look Back in Anger*, which set the pace in the 1950s.

Harewood goes on to back Gaskill's proposals: 'I also entirely support your idea that we should try to put together a season for 1967–8 which is in the highest Court tradition, full of new plays and recent revivals.' Referring to the Prague invitation, Harewood urges Gaskill not to refuse it, if the Council was unhappy about taking *Saved*, which Gaskill clearly wanted to do: 'Of course, one cannot put principle too high, but this seems to me to be an insistence on installing it as a Sword of Damocles above the stage.' The moment is almost symbolic: a safe play to Florence, or *Saved* to Prague. It was not until late 1969 that Gaskill got his own way.

In August, and by arrangement with the impresario, Michael White, the Court saw a group of plays by the Open Theatre of New York, performed for the English Stage Society. It was one of the first visits by a series of influential American companies which were subsequently to have such an impact on experimental work in England. The original intention had been to transfer the shows (under the general title of *American Hurrah*) to the Vaudeville theatre, but, according to the report at the December Council, the Lord Chamberlain had indicated very late on that he might institute proceedings, even if the Vaudeville was turned into a club for the occasion. Apparently, the reason for the threatened action was to do with 'unflattering references to a friendly head of state' [President Johnson].[44] Because of this, the Open Theatre stayed at the Court and Charles Wood's *Fill the Stage with Happy Hours* went to the Vaudeville.

If the Court had good cause to resent the interference of the censor, it was very soon to become engaged in the bitterest battle of all with the Chamberlain over Edward Bond's *Early Morning*. The play, which Bond had begun to write in January 1965, a few months after he had completed *Saved*, was delivered to the Court early in 1967. Since it had been clear from the beginning that the play would be subjected to demands for cuts from the Chamberlain, if not banned completely, the production was eventually announced for the English Stage Society for January 1968. The production was announced to the press on 3 August, but already the internal battles were beginning at the Court. At an Artistic committee meeting for 16 October, it is stated that the committee had been asked to read the play by the Management committee and by Neville Blond in particular. In effect, the Artistic committee was being asked if it wished more control over the decisions regarding main bill productions, a right which it had relinquished under George Devine. The committee 'saw no reason to reverse their previous decision not to circulate plays for the main bill with the rider that if the Artistic Director needed advice on controversial plays, especially those for Club performances, this would be given'. Further, the committee felt that the play 'showed new development of Bond as a writer and [it] was an exciting experimental work which should be seen'.

The difficulty at this stage was a consequence of the legal decision over *Saved* (see chapter 2). Any performance of an unlicensed play, club or not, was vulnerable to legal attack, if the Chamberlain wished to act. What was not clear was whether he would. He had not in the case of *American Hurrah* (although forbidding its transfer), nor did he in November over Charles Wood's *Dingo*. At the same time, the movement to remove from the Chamberlain his jurisdiction over the theatre was well advanced but at this point was not certain. For example, on 1 November, the government dropped its bill to end theatre censorship because of pressure of other business. Seven days later, the Chamberlain returned *Early Morning* to the Court with the single comment that 'his Lordship would not allow it.' By 16 November, George Strauss sponsored a Private Member's Bill to do what the government had decided it could not.[45] Thus in one way it seemed likely that the theatre would shortly be free of state censorship and it would have been a simple matter to have put back the production of *Early Morning* for a year or however long it took. Gaskill would not tolerate such an idea. It ran counter to the central Court tradition of nursing its writers and supporting them, often against the odds. It would also involve submission and the abdication of principle. But to struggle for the Bond play eventually came to mean taking on the Arts Council and some members of the Management committee, including the chairman. A letter from the Company's lawyers of 30 November indicates Gaskill's efforts to hold to the January main bill production. The lawyers indicated that the Court's licence was granted annually by the Greater London Council and that it could be revoked; that the Arts Council was under pressure for using public money to finance a club production; and that the fact that the Chamberlain was nearing his end 'may persuade him to prosecute what he considers to be a gross violation of his traditional powers, as a farewell demonstration of his authority'. On 5 December, the Secretary-General of the Arts Council, Nigel Abercrombie, replied to Neville Blond's letter requesting permission to turn the Court into a club for *Early Morning*. The application was rejected because the Council would not 'connive at an offence against the law'.

On 6 December, a special meeting of the Court's Council was convened. After announcing a trading surplus to the end of September of £11,700, the Council discussed the *Early Morning* affair. Two days before that,

Bond himself had given his view in a letter to his (then) American agent, Toby Cole: 'The Ld. Chamberlain has banned *Early Morning* completely! . . . And the Arts Council have tried to put pressure on Bill Gaskill to get him to withdraw his production. He won't do this (naturally) but it may be delayed about two months.' At the Council meeting, Joe Hodgkinson represented the Arts Council as somewhat belatedly realizing the full implications of the decision over *Saved*. He said further that if the implications had been understood earlier, the Arts Council would not have agreed to the club presentation of *Dingo*. All of which reflected poorly, it would appear, on the Arts Council rather than on the Court. Thus, the Arts Council would not be a party to another offence. Blond had already written to the Arts Council to inform them that *Early Morning* had been postponed. It is not clear whether Gaskill knew of this. He certainly would not have approved of it. The meeting clearly was of a critical kind. Gaskill was speaking for Court tradition when he argued that:

> it was our policy to present certain experimental plays and in the history of the English Stage Company there had been trouble over many of the plays that had been presented. Writers today were writing plays which would not be licensed by the Lord Chamberlain but they should still be put on. He thought that when the Royal Court could not put on new plays and certainly not the most important new plays, then the English Stage Company would cease to have any function . . .

Gaskill also made the point that, once the censor's powers had been abolished, there was the risk of a private prosecution and that 'it might be safer to put on an unlicensed play before the Lord Chamberlain's powers were annulled, rather than wait until censorship was abolished'. The Council eventually agreed to the postponement of the production and meanwhile to explore all possible ways of getting the play on, even in the face of the Arts Council warning that the grant would be withheld.

In some ways the December Council typifies the Court at work. On the one hand, the discussion was about the gravest crisis in its history, with both external and internal pressures to act in a way that would be regarded by some as capitulation. On the other, the Council formally approved a new two-year contract for its Artistic Director. Gaskill, championing Bond and his sense of the Court tradition at one moment, then reports on the development of the schools scheme, a programme of eight Sunday night shows for the next year and the possibility of plays in the club, with his assistants rehearsing them for one week. Importantly, in this last respect, he used the fact that the club was closed after the fire, to argue that when it reopened, it should be used 'more for our own internal use'. Gaskill was carrying a healthy financial surplus by now.

The season of four two-week shows was established, although he wanted them in future to operate on a three-weekly basis because of the strain on the staff. The year in many ways had gone very well.

However, the pressure increased over *Early Morning* from this point. Greville Poke wrote for legal advice on 22 January to Isador Caplan. In the letter he reveals that Lord Goodman, chairman of the Arts Council, was told by the Chamberlain that he might decide to prosecute if the production went ahead. If that came about, Poke, as company secretary, asks who would be prosecuted, what would be the size of the fine and would the licence be at risk? He says that Gaskill had written to the Chamberlain to try to find a way out. Caplan replied on 26 January to say that the maximum fine would be £50, the licence was at risk and the position was a very difficult one. Gaskill felt there was a clear attempt to stop *Early Morning* being done at all:[46]

> They tried to stop *Early Morning* being done, quite definitely. They being Neville and the Arts Council. The Arts Council was leaning very heavily, Goodman, I think, was leaning very heavily on Neville to stop it . . .

Part of the reason for the Arts Council's attitude was to protect the passage of the bill to abolish theatre censorship through Parliament. There was a feeling that a production of *Early Morning* at this point would make matters difficult to resolve. At the same time, the Council would not object if the Company found another source of finance for the production. It could then legitimately claim that public money was not involved.

At the point in January where the confrontation between Gaskill and his associates would inevitably have occurred, he fell ill with pneumonia. A hasty production of *Twelfth Night* was inserted into the programme, with predictable critical reaction, and good box-office. Once recovered, Gaskill continued to fight. He reported to the Artistic committee on 20 February, with Bond and David Storey there as recently co-opted members, that he had seen the Chamberlain's representative who had said that the play would be prosecuted if given for a run but that he would allow Sunday night performances. David Storey felt it was a battle worth fighting and that the Company should risk prosecution. Eventually, the committee agreed that, if the Theatres Bill got through its second reading on 22 February, Sunday performances should go ahead. If not, 'we should consider fighting for the play and call a Council meeting to discuss the matter'.

The Theatres Bill obtained its second reading and the Court issued a press statement indicating its intention to present *Early Morning* for two Sundays only. The statement added that 'The Management Committee of the English Stage Company were in complete agreement over this course of action.' It may have been publicly. Internally, the rows were furious and vehement. Gaskill, by this time, had watched a proposed three-week run of *Early Morning* dwindle to two Sunday night perform-ances, and he lashed out at the Chamberlain and the Arts Council in a letter of 10 March to the *Sunday Times*. Sarcastically, he thought it 'rather surprising that the Arts Council, whose Chairman is one of the most distinguished lawyers in the country, should have taken two years to find out that they were condoning a crime' and hoped that the current fuss represents the 'death throes of the censor who has so long interfered with our work'. On 15 March, Gaskill requested a meeting of the Artistic committee to discuss '*Early Morning* and his relationship with the Manage-ment Committee'. The previous meeting of the Management committee on 7 March had objected strongly to the fact that Gaskill had incurred expenditure and begun rehearsals before presenting his budget for the production. Some of these expenses, particularly for design, had been incurred when the play was to have been in the main bill, but the fact remained that the budget was much higher for *Early Morning* than for the usual Sunday night production.[47] The Artistic committee agreed that the expenditure was desirable (with the exception of Greville Poke) and that *Early Morning* should not be thought of in terms of a normal Sunday night show. It is noticeable in the minutes of the meeting that the committee was busily exercising its traditional function, that of calming everyone down and trying to make peace. Thus, while it was true that Gaskill should have submitted his budget, the committee felt 'that the Management Committee could have been more skilful in its reception of the budget, even though the Artistic Director should have shown it to the Chairman before the meeting'. The syntax of the sentence has Lord Harewood's stamp on it. From what Gaskill said in the meeting, Alfred Esdaile had threatened in the Management committee to veto the production entirely and the Artistic committee then had to discuss whether Esdaile had the power to do this. It was also revealed that George Strauss, M.P., was at present reading the play and that if he should disapprove of the presentation, then a Council meeting should be called. Finally on this, the committee reaffirmed the decision to produce the play as a Sunday night.

The committee then moved to the question of Gaskill's relationship with the Management committee, where, clearly, there had been an enor-mous row: 'Mr. Gaskill said that after the last Management meeting he had felt distinctly dispirited, and was definitely disinclined again to subject himself to a tirade of abuse.' The Artistic committee felt 'there was a degree of disingenuousness in making an issue of the high figures; the circumstances made these more or less inevitable and they should have been anticipated'. As always, when relations became strained, Lord Hare-wood was asked to speak to Neville Blond after the next Management meeting. The issue ostensibly was about the *Early Morning* budget. The real issue was that Blond wanted Gaskill removed. Harewood confirms this:[48]

> Yes, he wanted Bill out. I didn't think that he was right. He knew I didn't think he was right . . . they didn't really get on. They [tycoons] want in the end that their instinct prevails. . . . I believed in what [Bill] was doing. I believed in the responsible nature of a good Artistic Director, which Bill was. I thought he needed a lot of support . . .

Gaskill acknowledges Harewood's crucial interventions:[49]

> I remember Blond demanding my resignation at a meeting once, but George Harewood was so supportive. He was just so fair-minded and the times that Neville tried to get rid of me, he just talked Neville out of it.

Lord Harewood must have talked very persuasively since, on 13 March, after the Management committee row and before the Artistic committee meeting of 15 March, Neville Blond had set down his objections in a letter to Blacksell, in which he renewed his complaint regarding 'the management control' of the theatre, made on 12 January 1967. Blond's letter states that 'The situation in regard to Bill is becoming increasingly impossible . . . he seems to have adopted a totally blatant attitude towards the Management Committee. . . . He refuses to resign. I do not want a "John Neville" situation at the Royal Court, and that is why I have written to you.' Blond then summarized his objections in a document marked 'Private and Confidential':

> The issue at stake is Bill Gaskill. I am not concerned with the artistic merits of 'Early Morning'. I never interfere with the artistic policy of the theatre and do not wish to do so now – that is why we have an Artistic Committee.
>
> I am, however, concerned with the management of the Theatre and feel responsible to the Arts Council for the handling of the grant – which is in fact public money.
>
> My responsibilities have been added to owing to the fact that our General Manager is inadequate. I have mentioned this on many occasions. This position requires a much more experienced person who can deal with Bill and, if necessary, control and advise him.
>
> Bill has caused me endless trouble since he has been with us through his total disregard of any decisions taken by the Management Committee, i.e.
>
> 1. His attitude towards the critics
> 2. The trouble with Desmond O'Donovan
> 3. 'Saved' Court case
> 4. 'The Dragon' – overspending the budget

5. 'Early Morning'

The position re 'Early Morning' is as follows:–

(a) He was told to postpone the play, but he went ahead with auditions, scenery etc.

(b) He did not tell the Artistic Committee he wanted to do five performances which is a departure from our usual practice.

(c) The budget is fantastic for Sunday night performances and shows his total disregard for the finances of the English Stage Society.

To sum up – his attitude at the last Management Meeting was not only very stupid but extremely rude. He forgets he is an employee and as such must conform to at least some form of control – even Olivier had to do this (example 'The Soldiers'). I think he wants a situation similar to John Neville at Nottingham.

As things are at the Royal Court at the moment there is virtually no point in having a Management Committee and for the first time in the history of the theatre I feel I would not be justified in asking the Arts Council for money which I know will be spent in such an irresponsible manner.

I want a new Artistic Director and an Administrator to run the theatre.

The row over *Early Morning* spilled over into the next season and the performances (as such) began the new financial year (see chapter 5). Where the theatre had been totally united over the *Saved* affair, the reverse was to be the case over Bond's new play. Ironically, while these divisions occupied the theatre in one direction, in another, the productions were taking shape which were to be accounted one of the Court's greatest successes. Peter Gill had taken his company for the Lawrence trilogy to Nottinghamshire in the summer of 1967 and on 8 January 1968, Gill and his two assistants, Barry Hanson and Rob Knights, began rehearsals of *A Collier's Friday Night*, *The Daughter-in-Law* and *The Widowing of Mrs. Holroyd*.

4 · D. H. Lawrence's *The Daughter-in-Law*

The great success which attended the production at the Court of three of Lawrence's plays in the spring of 1968 had small and accidental beginnings. In 1958, Independent Television screened an adaptation by Ken Taylor of *The Widowing of Mrs. Holroyd*. Peter Gill recalls returning to his house and 'I bumped into Donald Howarth, and Donald and I saw a bit of *The Widowing of Mrs. Holroyd*, and I remember our saying, "Wasn't that interesting!" '.[1] At that stage, and for a few years, Gill was primarily an actor. He had auditioned early in 1958 for the Court's production of Ann Jellicoe's *The Sport of My Mad Mother*, understudied in Lindsay Anderson's production of *The Long and the Short and the Tall* in January 1959, acted in Wesker's *The Kitchen* in September 1959, and appeared in Gaskill's production of *The Caucasian Chalk Circle* for the Royal Shakespeare Company's first season at the Aldwych Theatre in 1962. By 1964, Gill had become an assistant to George Devine. Initially, he avoided the obligation of assistants to undertake a production by writing *The Sleepers' Den*, which Desmond O'Donovan directed as a Sunday night in February 1964. However, Devine's policy of training his assistants meant inevitably that Gill would have to find something. It was at this point that he recalled the television production and sent to the British Drama League for a copy. What was sent was the first edition (1934) of *A Collier's Friday Night*:[2]

> and this little green book, the original published copy . . . came, and I read it with enormous enjoyment. I had no experience of directing and had that feeling that somehow directing was more than it was, so, though I wanted to do it, I had no experience of any kind. . . .
> George read it and said, 'If you do it, I'll look forward to seeing it', which took away my nervousness and I think I enjoyed doing that show more than anything I've ever done since.

Gill rehearsed the production for two weeks, with the luxury of a real rehearsal room (the Old Vic rehearsal room in Aquinas Street) and some indication of an emerging directing style comes from Richard Butler, who

69

played Lambert, and Rosemary McHale, who played Nellie, his daughter. Butler recalls a good deal of improvisation and that Gill 'wrote little scenes that might have concerned the characters in *Collier's Friday Night*, and we used to act those as an exercise before we rehearsed. That was marvellous . . . a disciplined preparation'.[3] Rosemary McHale was nearing the end of her final term at the Drama Centre when she was cast:[4]

It was a very happy initiation into the professional theatre because Peter Gill's rehearsal procedures were very similar to those I was familiar with. He was keen that we should understand the unity of the family and what effect the pressures of the mining industry had on domestic life. We grew to realize how tiny the family's house was compared with our own homes and how much sweated labour went into every penny earned and every morsel eaten. We played the game of throwing a ball in a circle which I remember some of the older members of the Company thought absurd, and of passing objects carefully to one another as if they were made of fine glass, or very heavy, or likely to blow away. This helped us not just to get to know one another, but to start on the journey of exploring the physical world which was an important part of Peter's production.

Everything in the set was as real as possible, including the heat in the stove. My first professional appearance was to be discovered drinking tea, which is difficult if you're nervous, and very hot strong tea at that. I also had to wash the coal dust from my father's back, which he enjoyed less than I did.

Gill's worry about directing at all for the first time – 'I couldn't get out of it, and I was absolutely frightened'[5] – did not prevent his understanding of how the good Sunday nights came about: 'you had to be very shrewd because you had to wait until there was a set you could do it on'.[6] The first of the Lawrence productions was in fact played on the set of Osborne's *A Patriot for Me*. A run-through took place between the matinée and the evening performances of Osborne's play. Since Devine was entertaining after the matinée members of the Berliner Ensemble, he was not able to see Gill's production for, after completing his performance as Baron von Epp that evening, Devine suffered the first of a series of heart attacks. He never saw *A Collier's Friday Night*.[7]

It was during the rehearsals that Heinemann brought out Lawrence's *Complete Plays*, a publication which included the first appearance of *The Daughter-in-Law*.[8] Gill bought the volume 'and there, jumping out at me, was the extraordinary last scene in *Holroyd*. The play that really came out as a play was *The Daughter-in-Law*. . . . What happened was I read all of them and I think I did send *The Daughter-in-Law* to Hampstead, because I wasn't on the staff at the Court, and I don't know really how the production came about exactly.'[9] The plays seem to have been absorbed at the Court and, occasionally at this stage, there are references to them. Gill recalls a time early in 1966 when Desmond O'Donovan suggested *The Daughter-in-Law* as a possibility. As Gill puts it: 'I went off to get it and by the time I got back, they'd decided to do *The Knack*' (February 1966).[10] *The Widowing of Mrs. Holroyd* was put up as a possibility to open the 1966–7 season at a Management committee meeting of 22 April 1966. By 21 June, the Artistic committee was being told that plans for the entire season had become fluid, but as so often with the Court's programming, a gap opened up in the schedule which changed matters. Gaskill wrote to Blacksell on 3 January 1967 to tell him that a proposed production of *Three Sisters* had been put back. This was because Gaskill had to take over Soyinka's *The Lion and the Jewel*, when Desmond O'Donovan became ill. Since *Three Sisters* would now open in April, a six-week hiatus existed between Gill's production of *The Soldier's Fortune* and the Chekhov. Gaskill proposed to devote the first three weeks to a production of *Roots* for the Schools Scheme and for 'the second three weeks I am considering either *The Daughter-in-Law*, an unperformed play by D. H. Lawrence, to be directed by Peter Gill, or *The Restoration of Arnold Middleton*, a play by David Storey, which I have asked Lindsay Anderson to direct'. Gaskill believed that *Roots* and one of the others could be done for about the cost of one full-scale production. By 8 February, *The Daughter-in-Law* was scheduled to open on 16 March. The budgets were low. Out of a total estimate of £3,484, no more than £1,650 was to be spent on set and costumes. The set was to be built by an outside workshop because of the overlap with the production of *Roots*, and the opportunity was used to produce comparative estimates between the Court's own workshop and an outside workshop.[11] One result of the financial pressure existing at the Court at that time was that by 22 February, the budget had been reduced to £3,017, with weekly running costs of £1,767. A figure of £250 for costumes was queried on the grounds that the play was scheduled for only a four-week run. The Management committee insisted that the emphasis should be on hiring rather than making the costumes.

The first production of *The Daughter-in-Law* was rehearsed for only three weeks. What was learnt, however, in developing the production was to hold good for the group of three plays the following year and the approach to *The Daughter-in-Law* was to remain substantially the same. On 1 February 1967, Gill, together with his two designers, John Gunter (set) and Deirdre Clancy (costumes), visited Eastwood, on what Gill describes as the first field trip. Their purpose was both to locate the play's setting and also to visit local theatres in order to search for actors who could produce an accurate version of the play's dialect. As Gill said: 'It is a very distinctive dialect and it is very difficult to find the right cast.

I have a fairly open mind about it, because no play is worth sacrificing good actors to an accent – and this play is so written that the lines indicate the dialect to a certain extent. . . . But we do want something more than a general North country accent.'[12] Gill said of the trip that:[13]

> A very strange thing happened . . . We found a group of cottages that were incredibly poor and John said, looking into an empty house, 'I reckon this is the kind of thing he means', and we knocked on the door and an old gentleman let us in, and it was indeed very like the two sets in *The Daughter-in-Law*. John measured it up and we more or less used the basic size of the room. The man next door showed me a copy that his sister had given him of *Collier's Friday Night* in that same green cover.

Later, John Gunter talked of his shock at first visiting Eastwood: 'I remember the amazement for me, coming from a southern middle-class world, going up to Eastwood and Lawrence country with Peter Gill, and being invited in by a retired miner to see how one of those houses worked. It was deeply impressive. It taught me how beneficial research is, and how you get repaid a hundredfold for tracking down the right details.'[14] However, what was important was to translate what had been seen in Eastwood into theatrical terms and Gunter accurately catches the effect they all agreed on: 'The particular domestic situation, the environment and what the people did for a living were very much an influence upon it, but what was essential was to see those reactions trapped within that confined space. So you looked at it, like under a microscope. Of course, the Royal Court as a theatre allowed you to do that.'[15] The rooms they had found in Princes Street were effectively put into the Court, but with one important change, consequent upon the production of *A Collier's Friday Night*. Gill had followed Lawrence's stage directions very carefully in 1965:[16]

> and it was after that that I got the notion that one should see, when I came to do the plays again, the action offstage juxtaposed. . . . He had written with a conventional notion that you went into the kitchen and heard splashing when the father's washing, or whatever, so he had a box set in mind and that's how I did the first production. But when I did *The Daughter-in-Law*, I missed a wall out, so that you could see a little back kitchen. . . . I got it from *A Collier's Friday Night* that you should be able to see the room that it was set in, and you should somehow be able to see through, so there was usually continued activity in the scullery. It always met the sightlines, but it involved an enormously detailed working out . . .

Another problem to be resolved with *The Daughter-in-Law* settings was that Lawrence calls for a substantial change after one scene, where the action shifts from Mrs Gascoigne's house to the house of her son, Luther, and his wife Minnie. As Gill puts it:[17]

> I knew you had to get Minnie into the action before you took an interval. You had to have the balls as a director to take the interval after her entrance. It gives you a difficult problem because he asks for a lot in the first scene. . . . Once you're in Minnie's house, you never move. What do you do? Do you take some terrible little front cloth or do you do a big set [for scene one] and take an interval.
> Well, I knew you couldn't take an interval before the real protagonists came on . . .

In the event, the design for Luther's house was the reverse of the design for Mrs Gascoigne's house. By means of trucks and reversing the pieces of scenery, the change was accomplished very quickly: 'We brought the curtain down and they did a seventy five second scene change. They just zoomed it round and set it. There was a wonderful stage management and crew at the Court at that time.'[18]

By the time Gill went to Eastwood, he had cast only one part. Victor Henry had played in the 1965 production of *Collier*, and was now cast as Joe. The rest of the casting took quite a time:[19]

> I started with Victor Henry as Joe. I met Gabrielle Day through Barry Hanson and she was obviously Mrs. Purdy. I'd always liked Judy Parfitt, who had been in the Court's old filing system under blue for 'establishment' because of her early contact with H.M. Tennant . . . but I'd seen her play a crofter's wife on television and thought she was absolutely astounding. . . . I did endless auditions. I found it very difficult to cast Luther but in the end I went with Mike Pratt. I didn't cast Judy and Anne [Dyson] until the Saturday before we started. Initially, I thought I couldn't cast them up to standard . . .

Though none of the actors was from Nottingham, all, except Mike Pratt, were from the north.[20] The northern actors in the event formed the basis of the 1968 company when the three Lawrence plays were done.

As far as is known, Lawrence never mentioned *The Daughter-in-Law* in his writings. Precise dating of the play is difficult,[21] but it appears to be the one referred to in a letter from Lawrence to Edward Garnett, dated 12 January 1913:[22]

> I am going to send you a new play I have written. It is neither a comedy nor a tragedy – just ordinary. It is quite objective, as far as that term goes, and though no doubt, like most of my stuff, it wants weeding out a bit, yet I think the whole thing is there, laid out properly, planned and progressive. . . . I enjoy so much writing my plays – they come so quick and exciting from the pen – that you mustn't growl at me if you think them a waste of time. At any rate,

they'll be stuff for shaping later on, when I'm more of a
workman . . .

The play opens in Mrs Gascoigne's kitchen. She is a widow of sixty-
eight with two sons: Luther, six weeks married, and Joe, aged twenty-
six and still living at home. Joe has broken his arm. He's been to the pit
to claim his accident pay of fourteen shillings weekly. When he arrives,
he eventually discloses that, since he broke his arm by larking about
while at work, there will be no pay. The truth of the matter is gradually
dragged out of him, during which time his mother feeds him as if he was
a baby. Mrs Gascoigne's dominance over her younger son is established
as Joe takes refuge in jokes and impersonations of the pit managers.
When pushed, Joe disappears into whimsical versions of Biblical tags or
threatens to emigrate to Australia. This goes on against a background of
an impending strike. An already disgruntled Mrs Gascoigne is then faced
with Mrs Purdy, 'a little fat, red-faced body in bonnet and black cape'.[23]
Mrs Purdy reveals that her daughter, Bertha, is pregnant by Luther, and
the rest of the scene is a discussion about what is to be done, out of which
emerges Mrs Gascoigne's dislike for Luther's wife, Minnie. Mrs Purdy
departs after getting some agreement that a sum of £40 would enable
Bertha to stand a better chance of finding a husband. At Mrs Gascoigne's
urging, Mrs Purdy proposes to visit Luther and Minnie to settle the
matter. The scene ends with Joe sulking and Mrs Gascoigne in a rage.

The rage is brought about not so much by Mrs Purdy's news but by
the simmering resentment at Minnie felt by Luther's mother. Already
annoyed at Joe, she reluctantly allows Mrs Purdy to enter, and the initial
conversation is about a mutual dislike, that of the pit managers and the
repressions of the bosses. The conversation is formal, pauses, picks up
again, until Mrs Purdy gets the opportunity to introduce the real subject
of her visit. After the initial disbelief, it is Mrs Purdy who begins to
describe Minnie as a 'fine madam', a 'stuck-up piece', 'haughty' and 'a
woman wi' money'. Out of this prompting comes Mrs Gascoigne's attack
on Minnie. The initial subject of Bertha is put aside, as the real concerns
of the mother come suddenly into the foreground. She cannot help herself
as she 'turns half apologetically, half explanatorily, to Mrs Purdy', that
is to say, to another woman to find some commiseration. The history of
Luther and Minnie is retailed. Minnie cannot be forgiven partly for
keeping Luther dangling for four years, and partly for having ideas above
her station. That Minnie went off to Manchester to be a nursery governess
rankles immensely. Worse, Minnie agreed to marry Luther by letter, the
contents of which Mrs Gascoigne has off by heart. Despite Joe's attempts
at jokes during this sequence and his suggestion that Minnie has made a
'nice' home, Mrs Gascoigne dismisses the idea with the withering remark
that 'it's not serviceable'. The old mother wants Mrs Purdy to go to

Luther's house in order that the news will bring Minnie down 'a peg or two'.

The object of this anger first appears in scene two. The title of the play has suggested that it is concerned with the relationship between the mother and her son's wife and Minnie is described as 'a tall, good-looking young woman', set in a room which is described as 'pretty' and in 'cottage' style. Initially, Mrs Gascoigne's account of Minnie seems to have some force, as she complains at Luther's being twenty minutes late back from the pit, and tries to get him to wash the pit dirt off before eating. She tries to impose a certain style of proceeding upon a figure who resists it. A fussy housewife dealing in trivia, however, converts to a figure aroused and fascinated by the appearance of her husband. A bright, red mouth in a black face attracts her sufficiently for them to kiss and, momentarily, not to fuss about getting grime on her blouse. It's as if she discerns another person, 'a stranger' as she puts it, who does not resemble the other man, whom she describes as 'a tame rabbit'. This moment is a critical one for trying to catch something of Minnie's character, and needs to be placed alongside Mrs Gascoigne's version. The moment goes quickly as Minnie complains about Luther's lack of ambition. The subject veers around to the old mother's control over her sons. Plainly here, the centre of the animosity is another woman intruding into another domestic context. The developing fight is broken by Joe's arrival, who is intent on getting Minnie out of the house before Mrs Purdy arrives. Joe channels the tension in a different direction by deliberately dropping and smashing two of Minnie's best plates, as if to demonstrate that he cannot be ruled. But then Joe has nothing worth losing. Minnie, in a rage, hits Joe on his broken arm and, comically, Luther's view of it is that 'Tha shouldna fool wi' her.' She's viewed as a termagant, but seems helpless in the face of both brothers watching her.

Luther's reaction to the news about Bertha is to go to pieces. Urged by Joe, he cleans himself up, listens to Mrs Purdy's comments on the decor, and then, as his mother did in scene one, turns the account of Bertha's plight into a diatribe against Minnie. It's the second time Mrs Purdy has heard it (and will keep her in gossip for a good while). As with Mrs Gascoigne, there is an alliance between Luther and Mrs Purdy against what they see as the affectations of Minnie. The gap between Minnie and Luther, already large, grows further because of the new events, but at the end of the scene, Minnie on her return fusses around Joe, lights a cigarette for him and, as Luther leaves, breaks down to tell Joe: 'Why – you don't know. You don't know how hard it is, with a man as – as leaves you alone all the time . . . he leaves me alone, he always has done – and there's nobody. . . .' By the end of the act, Lawrence has balanced the action of the play. It could have been a crude account either of the domineering mother-in-law; or, equally crudely, an account of the fanciful daughter-in-law. Instead, perhaps as a consequence of the form itself, what is being achieved is presentational, a statement of the picture itself, where the sympathies of the audience are being deliberately manipulated. In a letter to Violet Hunt of 13 December 1910, Lawrence wrote of *The Widowing of Mrs. Holroyd* that:[24]

> I was trying to persuade myself that I had really got the tones flat
> enough for an act-able play: you know what I mean – as in a
> decorative picture the tones are flat . . . and the figures are parts of
> a design rather than individuals – so I thought these Holroyd folk
> were nicely levelled down. Woe is me!

Lawrence is uninterested in writing propaganda in the play but in recording figures within a particular context. The impulse to judge definitively is constantly kept at bay by a technique which allows judgment and then modifies it. It is a reductive process which forces something like objectivity upon an audience. Localized decisions are thereby supplanted as the play evolves. Unless that is achieved, the play becomes a sour story of warring factions, unresolved and vicious.

In the short second act, Luther cannot, does not want to contain the news about Bertha. The case of the hapless, pregnant woman is used, as before, as a means of doing something else. In this case, Luther uses it to try to hurt Minnie. Drunkenly, he flings the fact at her. Minnie, totally thrown when she finally realizes what is being said, ranges through shock to calmly deciding to go back into service, to angry accusation. The gulf between them seems insuperable. The act is about the inability of either of them to establish a vocabulary of co-existence. They use what resources they have, which at this stage, are few and destructive.

The longer act three finally brings the two women together against the background of the strike having started. It is a fortnight later. Minnie returns from Manchester to find Mrs Gascoigne in her house. The hostility is immediate, but since Minnie was away, the mother has arrived to provide food for Luther. Lawrence follows a recognizable pattern in letting Mrs Gascoigne give Minnie details of the strike (and the attempts to break it) before approaching the central subject, Minnie and her husband. Before it can develop, the men arrive. The subject of blacklegs at the pit occupies the men until, somewhat awkwardly, Luther tries to use the analogy by proposing a blackleg 'wife' to do instead of Minnie who has 'gone on strike'. The consequence of this is that Mrs Gascoigne resolves to 'mind my own business', but fairly quickly doesn't and at last the two women confront each other. The confrontation is brilliantly and naturally orchestrated. Each of them accuses the other, but Minnie's appears the stronger voice and Mrs Gascoigne recognizes the truth of what Minnie says about strong women, since she demonstrates that she is capable of the same strength. Minnie's judgment of the mother and her sons clearly affects Mrs Gascoigne but not as backbiting. The indictment is no more than a statement of the necessary truth and the contest slows down cleverly as Minnie, having said her say, comes to; 'We'll have some tea, should we?' The women come to some form of understanding at this point. Minnie, for the first time in the play, calls Mrs Gascoigne 'Mother', as they compare their housekeeping. As the scene slows, it flares again when Minnie reveals that she has spent all her money. The £120 has gone on rings and prints. Minnie has decided that 'I was sick of having it between us' and in one action has brought herself the chance of making the marriage work. The effect upon the Gascoigne family is comic and enraged. Mrs Gascoigne is reduced to speechlessness and tears, and Luther completes Minnie's action by hurling the prints into the fire. At the curtain, Minnie 'stands with her hand on the mantelpiece', alone. It is yet to be resolved.

The very brief final act brings the two women together again. Mrs Gascoigne arrives to try to find Joe who has not been home. Neither has Luther. The two women sit in the silence of the dawn and the silence from the pit not working and, as a consequence of the row the previous day, Mrs Gascoigne begins to share her experience with her daughter-in-law. She describes men as 'revengeful children' and her account of a life built around men gains a tragic force. She is teaching Minnie what she knows and any account of the mother built upon the first scene of the play must consider what she says in the last scene. Mrs Gascoigne gives Minnie her experience and her son: 'An' tha can ha'e Luther. Tha'lt get him, an' tha can ha'e him.' In that is the recognition on Mrs Gascoigne's part of Minnie's strength and Minnie understands it. When Luther arrives, it seems for a moment as if nothing has changed for he goes immediately to his mother. But the mother leaves to find Joe, and the husband and wife finally come together. It is not said that they will be happy. It is said only that they may be. The final image is still of the men as 'children' as Minnie supplants the mother-in-law.[25]

The main thrust of the 1967 production at the Court, which held good for the 1968 group of Lawrence plays, was to do with the physical environment of the world of the play. Initially, the approach came from the 1965 production of *A Collier's Friday Night*:[26]

> it was to lay down the rules, which is where all the detailed business
> that it became famous for sort of started, but quite unconsciously.
> It was not deliberate . . . it was that I knew you had to go through
> all these things that were being done and I didn't like slapdash,
> pseudo-naturalistic business at that time. It used to get on my nerves.
> It was all very orchestrated in those productions. It was all too

ceremonious, if you like. It had a kind of poetic, heightened quality, whatever the word is one says after the event.

What was stressed was the importance of the physical activity going on throughout the play. Anne Dyson, who was to repeat her role as Mrs Gascoigne in 1968 and also play Mrs Lambert in *A Collier's Friday Night* and the Grandmother in *The Widowing of Mrs. Holroyd* recalls that there were:[27]

> a lot of silences while I was just getting on with the work. They [the audience] had something to look at. There was no question of just getting on with the dialogue. It's worked out in sequences . . . doing it over and over again until you find the timing which becomes part of the rhythm of the play . . . it could become mechanical but it doesn't because it's part of the action of the play, so the whole thing becomes quite natural . . . when it all clicks into place, it's a wonderful feeling.

Edward Peel, who was persuaded by Gill not to leave the Court and to stay for the Lawrence plays, initially had to understudy the two men in *The Daughter-in-Law*, and play a miner, as well as understudy the other men in *The Widowing of Mrs. Holroyd*. When *The Daughter-in-Law* of 1968 was extended for two weeks, Victor Henry left the cast, and Peel played Joe:[28]

> Rehearsals were very exacting. Gill was a stickler for detail and the realism was such that it was absolutely spellbinding. I can still vividly recall a sequence when Luther was washing off his pit dirt and Joe was eating some jam and Yorkshire pudding. Luther had just been told of his former girl's pregnancy and he realises the shattering effect that it will have on his marriage. It was followed by a silent sequence of preparing for washing and the ritual of washing with Joe silently nodding in an armchair by the fire. It was something like a twenty minute sequence which in rehearsal the actors felt would never hold but always, always did and was magical. The baking of bread, the washing of bodies were practicalities which Gill was absolutely meticulous about. Whatever the crisis, the hardships, the dramas encountered by these working class people, the practical, everyday duties still had to be performed and were the cornerstone around which these plays were built . . . water steamed when it came from the hob, meals steamed and there was a wonderful smell of freshly baked bread and Yorkshire pudding. Gill worked like a madman and consequently made himself ill, but he was a wonderful director.

Gill, deliberately to begin with, did not concentrate on the play's dialect. Anne Dyson remembers that the Company did have a record of the dialect but 'we ignored it to start with. Peter didn't emphasize it too much to start with',[29] and Gill had a good reason: 'I didn't encourage a Nottingham accent, because a lot of Nottingham is to do with that very beautiful Derbyshire, creamy tone. Not in the accent, but in the vocal quality. We didn't do a lot on that, we just kept faith with how it was written.'[30] What was done, however, was a good deal of improvisation where 'We had days out going to the fair with the boys when they were young, all based on the plays themselves. They were used to get a feeling of the characters, the sort of things that they would do. It was a release, it helped you to relax . . . we usually did that at the beginning of a rehearsal, a sort of loosening up process.'[31]

The 1967 *Daughter-in-Law* received twenty-five performances and achieved a 48 per cent box-office, with 61.1 per cent of the seats sold. Critically, the play was quite well received but as Gill said 'it was a sleeper in people's consciousness because it did relatively good business. It was a typical Court thing . . . because of the curious hierarchy at the Court and me being one of the younger directors, nobody pounced on it. It sort of seeped in that it had gone very well. . . . It struck a chord.'[32] Nothing happened, however, until Gill proposed the idea of a group of Lawrence's plays: 'Having read the plays, what occurred to me was that here were three plays all set in Eastwood, which seemed to cleave together. They were quite different, but they yielded up a company, for example. You can always get a company built round an author. . . .'[33] By 31 May 1967, Gaskill reported to a Management committee that Gill wanted to do a short season and felt that the Court should take up the options on the plays.

The three Lawrence plays were performed by eighteen actors, of whom five had been in either or both of the earlier productions. There existed therefore a nucleus of actors who were familiar with Lawrence the play-wright and Gill the director. This alone became a central feature of the great success of the plays. The casting process was still difficult. For example, having cast Anne Dyson in two of the plays, Gill, as late as the Saturday before rehearsals began, decided that she ought to play in *A Collier's Friday Night* as well. After another field trip to Eastwood, work began on 8 January 1968. Since only seven weeks were available for rehearsal, Gill divided part of the responsibility for the shows among his two assistants, Rob Knights and Barry Hanson. The former took charge of *The Daughter-in-Law*, the latter took *A Collier's Friday Night*, while Gill himself concentrated on *The Widowing of Mrs. Holroyd*. *The Daughter-in-Law* initially received less attention because of the 1967 production. The pressure on all concerned was immense over the seven weeks and what was to prove the single most affecting scene turned out to be the final sequence in *The Widowing of Mrs. Holroyd*, where Holroyd's body lies dead on the floor and Mrs Holroyd and the Grandmother prepare to wash the body. For a long time in rehearsal, the two actors (Parfitt and Dyson) could not prevent themselves from weeping:[34]

> Peter used to go mad because we used to cry, couldn't help it. Peter
> said the audience would never take it, stop crying, get on with it,
> do what you have to do, practical things. . . . Finally, Judy cried,
> but not the mother because the mother had lived through this sort
> of thing; she just reminisced. The audience were stunned by it. When
> the curtain came down, there wasn't a sound. Nobody came round
> after the show . . . it took practically the whole of the rehearsal
> period.

The effort involved in mounting three productions eventually told. Gill fell ill at the end of rehearsals and after the technical run of *A Collier's Friday Night* which, remarkably, did not stop and became a full run-through, he ended up in hospital the following day. Slightly earlier, each of the plays had had a run-through. The run of *Holroyd* 'was rather a famous thing. It was full of people and everybody started crying at the last scene. . . .'[35] With Gill in hospital, Gaskill took over *A Collier's Friday Night* and Jane Howell *The Daughter-in-Law*, with the two assistants co-ordinating the third play. As Judy Parfitt says: 'It's enormous credit to Peter that the plays got on as he wanted them to, and to the attitude at the Court, that the . . . actors didn't feel left, but were looked after with warmth, respect and understanding.'[36]

The three plays opened at weekly intervals and continued in repertory for a total of sixty-one performances. Critical praise reached a rare degree of near unanimity. Over 21,000 seats were sold, an average of 86 per cent. The Management committee was told on 15 October that the touring production of *The Daughter-in-Law* had won first prize in Belgrade at the annual BITEF Festival. What had begun in 1965 as a Sunday night production which Gill could not get out of became in 1968 one of the Court's best moments during the period.

The process for Gill did not conclude once the plays were running. Towards the end of the season, at the point where Edward Peel was to replace Victor Henry as Joe, Gill watched *The Daughter-in-Law* and was not pleased with some of what he saw. He issued a long note designed to halt something of a decline in the playing. After complaining generally about the tiredness visible on stage and attributing it in some cases to 'perhaps their private life or outside professional commitments . . . for which I think it unreasonable to suppose that *The Daughter-in-Law* should suffer', Gill concentrated upon the playing of the first two scenes:[37]

> After these scenes the play itself is simply strong dramatically and
> will produce energy whether or not you have it – and that said I
> must say I was quite impressed with a lot of the playing in the
> subsequent scenes. The first two scenes, however, demand a great

deal from the audience. . . . It seemed in these scenes that you also have believed the press: it was *slow*, except where you were shouting or getting laughs, it was often too *sotto voce*, too significant. The business was being dreadfully *shown off* rather than *experienced* by you for its sake and not for any nonsensical ritual or whatever. The second scene is always difficult: it is a lovely scene but very long and the orchestration and feeling must be adhered to or it goes down the drain . . .

Part of Gill's concern centres on the playing of the women:

Judy and Anne, on last night's showing, seem to have believed the press, indeed seemed determined on proving that Lawrence was Strindberg. *He was not*; *he was Lawrence.* . . . Judy, I know, when she is tired, feels a nervous response to over-energize. But on Saturday both she and Anne really supported those people who find Lawrence's women ball cutters. They are both (the actresses I mean) extremely nice women and the women they play are extremely high class cookies and should not falsely over attack. . . . Minnie Gascoigne is a working class girl who actually changes a situation. . . . I wrote down *every single* line in the first Minnie/Luther scene on account of each one of hers being quite so unpleasant. It must not go that far because with the way Michael plays it, it seems incredible to begin with that there is *anything* between them, and there really *is*, they really are attracted to each other. The kiss is good, however: but when Judy sits down before it, she must modulate – sensually and tired and potentially sexy, look indulgently and idly at her washing (there must be more white washing for her to look at).

Gill also, and this is at a point where the productions are already massively successful, argues about details. Of Minnie, he says:

I know she doesn't wear much make-up, but because no one else does, even a little shows up and I think if you check, Judy, you will find red lipstick was worn in 1912 only by women in service of a quite different kind to Minnie Gascoigne's. Also I realize the wig was over-dressed but please insist, Judy, that it never looks as though Minnie's own private hairdresser pops in twice a week. Also remember that while I'm sure you'll be wearing charm bracelets in *A Hotel in Amsterdam* you shouldn't appear to be wearing them now.

The details are the essence of the productions. Gabrielle Day is invited to help the other actors in scene one 'to overcome a tendency to present it as if it were J. B. Priestley rewritten by Harold Pinter'; Michael Coles should not react to Mrs Gascoigne's saying, 'Where's Joe?', 'as if she were in the SS' and Edward Peel is asked to 'play with your own passion and life and remember you look very much as Lawrence imagined Joe'. The notes end with the assertion that:

It is a magnificent play, the best of the three, but it only just scraped
home and compared to the playing of *A Collier's Friday Night* the
other night some people would certainly think it an inferior work. I
only want these notes to make these last performances try to re-
create some of the fine playing I have seen in the show.

Even a cast of the calibre of *The Daughter-in-Law* was not immune from
real and constructive criticism. As Anne Dyson remarked of other
productions she had been in: 'There are so many things done which are
unnecessary and so many things asked which are unnecessary.'[38] Lawrence had asked, in his 'Preface' to *Touch and Go* (written June 1919), for
plays about people:

> Not mannequins. Not lords nor proletarians nor bishops nor husbands
> nor co-respondents nor virgins nor adulteresses nor uncles nor noses.
> Not even white rabbits nor presidents. People. Men who are
> somebody, not men who are something.

For Gill, Lawrence 'seemed to be a completely natural Royal Court writer.
I think that was the curious thing about it, this bloke that people either
liked or didn't like, who I happened to be very influenced by, reading
The White Peacock by chance when young, and then *Sons and Lovers*, and
the productions and the plays seemed to be proper home.'[39]

5 · From April 1968 to March 1970

Early Morning finally reached the stage in a Sunday night performance on 31 March 1968. The publicity leaflet announced that the production 'celebrates the twelfth anniversary of the English Stage Company'. Ironically, the celebrations were via a writer whose work had yet to receive a public performance in his own country. Despite the verbal assurance by the Chamberlain that he would not proceed against a production for Society members, John Calder, the publisher, noted that in the audience was the same police officer, Detective Chief Inspector Alton, who had served the notice of prosecution on Calder for his publishing Hubert Selby's novel, *Last Exit to Brooklyn*.[1] Unsurprisingly, the performance was not a success. Bond wrote to his American agent, Toby Cole, on 8 April, that on his return from filming in Czechoslovakia:

> I got involved in the last stages of rehearsing *Early Morning*. . . .
> Because of rehearsing difficulties (the actors were all earning their
> livings in other rehearsals!), [it] was cut down to two performances.
> One performance was given – but after that the police visited the
> theatre, and the licensee banned the second performance. So a hurried
> performance was given for the critics in the afternoon – and it was a
> disaster, badly under rehearsed and unconvincing. This isn't Bill
> Gaskill's fault – if he'd had time it would have been one of his best
> productions. Inevitably, after this, the notices have been terrible –
> but I don't care.

The evolution of the production was under impossible conditions. Gaskill was not fully recovered from his illness, internal rows were continuing and, as Bond notes above, the amount of rehearsal time for a Sunday night is always very limited. Jane Howell, Gaskill's Associate, was in the 1968 production and recalls the time as one of frayed nerves and great pressure:[2]

> we never cracked *Early Morning*. I did see two rehearsals when *Early
> Morning* was nearly cracked, and then it all went back to the beginning
> again and in those two rehearsals the actors were very tired and there

was a lot of pressure . . . they started playing it rather fast and
nervously, and it started to become farcical, and it was very funny
and very fast, and you didn't have time to think because you were
laughing too much . . .

She also recalls that Gaskill was still unwell and refused to rehearse one
morning because someone was two minutes late. She herself was threatened with dismissal by Gaskill when he realized she was rehearsing the
cast when he was absent.[3] The Chamberlain was effectively damaging the
production without taking further action but he was to be helped by the
Court's licensee, who was profoundly alarmed when, a few days after the
31 March performance, two police officers questioned Gaskill and Alfred
Esdaile. Scotland Yard admitted that an investigation had been launched
that might lead to consultations with the Director of Public Prosecutions.
Consequently, the Court sought legal advice, 'at which conference Mr.
Esdaile was present, and the Management Commitee of the English Stage
Company decided to ask the English Stage Society to continue with the
second performance. Mr. Esdaile, however, later exercised his legal right
as the licensee of the theatre, and banned the second performance.'[4] Not
for the first time had Esdaile acted against the wishes of the Company
and, as before over *Macbeth*, his views were finally dismissed. In place
of the second scheduled performance, a teach-in on censorship was held
with Tynan, Gaskill, Bond and Calder. In the afternoon, a private
performance was given and described as 'a dress rehearsal', with guests
being screened before admission via a side door. The idea of proceeding
in this way came from Greville Poke. The Company had received a letter
from Esdaile's lawyers threatening the withdrawal of the licence[5]

and we were frightened of it, obviously, though dubious as to whether
he would really succeed. . . . I was puzzling out how we could deal
with this thing and then I suddenly thought, why couldn't we have
a non-paying, private production and call it a dress-rehearsal. It was
an absolutely phoney thing of course, and I rang up Neville Blond,
who had got Robin Fox with him at the time . . . and they said,
good idea, go ahead and do it. So that's what I did. It was an
extraordinary situation. The only sad part of the story was that the
notices which were eventually published were so bad.

The reviews were indeed loud in their condemnation, but John Arden
defended the importance of Sunday night performances in a letter to *The
Times* dated 8 April:

The whole point of Sunday evening performances at the Royal Court
is that works which may well be untalented, or muddled, should
nevertheless be given an inexpensive and experimental production in
the only way that matters to a dramatist – on a stage, before an
audience.

Mr. Bond has already shown in his earlier writings that he is a playwright who knows his business. But he will never be able to develop himself further in his craft unless he is given the opportunity to make his own mistakes. . . . It is therefore all the more horrifying that the work of an obviously talented writer should be snuffed out in its very beginnings by a sinister confederation of the Lord Chamberlain (and his bravoes, the police) and the licensee of the Royal Court – a gentleman whose interests in the bricks-and-mortar of the building should weigh in the scales alongside those of the artists concerned, not against them.

Arden spoke from direct experience of the advantage of Sunday night shows and of damning critical reaction. On the same day as the letter was written, Esdaile demanded the suspension of Gaskill for a month, pending discussions about his future. He also offered his own resignation and complained that 'Mr. Gaskill had gone behind my back and put the play on, under the guise of a dress rehearsal. I have been against putting it on from the start. It has no artistic merit and I think Mr. Gaskill and Mr. Bond are doing it just for the publicity.'[6] Esdaile's views were discounted by the Court. In the same newspaper report, Poke gave his view that if the question of Gaskill's being fired came to a vote in the Council, Esdaile would find himself in a minority of one. Nevertheless, the affair had its damaging effect. Though the governing bodies of the Company had, as always, closed ranks in the face of external attack, the hostility within the Court's walls remained. Gaskill recalls that the episode 'was too fraught and I'd lost the support of the Council really on that. It all became too tense. I don't remember it as a period of great solidarity. I remember it more as a period of hysteria.'[7] Yet the absolute tenacity of Gaskill in driving *Early Morning* through to a production of sorts provided the clinching argument against the Chamberlain. It was the last play to be banned in its entirety in English theatrical history. On 28 September 1968, George Strauss's bill, the Theatres Act, became law.[8] Though the struggle against the censor had by no means been confined to the Royal Court, it is undoubtedly true that Gaskill and his associates conducted the main campaign. They brought to a conclusion in this way one of Devine's main preoccupations.

The programme for the 1968–9 season, unlike earlier seasons, was reasonably well fixed at the beginning of April. At a Management committee meeting of 3 April (exactly in the middle of the *Early Morning* crisis), Gaskill proposed to extend the Lawrence season for two weeks, to bring into the main bill Michael Rosen's *Backbone*, which had appeared as a Sunday night production on 11 February (the play had won a prize at the National Union of Students Drama Festival) and to follow this with John Osborne's new plays, *Time Present* and *The Hotel in Amsterdam*.

The new play season of four would follow. At this stage, they were to be John Antrobus's *Trixie and Baba*, Christopher Hampton's *Total Eclipse*, David Cregan's *The Houses by the Green*, and a new play by David Storey, *In Celebration*. The last of these in the event was delayed until Lindsay Anderson was available to direct it. It was finally replaced by a revival of *Look Back in Anger*, thus making the main bill very much to do with Osborne. When, eventually, the season also included a group of three of Bond's plays, the list of main house productions seemed to reflect present and former regimes at the Court. There is no doubt where Gaskill's loyalties lay and what his mood was during the 1968–9 season:[9]

> I remember vividly thinking that, whereas at one time I felt very centred in the theatre, I became very ambivalent about the kind of theatre I was running. For instance, the Osborne plays we put on, which made money and financed the Bond season, were two plays that I particularly disliked. I thought they were sub-West End plays and well suited to the West End but I didn't think they broke any new ground at all.

However, despite Gaskill's views, the name of Osborne in the minds of some at the Court still reflected the former days of glory and of financial security. And the question of finance was omnipresent. Neville Blond at the 3 April meeting requested that in future the running costs of productions (as opposed to the production budget) should accompany the budgets themselves and clearly was determined to keep a close eye on expenditure.

The matter of finance arose in connection with the development of the club. By 3 April, three short plays had been performed, since its reopening in March. It has already been seen that Gaskill had definite ideas about the use to which the space could be put, but at a Management committee of 19 April, a proposal surfaced via Alfred Esdaile that the club be used 'for the purpose of providing club facilities for young accountants'. Thus stated in the Minutes, the proposal assumes an irresistibly comic tone but the real point is that it would bring in around £2,000 each year. It would also spell the end, inevitably, of serious theatrical development for, although it was said that the short plays could continue, those running the club for the accountants said that they would like three weeks' notice of a production. After discussion, the proposal was not accepted, although Neville Blond, somewhat ominously, felt that the theatre could not afford to forego the money involved. By the end of April, Gaskill reported to the Artistic committee that six plays had been seen at the club and that he would like to keep up this intensive work, perhaps at the rate of one production each week. It was agreed that the performances should be advertised. With the three Osborne plays scheduled for the main bill, what is noticeable at this stage is the extent to which Gaskill sought other outlets. At the same meeting, he suggested the planning of a project, 'either of an experimental studio or of a play rehearsed for a long period'. The finance should come from the annual budget. Harewood suggested that such a scheme could well come into existence towards the end of a financial year, when the figures would be clear. It is therefore at this meeting that what was eventually to become the Theatre Upstairs was first aired. On 4 June, as Gaskill told the Council meeting the following day, a studio had begun in the club, financed by the remnants of the original Gulbenkian grant. It would run for six weeks and involve, as well as writers, actors and directors, painters and musicians.[10]

While this development was taking place, echoes of the *Early Morning* performances were still very much to be heard. It had become clear that the visit of police officers to the theatre on that occasion had been prompted as a result of the Chamberlain's supplying information to the office of the Director of Public Prosecutions, notwithstanding the censor's assurance that he would not interfere with Sunday night shows. The Management committee of 19 April discussed the future of Sunday nights in the light of police action over *Early Morning* and it was decided to see whether Neville Blond, together with Greville Poke and Lord Harewood, might see the Chamberlain to discuss the matter. Meanwhile, the double-bill, planned for Sunday 28 April should go ahead. The uncertainty of the Company's position was now extremely irksome as regards planning. Two days later, the Artistic committee recommended that no such meeting take place, in case the Chamberlain used the occasion to ask for the submission of Sunday night scripts in future. Better, the committee decided, to carry on nearly regardless. The immediate future seemed very uncertain, particularly as regards whether the Chamberlain would produce a final flourish as the Theatres Bill moved towards receiving the Royal Assent. Equally, there now arose the problem of the position once the Bill became law. Theatres would face potentially a prosecution under common law. Greville Poke wrote to Lord Harewood on 30 May, pointing out that a successful prosecution could render the entire theatre board liable, and that this in turn raised the question of the relationship of the Artistic Director to his board. It became a question much discussed over the coming months.

The disputes within the Company surfaced at the Council meeting of 5 June. The chairman asked all those 'in attendance', except the Artistic Director, the Arts Council and the representative of the Royal Borough of Kensington and Chelsea, to retire. Then Neville Blond expressed his concern about the management of the theatre, and in particular about expenditure upon certain productions. He referred specifically to unauthorized expenditure on *Early Morning*. Whilst stating that he never had or would interfere with artistic policy, he stressed that his duty lay in how the funds produced by the Arts Council were used by the Company. What obviously rankled was the money spent on *Early Morning* before the budget had been presented. Eventually, everyone reaffirmed where the different responsibilities lay and the meeting moved on. It cannot, however, have done so happily, for while it was no doubt true that Blond did not overtly interfere with artistic policy, it is also the case that by this stage he and Gaskill simply did not agree as to the nature of the theatre for which in different ways they were responsible. Blond can hardly have been delighted to hear in the same meeting that *Early Morning* was scheduled for an autumn production. In addition, Council accepted that the George Devine award for 1968 should go to Edward Bond. The Council also reviewed the progress of the Schools Scheme. In the middle of May, Gaskill and Jane Howell had held a meeting with the Arts Council and discussed the Scheme in detail. Amongst the suggestions were: five plays to be presented for schools, two main bill and three Sunday nights; the continuing of demonstration work; the transfer of school shows to Sunday night productions; the commissioning of new plays for children to be performed at the theatre with schoolchildren; a teachers' course and the continuing of the student card scheme. In response to a request for £4,800, the Arts Council produced £4,300 and suggested that an assistant be found to work on the Schools Scheme.

By June, Gaskill, happily, had a backlog of plays demanding some attention. He told the Artistic committee on 11 June that a number of plays deserved more than a Sunday night or were, alternatively, too short or too problematic for the main bill. Amongst these were Michael McClure's *The Beard*, which Michael White and Tony Richardson wished to import from America, *AC/DC*, which Heathcote Williams had rewritten, *The Diary Plays of Franz Kafka* and Bond's new play *Narrow Road to the Deep North* (if it did not go into the main house). Gaskill's idea was to present some of these plays as late night performances on Thursday to Saturday and as Sunday nights for two or three weeks. He ran into difficulties almost immediately with *The Beard*, a play which had been prosecuted a number of times in America. At the 11 June meeting, the play and its implications were discussed. John Osborne had read the play and thought it was 'rubbish'. He was not opposed to its production except that, given the liability of the theatre board to prosecution under common law once the Theatres Act became law, he was not prepared 'to go into the witness box or risk being fined for a play that he did not particularly like'. Osborne further stated that *The Beard* was not the right play to test the new legal conditions obtaining for the theatre. The clear implication of this is the attempt by Gaskill to meet head on and to clarify those new conditions. Gaskill's view was that the play was 'a wonderful, poetic play', but the Artistic committee now wished for the right to read plays for which the members might personally be prosecuted. The meeting agreed to circulate the play and to discuss it further. In other words, the uncertainty of how the law would now operate was effectively providing a censorship of its own, and at this stage there were some who perhaps felt that, odious as the official censor had been, at least he was identifiable. The general public's reaction, by definition, was unknowable.

While the discussion developed over the quality and extent of the new freedom in the theatre, the Court's main bill productions reflected a characteristic pattern. The two Osborne plays were a box-office success. *Time Present* achieved 75.5 per cent, and *The Hotel in Amsterdam* reached 96.2 per cent. Both plays transferred to the West End, the first to the Duke of York's Theatre on 11 July, the second initially to the New Theatre on 5 September, and subsequently to the Duke of York's on 12 December. The critical reaction was muted and talked of consolidation rather than progress. Martin Esslin reflected that 'Thus do the angry young men of 1956 turn into the Edwardian high Tories of 1968, the iconoclasts of yesteryear into the satisfied upholders of established values of today.'[11] The new plays in the main bill fared less well at the box-office. Antrobus's *Trixie and Baba* managed 22.5 per cent, Hampton's *Total Eclipse* got to 45.0 per cent and the new David Cregan, *The Houses by the Green*, dropped to 18.6 per cent. Hampton's play was his first as the Court's Resident Dramatist. On 10 July, Gaskill told the Management committee that Hampton had completed his studies at Oxford and, with Arts Council agreement, could be appointed to the post. Hampton thus became the first of a long line of writers to be attached to the theatre in this way. Interviewed a few months after taking up the appointment, Hampton described the job: 'I'm in charge of the script department. We receive about twenty scripts a week and apart from myself there are half a dozen readers. I read about ten scripts as second opinion. . . . We're going to open up a studio theatre here, you know, which will make it possible to put more new plays on. It has 100 seats. But the policy is not definitely formulated yet.'[12] If the new plays had had mixed fortune, the third of Osborne's plays, a revival of *Look Back in Anger*, raised the box-office to 66.9 per cent and transferred on 10 December to the Criterion Theatre. As ever, Osborne's work produced funds for the theatre but by now Gaskill was developing ideas about a way of breaking the pattern of main bill shows with established stars, on the success of which new plays were to be launched. He was also attempting to define where his real responsibilities lay.

At an Artistic committee meeting of 17 July, Gaskill spoke of the difficulties of dealing with the backlog of new work by putting them on as late-night additions to the main bill production. One was clearly that if a show ran past midnight, it would involve problems with the licence. Another was the consequent problem of finding an audience. He proposed an alternative. Since the performances upstairs were becoming very popular, he asked for permission to make some structural alterations to the club. He thought that, if rostra levels were installed and the bar taken out, up to 150 people could be seated. Shows might then run for up to three weeks at a time. Gaskill's reasons for this idea are complex. He had become conscious that, unlike Devine, he had not developed a group of assistants who could take over the Court's direction when it arose: 'In fact, the Court lived off George for all that period really. I don't think I was anywhere near as successful in developing people.'[13] His attempt to develop assistants, as has been seen, began initially with studio work and was then moved into shows in the club in the spring and summer of 1968. Gaskill was also reacting to the steady growth of small theatres in London in 1968, as Nicholas Wright recalls:[14]

> Bill said he was fed up with some of these people, these kinds of
> students and people, doing perfectly good productions of plays in
> attics and cellars. Why couldn't we, the assistant directors, do plays?
> And we said, 'All right.' He said, 'You can't spend any money.' 'Really?
> How much?' He said, 'No, you really can't spend any money.' We
> just had to get people who would do it, put on plays for nothing. . . .
> Victor Henry put on a play called *Booze*. . . . Bill put on an
> improvised play called *A Show of Violence*, starring him and Barry
> Hanson . . . it was a sixties going on. It was Bill thinking, 'What is
> all this? There is something to all this . . .', and then the Theatre
> Upstairs was very much an extension of that.

The performances were often quite lively. Edward Peel, whose first part at the Court was in *The Dragon* (December 1967) recalls:[15]

> trying to perform *Tube Boobs* to an audience of well-pissed Chelsea
> guardsmen who'd spilled in from the pub next door. Bill Gaskill,
> Jane Howell, Bill Bryden, Bob Kidd, Philip Hedley, Barry Hanson,
> Rob Knights and others performed a directors' improvisation
> evening to a mixed audience who were throwing half crown drinks
> down their throats and barracking. . . . I was sometimes thereafter
> employed as a bouncer. . . . Directors don't like the piss being taken.

It was also simply the case that there was great pressure to keep the theatre solvent via the main bill and that the development of work upstairs could provide some kind of solution but at this stage there was no thought of a second auditorium playing a regular programme. For one reason, the money was not available. For another, even a smaller space still ran the risk of the drying up of new work. However, the proposal was received reasonably and no doubt some figures at the Court felt that, whatever else, the more risky work could be siphoned off in this way.

By July, Gaskill had proposed a season of plays by Edward Bond, prompted by the success of *Narrow Road to the Deep North*, which had opened at the Belgrade, Coventry in June. Thus the intention of reviving *Early Morning* expanded into a full-scale small season of Bond plays, both to continue the support for Bond, to be the theatre which first offered Bond's plays to the public in the UK, and also to celebrate the abolition of state censorship. At the same time, Gaskill was threatening to resign over *The Beard*. The play was discussed in the same Artistic committee of 17 July. The issue, for which *The Beard* provided the occasion, was to do with the freedom of the Artistic Director to choose the plays to be put on in the theatre, and the demand that that freedom be supported by the Artistic committee. The committee in turn was attempting to secure its individual members from the threat of prosecution and also to provide the very freedom which Gaskill was demanding. In urging his point, Gaskill argued the importance of not neglecting new work:

> the standard of plays from America is getting better. We cannot ignore certain kinds of freer, more experimental work which is now being shown. We must let in this new element. At one time we were aware of Brecht and Ionesco and to cut off the Court from this type of play would be a very crucial decision.

Greville Poke spoke for the Council when he worried at the possible prosecution of all of the theatre's permanent staff. After a lengthy discussion, the committee affirmed its confidence in Gaskill's position 'but their decision would not affect the action of the Management Committee. Mr. Gaskill felt he would have to resign if his freedom was limited in this way.'

The Beard eventually appeared as a late night production from 4 November, after performances of *Look Back in Anger*. The Company accepted legal advice that, provided that there was a separate contract between the theatre and the producers (White and Richardson), and that the play was not jointly billed with *Look Back in Anger*, and that seats were not sold jointly, there would be no action taken against the Court. The discussion over the Artistic Director's freedom, which the play provoked, continued. Eventually, the Artistic committee for 17 September agreed to recommend that Gaskill's contract be amended to show that he had freedom of choice as regards plays, subject to budgetary control, but that a successful prosecution 'would be a reason for terminating his contract'. Though this revision did not remove the possibility of individuals on the committee being prosecuted, the device did resolve the matter to the committee's satisfaction. The Company's lawyers were to be consulted further. Thus an important precedent for the freedom of artistic directors generally in the theatre may be seen in the making on this occasion.

The Company accounts to the end of September 1968 showed a very successful six months in financial terms. The amount by which the surplus exceeded expectations came to £19,350. The Lawrence season and the two Osborne plays had been the main contributors to this state of affairs. The high reputation of the Company was demonstrated when in September, Gill's production of *The Daughter-in-Law* won first prize at the Belgrade Festival. And the conversion of the club was proceeding. Gaskill secured the agreement of the Management committee on 15 October to present four plays for three weeks each early in 1969. The estimated loss was £5,000 (the average cost of a main bill production). The possibilities for structural modification had been discovered in the first instance by Nicholas Wright (the Theatre Upstairs's first director) and Peter Gill. According to Wright, Gill at this stage had been influenced considerably by studio work going on in America and thought of the club space as a potential research studio with no particular obligation to present a running repertory of plays:[16]

> Peter Gill and I used to like the space very much and once I remember
> we climbed on the roof and found a window which didn't seem to
> connect with anything. We looked through it and what we saw was
> the inside of the roof. The ceiling had been levelled off . . . a secret
> garden. . . . There was a lot of new work being shown in smaller
> auditoria . . . we saw an enormous amount of it, specifically the
> work that Jim Haynes was doing, and Brighton Combination. . . .
> Bill wanted to put the work on, but he didn't want to put it on the
> main stage, partly for commercial reasons. Also, it seemed to fit that
> space. . . . There was an enormous rush to convert it, because it
> had to present its first season within that financial year . . . the whole
> idea was that if it was successful, it would go on, become an
> intermittent theatre at least, and if it was a flop, it would go back to
> being a club again.

By 12 November, the club had been named the Theatre Upstairs. According to Gaskill, the name came from Joe Hodgkinson of the Arts Council, which was asked for a capital grant of £6,000, the cost of the conversion. Meanwhile, the English Stage Society loaned the Company £4,000, so that the work could begin. Gaskill intended the theatre to operate regularly if all went well and planned to include its costs henceforth in the Company's application to the Arts Council for its annual grant. At the same time, Gaskill reported to the Artistic committee on 12 November that he was very excited at finding two new writers. These were Jeremy Seabrook and Michael O'Neill, whose play, *Life Price* (originally titled 'Wergelt') would now follow *This Story of Yours*, the first stage play by the television writer, John Hopkins. The latter, after an initial week in Brighton, opened on 11 December and played to 43.1 per cent, and generally favourable notices. *Life Price* was a different matter. After eleven performances (which produced 14.4 per cent at the box-office), Gaskill decided to give all the seats away free for the rest of the run (another fourteen performances). As he explained in *The Times* (18 January), 'Free theatre was very much a part of my thinking for the future. But at present we are straddling a gap between experimental and commercial work.' The Arts Council, when asked for permission to offer free seats, refused to give a ruling. What did emerge from the decision was a packed house for the rest of the run. Yvonne Antrobus, a member of the cast, said 'We're getting marvellous audiences of young people, students who couldn't normally afford to go to the theatre', a view endorsed by Michael Billington who saw 'the stalls packed with young couples in their early twenties who, to judge from their conversation, were not regular theatregoers but who were visibly gripped by the performance. In fact, it was the most attentive audience I've come across for ages. . . .'[17] According to Billington, Gaskill, on television's *Late Night Line-Up*, argued that the Arts Council should set up something like six free theatres throughout London. The core of the action is, of course, the familiar attempt by the Court to find a wider audience and Gaskill pressed ahead with proposals to attempt one or more productions in the future free of charge. As he remarked at the time, 'This is the biggest step we have to take in the years ahead if the theatre is to remain alive.'[18] It was, however, a step he was never able to take.

The two major events at the beginning of 1969 were the presentation of the Edward Bond season and the opening on 24 February of the Theatre Upstairs. For the first time in England, the public could see *Saved* and *Early Morning*, as well as the London première of *Narrow Road to the Deep North*. If Bond acknowledged, as he did subsequently, the importance of the Royal Court to him, it is no less true that the Royal Court owed a comparable debt to him and to his tenacious director. The essential integrity of the Court during this period revolves around the struggle to free Bond's plays from the censor. It was both a battle for Bond and on behalf of the life of the theatre itself. Nowhere is Gaskill's quality as an Artistic Director shown more vividly, and many reviewers found themselves reconsidering earlier judgments. Bond's reputation, already established outside England, began its slow climb from this point in his own country.

The Theatre Upstairs survived some worries on the part of the Arts Council to open with David Cregan's play, *A Comedy of the Changing Years*. The Arts Council wished to be clear that the new auditorium would neither compromise nor dilute the main bill programme. Equally, it did not want a duplication of the work already in existence at theatres such as Hampstead and the Open Space. Gaskill, in a Management committee of 14 January, explained the need to accommodate 'a mass of young directors, writers and actors' currently available and that with a second theatre, 'the Court would be in the privileged position of being able to form a bridge between traditional and experimental theatres'. The Company further wished to change the Arts Council method of awarding the grant. Currently, it consisted of an outright grant, together with a guarantee against loss. The guarantee was obviously lost if shows were successful and particularly if they transferred to the West End. What the Company wanted was an increase in direct grant at the expense of the guarantee. Though the reported surplus at the end of December 1968 was £27,600 the request to the Arts Council was in order for experimental work to develop, rather than, as usually happened, fall the first victim in a lean period. Eventually, after Blond, Fox and Gaskill talked to the chairman of the Arts Council, the balance was altered, giving the Company £89,000 outright and reducing the guarantee to £5,000. A separate grant, as such, for the Theatre Upstairs, was not given. Nicholas Wright's view of the opening productions was that critical reaction was conditioned by the fact that reviewers were unused to small house productions, particularly small houses in larger theatres. Though the Theatre Upstairs was presenting new and important work, there seemed to be a lack of preparedness to judge that work in its particular context. Wright was not alone in his opinion. Irving Wardle in *The Times* (28 December 1968) had suggested that critics should 'Get out more to the provinces and the basements' and be prepared 'to make appropriate adjustments to assess productions designed for a particular locality'. And Helen Dawson argued that it was time 'that the whole role of criticism and how it relates to theatres, audience and newspaper readers *now* be discussed. . . . Plays have changed in construction and in subject matter . . . but journalistic criticism has hardly altered. Sometimes it seems out of touch: often the standard just isn't high enough.'[19] That two reviewers themselves should be sensitive to the problem goes some way to vindicate the feelings of some of the members of the Court. Robert Kidd's reaction to the notices received for Hampton's *Total Eclipse* (September 1968) was to voice the idea, shared by others at the Court, that the critics as such be replaced by other artists. The public might accept an improvement: 'lose Hobson, no – but lose Hobson for, say, Henry Moore, yes'.[20] The antagonism is familiar and was longstanding. Gaskill requested at a Management committee of 6 March that Milton Shulman of the *Evening Standard* should not be invited to review *Early Morning*. Gaskill had written to Greville Poke to say that if Shulman were invited 'we would be deliberately harming the work of the Theatre . . .'. The committee, however, decided that the Court should not differentiate between critics and told Gaskill he should not write to Shulman. The exchange was to prove a trailer to a more spectacular row later in the year.

The new financial year began with David Storey's *In Celebration* and marked the return of Lindsay Anderson as a director to the Court. His last production before this had been *Julius Caesar* in November 1964. Anderson had been invited by Gaskill to direct the play when he was involved in editing his film, *If . . .* and Anderson's response was that it was 'Something for which I shall always be grateful to him.'[21] The play was extremely well received and produced a box-office figure of 62.0 per cent. While Storey's play continued, Upstairs saw a revue about Enoch Powell, *The Enoch Show*, disrupted by members of the National Front, in which one actor, Henry Woolf, was knocked off the stage.[22] This was minor in comparison with what arose in June. At a Management committee for 12 June, Gaskill, after announcing the programme up to October, delivered without warning his intention to go on leave. He proposed to direct in Hamburg at the end of August and rehearse at the National Theatre in November for a production of *The Beaux' Stratagem*, which would open in Los Angeles early in 1970 before coming to London. The minutes record that the committee expressed 'surprise and concern' that Gaskill had not discussed his intentions beforehand. The question as to who would take over was raised and Gaskill thought he could still run the Court but, under pressure, agreed to consider the idea of another director taking charge during his absence and presenting a season. The names of Lindsay Anderson (who was at the meeting to discuss future plans for *In Celebration*) and Anthony Page were mentioned.

There is no doubt that Gaskill felt at this point that there had come a natural pause in the life of the Court as far as he was concerned:[23]

Funnily enough, I think when the battle against the censor had been won and we did the Bond season . . . the four years of work were justified. We'd got rid of the Lord Chamberlain. It's so difficult to imagine now, but it did loom enormously large over our lives. He had in a strange way given us a kind of *raison d'être*. There was a line through our work, that, if nothing else, we were fighting the censor and, in particular, we were fighting the censor on behalf of Edward Bond. If the Court meant anything, his plays had to be done . . . we did his plays and it was for me really as if something was over and I felt very empty and directionless. And it was in that kind of vacuum that the idea of Lindsay and Anthony being part of the theatre started and that created a completely different situation.

He felt that the process of renewal could be found in a period of leave to direct at other theatres. What obviously upset the committee was the lack of respect for observing the normal procedures. As Greville Poke observes:[24]

George Devine went to New York to direct *The Country Wife*. I think
there was always an understanding with George that if he wanted
to go off, provided he made suitable arrangements for the Court, he
could go off and do a production or take a sabbatical . . . if [Gaskill]
had said . . . I need a sabbatical after four years, I don't think there
would have been anybody on that committee that would have denied
him the right.

Far from agreeing with the committee about finding a replacement,
Gaskill felt that Jane Howell could stand in for him. Oscar Lewenstein
recalls that the suggestion regarding Jane Howell alarmed the Council:
'they insisted that instead he should ask Anderson and Page to come
in. . . . He was told by the Council that if he wanted to go off, he must
do that. They wouldn't have [Howell] take over that position.'[25] Clearly,
Gaskill in suggesting Jane Howell, was intent on maintaining the line of
work of which he spoke. However, the opportunity to modify the line
was seized when it presented itself. One cannot suppose that Neville
Blond did not suddenly see the possibilities. As Poke says:[26]

things weren't going at all well and Robin Fox, Oscar and Neville
had discussions amongst themselves as to whether or not we were
going to continue with Bill as Artistic Director or whether we should
try out another scheme. I was never quite sure whether it was Oscar's
or Robin's idea, the formation of the triumvirate, which was highly
successful and quite different . . .

According to Lindsay Anderson, the Council 'made it a condition of his
departure that he should invite someone of the status of Anthony Page
or myself to take over the running of the theatre. Bill chose Anthony
Page – who then asked me to join him. This is how both of us returned
to the Court after some years of virtual exclusion.'[27] They returned on
their own terms and not Gaskill's. At a meeting of the three directors,
Anderson and Page made it clear that they were not interested in a short
term appointment. The Management committee of 28 June was told that
their wish was for 'a continuing relationship' with the theatre. Anderson
in particular had not forgotten what had happened in 1965:[28]

That was simply our reaction to having been elbowed in 1965, which
I think we weren't particularly pleased about. We felt we had as
much to do with the Court as Bill did and, feeling that, to hell with
this, if they'd got into a jam, we're not going to just go in there and
hold the fort so that he can have a holiday and then be excluded when
he comes back again. So we made that a condition.

Whereas in the 1965 triumvirate, there was no question as to who was in
charge and what functions each of the three was responsible for, in 1969
the lack of an overall figure in authority was the basis for a good deal of
difficulty. The 'solution' of three directors such as Gaskill, Page and

Anderson was dictated not so much by good sense as by a strong feeling in some quarters that the theatre under Gaskill was not flourishing. When the Artistic committee met to discuss the proposal on 7 July, Lindsay Anderson's impact was immediate. He stressed his and Page's long-standing relationship with the Court and felt that, in spite of the difficulty of managing an equal division of responsibility, he was ready to commit himself 'to ensure that the traditions and future programme would be carried on for the immediate future'. Yet even at this stage, Anderson was doubtful whether a triumvirate would work in the long term and suggested it should not be immediately implemented. Rather, there could be an 'Artistic Council/Committee' which would meet regularly to consider the creative work of the theatre. Lord Harewood's response was to stress the importance of the Artistic committee and that if Anderson and Page did not wish the triumvirate to begin immediately, the arrangement would be described as 'a continuing relationship'. Anderson is intent here on defining the precise limits of the relationships. He remarks that 'absolute goodwill existed between Mr. Gaskill, Mr. Page and himself, but . . . creative impulses could be stronger than friendly feelings'. Anderson is also concerned at the work of the Artistic committee and felt that it had 'been reduced to a kind of impotence and although things had been difficult in the past he did not think this was an excuse for the inertia of the present'. The aim is obviously to administer a thorough shake-up. Amongst Anderson's plans for the autumn season were Storey's *The Contractor*, a new Donald Howarth play, *Macbeth*, *Sweet Bird of Youth* and *Hedda Gabler* (the last two as possibilities for a later season). That matters were unresolved is indicated by the fact that the Artistic committee met again the following day. All that had so far been resolved was that Anderson and Page should do a six-month season. Harewood was worried about the potential for breakdown in the administration inherent in a triumvirate. John Osborne was concerned about the potential 'clash of personalities'. Robin Fox was 'somewhat depressed' by the suggestion of an Artistic 'Council' at yesterday's meeting. Gaskill was very occupied 'with the emotional feelings of the staff'. The committee, faced with all this, decided that a long term solution had to be reached by the end of the year. When the Management committee met on the same day, it was told that both Council and the Artistic committee welcomed the prospect of Anderson and Page running the theatre while Gaskill was away 'with enthusiasm'. This became 'with much enthusiasm', when Harewood reported to the Council, again on 8 July. But all that had been settled was to do with the period when Gaskill was absent. The major matter of the continuing triumvirate remained for a future agenda.

Inevitably, the worries of the Artistic committee reflected a knowledge of the personalities involved. Anderson, as shown, was well aware of it, as was Gaskill:[29]

> my knowledge of Anthony and Lindsay made me already know that it would not altogether be easy. Also, when you run a theatre absolutely by yourself, with all the authority, to suddenly share it is, for someone who comes from where I come, quite difficult. It's foolish, really, because if you look at those years, they were also good years, in which quite a lot of very rich work was done . . .

And Oscar Lewenstein points out that Anderson and Page's situation was not easy, since 'The whole staff of the theatre had been recruited by Bill by that time and so most of their loyalty was to Bill.'[30] A group of theatre workers had been forced together by the events of four years' work and that period was about to end. After the American group, Bread and Puppet Theatre, had appeared in the main bill in June, Gaskill directed Congreve's *The Double Dealer* in July, the bookings of which were badly affected by a heatwave. Gaskill was not to direct again in the main bill until March 1971, though he worked in the Theatre Upstairs. The smaller house opened for a new season in July with a double bill by Peter Tegel followed by Peter Gill's *Over Gardens Out*. While *Saved* and *Narrow Road to the Deep North* were revived briefly in the main bill prior to a European tour, Howard Brenton's *Revenge* made its appearance Upstairs. In another area of the Company's work, Christopher Hampton had recruited David Hare as organizer of the script department. His view of the Court, coming new to it, seems to catch something of the atmosphere:[31]

> Nobody's work in the English theatre since 1945 had been so misrepresented as William Gaskill's at the Court. A small group of loyalists had ridden out the storm, and in all the important things had been proved right. . . . But the psychological cost of surviving the constant critical abuse had been very great: the staff were arrogant, touchy, entrenched. And a boy from university, as I was . . . found their prickliness incomprehensible.

While the Bond plays went abroad (where *Saved* won second prize in Belgrade on the grounds that festival rules made it impossible for the same company to win first prize in successive years) and the celebrated Compagnie Renaud-Barrault opened at the Court, Anderson and Page worked hard to establish the ground rules of the new arrangement. Both directors wanted included in their contracts a clause to the effect that their continuing influence on Company policy be effected via meetings of a small Artistic committee. The Management committee evaded the issue by arguing (on 17 September) that only Council members were eligible to serve on the committees. It is hardly surprising that Anderson and Page wished to identify their position as firmly as possible in a theatre which they perhaps saw as being in need of fairly radical change.

However, the new season, opening with Storey's play, *The Contractor*, on 20 October, had barely begun before an enormous row arose regarding critics.

On 2 October, a Company press release announced the withdrawal of press facilities from Hilary Spurling, the theatre critic of *The Spectator*. The release said: 'There is no question of our barring Mrs. Spurling: we are simply not inviting her to review our work. We do not find Mrs. Spurling's attitude to our work illuminating, and we don't believe that it furthers our relationship with the public.' The statement came from the Artistic Directors and was not at this point endorsed by the Management committee. However, there is no reference to the matter at the committee meeting of 15 October. Not until 29 October did the item, which was to feature in the minutes for several months, finally appear, although the newspapers carried the press release on 3 October. What began as perhaps a small element of skirmishing rapidly developed into a major battle. On 29 October, Anderson presented a memorandum on the affair so far. Describing what he called 'a slight fracas', Anderson told the committee he had received a letter from Nigel Lawson, the editor of *The Spectator*, 'rather like a summons from a headmaster to a fifth-former, who had not reported to him for cheeking Matron'. No reply had been made to Lawson until, as Anderson rather disingenuously remarks, 'the whole matter could be discussed by the Management committee'. Anderson then detailed the events leading to the decision not to offer Hilary Spurling free tickets. She had, he said, walked out of Peter Gill's *Over Gardens Out* in the Theatre Upstairs in August. Gill's play ran for approximately one hour and ten minutes and no review of it appeared. *The Spectator*, when telephoned as to why the play had received no review, said that Hilary Spurling had not liked the piece. Mrs Spurling, a newcomer to reviewing, thus became the latest in a long line of critics to incur the anger of the Court's directors. In one sense, the reaction, fuelled principally by Anderson, perhaps indicated the hypersensitivity and insecurity of the directorate; in another, there was some justice in what was felt to be ill-informed and patronizing notices. But what might have subsided as a local irritation became unstoppable and was stoked up by most of those concerned. Thus it was initially decided not to invite Mrs Spurling to Upstairs productions. Then, in a discussion of press arrangements for *The Contractor*, it was seen that Mrs Spurling reacted violently against Storey's writing and, Anderson alleged, she had a considerable prejudice against aspects of the Court's work, and in particular 'anything with a Northern working class setting'. After appending extracts from some of Hilary Spurling's reviews, Anderson (and his co-directors) felt it would be 'masochistic folly' to invite her to review *The Contractor*. Anderson further stated his outrage that Lawson had contacted 'his friend', Lord

Goodman, who had then contacted the Court to argue that a theatre in receipt of public funds should allow the press to report the plays to the public. It implied, argued Anderson, an unwarranted right of interference in the Court's work by the Arts Council.

Behind the reaction of the Artistic Directors stood a long series of battles with the critics and Anderson presumably spoke for the others when he argued that the Court existed 'in a different relationship with the press from the other two main subsidized theatres, since our prime object is the presentation of new work – a policy to which critics, taken as a whole, are traditionally and notoriously resistant'. There should be a rationalization of the list of press invitations and a greater emphasis on 'public relations' rather than 'press relations'. When the memo came to be discussed in committee, Anderson found broad agreement. Fox, Lewenstein and Blond backed the action. Neville Blond, according to the minutes 'thought that Mrs. Spurling's criticisms were not of value to the theatre, and that Mr. Anderson's action was justified'. The lone voice in opposition was that of Greville Poke. Poke was totally against the exclusion of Hilary Spurling: 'it had been done against his instructions and without the permission of the Management committee'. Poke also argued the right of the press to attend productions. The theatre had affirmed that right over *Macbeth*. Nevertheless, the committee supported Anderson who was asked to write to Lawson at *The Spectator*. He did so on the same day, and was now able to say that he and his co-directors had the backing of the Management committee. As the news of the affair began to circulate, the reaction of the critics began to show. Hobson in the *Sunday Times* for 2 November protested and the newspaper announced it would not review Court productions until the theatre reversed its decision. The *Daily Express* and the *Evening Standard* joined the boycott, as did eventually the *New Statesman*. To the latter's theatre critic, Benedict Nightingale, who wrote to Anderson, came a reply on 3 November defending the decision, in which Anderson argued that 'We are *not* preventing Mrs. Spurling from either coming to this theatre or from writing about it. We are just not going to invite her to do so, and we would be hypocritical if we did.' At the same time, Greville Poke had complained to Blond that in backing the Artistic Directors in this, the Management committee had gone against its policy decision of press freedom, which had been decided in the case of *Macbeth*. Blond wrote to Poke on 3 November to say: 'You are quite right in your assumption that we did interfere with the policy. We were quite wrong and we should put it right at the earliest opportunity. The policy is laid down and we have had enough trouble, so should not interfere with it. . . . I am extremely sorry we did not take your advice in the first instance.' Part of Greville Poke's worry was to do with what the press generally would make of it all. As a former journalist, he knew what could potentially be done with the story. By 4 November, Anderson was writing to Lord Goodman to give an account of the Court's decision, in the middle of which he complained, justifiably, that the press 'insisted on using words like "banned", "barred" or "excluded" '. The real point of the letter, however, is to try to take the name of the Arts Council out of the dispute. What was opening up was to do with the relationship between the Arts Council and those theatres which received public money. On the same day, Anderson wrote to the editor of the *Sunday Times*, whose decision not to review Court productions had been communicated in a letter to Neville Blond. Since Blond was in Israel, Anderson, 'with what propriety I am not sure', goes through the details and adds that 'We are happy to say that Lord Goodman supports us in this view'.

Nigel Lawson replied to Anderson's letter of 29 October in an article in *The Spectator* of 8 November. Headed 'Anderson's Complaint', the piece identified the 'complaint' as 'A disorder in which an innate authoritarian mentality is in conflict with strong iconoclastic urges. The best-known symptom is an acute hypersensitivity to any form of criticism other than that which the patient has deliberately set out to provoke.' Lawson then printed a pacifying letter from Goodman, who was obviously attempting to prevent the issue gaining any more ground. The article concludes with the idea that Anderson is 'little more than an inverted Mary Whitehouse'. What had begun, somewhat optimistically as a small matter, rapidly assumed the character of a major row. Anderson and Gaskill met the Arts Council, as reported to the Management committe on 12 November, twice, on 7 and 11 November. Greville Poke objected that the report of 7 November was inaccurate and he was given the task of redrafting it. By 27 November, the committee learnt that Anthony Page was lunching with Harold Hobson and it agreed that tickets for Frank Norman's play, *Insideout*, which was to open on 24 November, should be sent to Lawson with a note to the effect that a critic other than Hilary Spurling should review the play. *Insideout* was caught in the firing line and was not reviewed by some critics, which was probably a factor in its poor showing at the box-office (28.0 per cent). According to Frank Norman, the play was cut severely by Anderson who virtually took over the direction from Ken Campbell and there were further cuts suggested by Anthony Page. Reflecting on the production, Norman complained that 'What seems to me to be so unfair about the Royal Court's policy is that it is their playwrights, directors and actors who are the real victims of it. . . . It was nice having my play on in Sloane Square; I only wish that it had been a more rewarding experience.'[32]

The Council met on 3 December to be told that the financial projection to the end of March 1970 suggested an overall loss of over £7,500. To

December, the box-office had averaged 49 per cent; seats sold came to 63 per cent. What was facing the Court was not particularly a lack of success, but a steady increase in overall costs. Though there had been successes, particularly from the Compagnie Renaud-Barrault and *The Contractor* (which transferred to the Fortune Theatre in April 1970), the outlook was not a good one. Blond's response was to propose the closure of the Theatre Upstairs, once its programme was completed in January 1970. Gaskill defended the new theatre. After a difficult start, the work was proving 'of great value. We should not close it just because the Arts Council was not supporting it. Mr. Hodgkinson [for the Arts Council] said that the Arts Council regarded it as of great artistic value.' The matter was deferred, but the threat remained. At the same meeting, Greville Poke reviewed the Spurling affair. He had met Lawson the previous weekend with a view to a compromise, which involved an apology from *The Spectator*. By now, Lawson was stressing that the incident occurred way back in August and that no complaint had been made about it until October. After a long discussion about the matter, Blond acted in accordance with his letter to Greville Poke of 3 November. Council 're-affirmed its policy towards the Press of critical freedom, while also expressing its disapproval of any action by a critic which could disturb the actors or audiences'. A press release was prepared using the above words and sent out on 3 December. The moment of settling the matter arrived but was not accepted. Lawson made it clear that he did not accept the press release. Neither did Hilary Spurling. Accordingly, Neville Blond wrote to *The Times*. His letter was published on 6 December and, characteristically, once his Company was treated with disdain, he revoked the Council decision: 'In view of . . . the basic disagreement on essentials of principle, there can be no question of our renewing invitations to his paper at present.' Greville Poke, meanwhile, was desperately unhappy at the escalation of the row. He wrote to Blacksell on 4 December retailing the details:

> When this matter was discussed at the Management meeting on October 29th I warned the Management and the Artistic Directors where this would lead us to, *vis-à-vis* the press, though I am bound to admit that I did not foresee at the time that we could be in danger of having questions asked in the House of Commons about our actions, and of course, this would lead inevitably to questions as to whether our grant should be continued. Entirely between you and myself, though the suggestion is pooh-poohed by our Artistic Directors, there was more than a hint from certain quarters that a continuance of this kind of behaviour would lead to the sacrifice of our grant.

Poke adds a postcript in the letter that he had seen Hugh Willatt on 8

December (the Secretary-General of the Arts Council) and had arranged to see Lord Goodman on 9 December. He urges Blacksell to write to Blond to try to get 'this childish business stopped'.[33]

However, the cumulative effect of the hostilities having begun made cessation difficult. The Management committee of 18 December decided not to invite *The Spectator* to the Court's Christmas show, *The Three Musketeers Ride Again*, and called for a Council meeting to discuss it all again. Some figures were, however, taking it very seriously. Norman Collins, a member of Council, wrote to Blond on 22 December to suggest that he talk to the Arts Council 'because at the moment things are developing along the classic lines of the Nottingham affair'. And Poke, writing to Blacksell on 30 December, was clearly very alarmed to see that Paul Channon was waiting to put down a question in the House of Commons. While some Court members saw the fight as the culmination of all their animosities towards critics, others saw the potential demise of the Court. Poke told Blond on the same day that the Arts Council was 'extremely restive' about the position and will find it increasingly difficult 'to maintain the apparent present mild attitude' unless the Court resolves the problem. The Arts Council hardened its attitude by 1 January 1970 when, at a Management meeting, its representative stated that the committee had acted unconstitutionally in changing the decision of Council and that a decision should be reached. Fox was to meet Lawson to see what could be done, but the Council reacted angrily to the change of view emanating from the Arts Council. The Company was becoming isolated. Some of the Council now felt that the situation was out of hand and needed drastic measures. Blacksell wrote to Poke on 2 January:

I have spent a couple of days with Neville and I have done all that I can to impress on him the seriousness of the situation. . . .

The things that I am recommending are as follows: that we quietly move towards the termination of Bill Gaskill's contract and along with that, we also look for replacements for Lindsay Anderson and Anthony Page. I feel that the sooner the whole of the Spurling affair is allowed to die, the better; but at some juncture the artistic people should be told that they are not at liberty to use a trivial incident as a stalking horse for their anti-critic behaviour, which we as a Council find quite intolerable.

While this was dragging on, and kept going by both the Artistic Directors and by Lawson, there was still the problem, left unresolved from the middle of the year, of the triumvirate and the arrangements for the future programme of the theatre. At an informal meeting of 8 January, Gaskill said that he would be returning to the Court in the first week of February, but that he could not plan a programme until March and nothing would be set in motion until the middle of May. Anderson said his contract ended in March and he had a film in mind. Page would probably be unavailable, since he would be occupied with a production of *Uncle Vanya*. Hampton's new play, *The Philanthropist*, down for Gaskill to do, would have to be postponed, unless another director took it on. There was a possibility of bringing in Nottingham's *Widowers' Houses*. Gaskill wanted, when he returned, to tour the country looking for new talent for an experimental season in the autumn of 1970. At the root of all this was the question of who was to run the theatre. Anderson renewed an earlier argument when he said 'that it was difficult for the three Artistic Directors just to sit down and plan a programme as they have differences and needed the help of some form of permanent committee to make decisions'. What Anderson wanted was a release from the overall burden of administration. He had said straightforwardly:[34]

> I'm the sort of person who can only do one thing at a time. For
> example, I couldn't be directing another play at the same time as
> fighting this thing out with the press. Which means I don't have the
> natural talent for organization – thinking of everything at once,
> balancing future plans against present necessities, and so forth. Nor
> do I have the urge to build empires. . . . When occasion demands, I
> can go into a meeting and be very good, but I am subject to feelings
> of revulsion. I'm also capable of ruining things with sudden
> outbursts of emotion.

The kind of honesty contained here suggests very clearly one source of the Court's difficulty. Nor is there any evidence that Page was interested in administration. Rather, his main concern was to operate as a freelance director. Which is perhaps why the concern of the informal meeting of 8 January was to find out when Gaskill might be available. Four days later, the Artistic committee met to try to find agreement among the three Artistic Directors. It proved difficult to find a solution upon which all could agree, despite Lord Harewood's best efforts. Anderson would say only that he would take over when free. Page would be happy to take over for at least six months 'twice in three years'. Gaskill said if he committed himself for three years he would want a substantial amount of time off. Peter Gill's name was considered as overall director but it was thought inadvisable. Eventually, a solution of kinds was reached, whereby Gaskill was to be Artistic Director, with Anderson and Page as Associates. The meeting was clearly a fraught one. When Gaskill referred to the Theatre Upstairs, Anderson suggested changing its name to 'The Gaskill'. Robin Fox wanted some recognition from all three of 'responsibility to the theatre' and wished to know 'if there was an artistic director with whom to discuss a future programme'. Anderson at this point proposed 'that an element of instability of temperament be acknowledged in the set up'. He also urged the acceptance of the need for success for the Court and that the directors must dedicate themselves to success. The directors then agreed that some way of sharing the future artistic direction of the Court be found by June 1970.[35] Internally, matters were extremely difficult, with no one director taking the lead and with Anderson, in talking of success, perhaps indicating a potentially different route for Court policy. Publicly, Anderson was seeking to dispel the current image of the theatre. At a party given for the present and future companies of the next two productions, held on 9 January, he announced productions of Howarth's *Three Months Gone*, *Uncle Vanya* and *Widowers' Houses*, and added: 'We are sometimes characterised as gloomy, always doing plays about dustbins and all sorts of other, rather grey ideas. But I would like to reassure you that we are quite human. It is not a surprise to hear laughter in the Royal Court. . . .'[36]

There was not much laughter at the Court at this time. Robin Fox had seen Nigel Lawson, as he told the Management committee on 15 January but it had proved unproductive. *The Three Musketeers Ride Again* had produced only 23.7 per cent at the box office. It was anticipated that the loss could be over £13,000, against which the Arts Council grant was only £6,800. By the time the Council met on 23 February, and despite full houses for *Three Months Gone* and *Uncle Vanya*, the projected loss for the year would be in the region of £11–12,000.[37] At the same Council meeting, the Arts Council referred to the decision made by Council on 3 December to reaffirm its policy of press freedom. Its representative made it clear that the decision should stand and that 'the Arts Council's relationship with the English Stage Company was seriously affected by this affair'. After a long discussion, Blond called for a vote. In favour of reinviting Hilary Spurling were Poke, Collins and Blacksell. Against were Peggy Ashcroft, Fox, Jocelyn Herbert, Mrs Sieff, Osborne and Lewenstein. Council thereupon resolved to continue to withhold tickets from *The Spectator* and expressed its concern at the interference of the Arts Council. The fundamental problem remained, and stretched on into the new financial year. The final immediate stage of the business came at the Council meeting of 9 April, when Neville Blond reported the contents of a letter of 24 March from the Arts Council. The letter threatened the withdrawal of the grant for 1970–1 unless Hilary Spurling was issued with free tickets to review Court productions. After considering the alternatives, the Council decided to accept the terms stated in the Arts Council letter, to write to the Arts Council and to issue a press release. The letter regretted 'that the Arts Council should appear to show more concern for the susceptibilities and privileges of the Press than for the independence and integrity of the artists whom they exist to support'. The press release barely contained the Company's anger:

Under duress, the Royal Court has agreed once again to give free

seats to the critic of *The Spectator*. The Arts Council having
threatened to withhold its grant if this was not done, and as it did so
one week before the grant was due to be paid, the theatre had no
choice. After all, the privilege of not inviting *The Spectator* was not
worth the closure of the theatre. Once again the tanks have rolled
and principle has had to give way to force . . .

When the letter arrived at the Arts Council, the reply, on 14 April,
regretted that both the letter and the press statement 'should be written
in such tendentious terms'. A period that had begun with Arts Council
pressure over *Early Morning* ended with comparable pressure over critics.
If nothing else, the affair highlighted the paradox of subsidized theatre
and illustrated rather well that, if the state censor had departed, there
were other forms of repression still very much alive.

Plates

1 The English Stage Company at the Royal Court, London: opening of the 1965-6 season (Photo: Edward Bond)

2 The stage seen from the auditorium (Photo: John Haynes)

3 The Royal Court auditorium (Photo: John Haynes)

4 John Castle as Len, Barbara Ferris as Pam, and Richard Butler as Harry in Edward Bond's *Saved*, which opened on 3 November 1965 (Photo: Zoë Dominic)

5 Ronald Pickup as Pete, Dennis Waterman as Colin, and William Stewart as Barry in *Saved* (Photo: Zoë Dominic)

6 The set for Minnie and Luther Gascoigne's home in D. H. Lawrence's *The Daughter-in-Law*, which opened on 7 March 1968 (Photo: Douglas H. Jeffery)

7 Victor Henry as Joe Gascoigne, Michael Coles as Luther Gascoigne, and Judy Parfitt as Minnie Gascoigne in *The Daughter-in-Law* (Photo: Douglas H. Jeffery)

8 Matthew Guinness as John Clegg, Edward Peel as Mic Morley, and Warren Clarke as Kendal in David Storey's *The Changing Room*, which opened on 9 November 1971 (Photo: John Haynes)

9 Dinah Stabb as Veronica, Peter Postlethwaite as Cliff, Kenneth Cranham as Jed, Carole Hayman as Mary, and Michael Kitchen as Will in Howard Brenton's *Magnificence*, which opened on 28 June 1973 (Photo: John Haynes)

10 John Barrett as Harry, Warren Clarke as Kendal, and Brian Glover as Sandford in
The Changing Room (Photo: John Haynes)

11 Geoffrey Chater as Alice and Kenneth Cranham as Jed in *Magnificence*
(Photo: John Haynes)

6 · David Storey's
The Changing Room

Between July 1967 and November 1971, five of David Storey's plays were shown in the Court's main bill. These were: *The Restoration of Arnold Middleton* (1967); *In Celebration* (1969); *The Contractor* (1969); *Home* (1970); and *The Changing Room* (1971). All of them, with the exception of *In Celebration* transferred to West End theatres. At the Court's box-office, the lowest figure returned was 57.6 per cent (*The Contractor*) and the highest was 94.0 per cent (*Home*). It is a record of success only exceeded by John Osborne.

Initially, the series of plays started life as a more attractive alternative to the solitary business of writing novels. *The Restoration of Arnold Middleton* (originally called 'To Die with the Philistines') was written during work on Storey's novel, *This Sporting Life*:[1]

> I think *Sporting Life* was about the eighth novel I'd written and I got so tired of trying to get them published that after *Sporting Life* had been turned down about eight times, I thought 'Well I've got nothing left here, perhaps I'm really a dramatist.' I was then teaching in Islington and during one half-term I took time off and wrote a play. I didn't feel I'd got very far, and left it and went on with *Sporting Life*. Two years later it was published. Then there was a backlog of novels, two of which came out during the next three years, *Flight Into Camden* and *Radcliffe*. Then I set to work on another novel which took me about four years to write and got nowhere.

The play finally reached the stage at the Traverse Theatre, Edinburgh in 1966, and at the Court in 1967 (see chapter 3), by which time Storey had gone through the experience of scripting *This Sporting Life*, and had also written two further film scenarios, one for Lindsay Anderson and another for Karel Reisz: 'and doing this taught me a lot about the technicalities of dramatic dialogue'.[2] Storey, at the time of the Traverse production, was not inclined to regard play writing as particularly important or central to his work: 'I was resigned that that was the end of it. It was really still a diversion, in the background in relation to the novels.'[3] However,

the actual experience of seeing the play in performance quite quickly
engendered a series of works for the stage:[4]

> And the plays really came out after that. Having been bogged down
> with a novel which I'd worked at obsessively for three or four years,
> when *Arnold Middleton* came, it offered an alternative – just seeing it
> on the stage resulted in several more plays popping out, six or seven.
> We're gradually working through them at the moment. *The Contractor*
> was written immediately after *Arnold Middleton* had been on at the
> Court, and when I'd finished *The Contractor* I was struck by the image
> of the white table at the end, a white metalwork table which is left
> on the stage. I went back to the novel and perhaps two or three weeks
> later sat down one morning and thought of the table sitting by itself
> and thought 'Well that's the beginning of something' and wrote a
> description of a metalwork table sitting by itself on a stage with two
> white chairs, bringing on a chap after a little while – somebody has
> to appear – he can't sit there alone too long. It really began like
> that, and it was written about the same time. *In Celebration* was also
> written either during or just before – in a few days. I wrote two
> plays called *Home*, and this is the better of the two, I believe. And
> then I went back to the novel.

Though the plays up to and including *Home* were written at about the
same time, two years elapsed before the next, *In Celebration*, was produced at the Court. It was for this production that the partnership of
Storey and Anderson was formally renewed, although in some ways the
connection was already well established. Storey has identified the early
influence of Anderson upon him when making the film of *This Sporting
Life*, particularly as regards essential differences between the writing of
a novel as opposed to a play. Of some scenes for the film, Storey said:[5]

> We discussed them and he said 'Yes that's good, but what are these
> other three characters doing while these two are talking?' In my
> naïve literary fashion, I'd shoved them to the back of the room. In a
> novel you tend to forget the silent characters while you get on with
> the active ones. If no one speaks for five minutes it doesn't matter,
> whereas you can't have people fidgeting around on a stage waiting to
> come out with a line whenever it's required. It was only then I
> appreciated that when you're actually watching dialogue, it has to
> have a completely different inner dynamic, that everyone has to be
> engaged in some way or other even if they are passive . . .

The learning process implied in these remarks in effect continued to show
in the first few plays which were put on the stage. Watching *Arnold
Middleton*, Storey felt it was 'pretty close to a novel. It exists in its own
terms perhaps as a play, but when I watch it, I get the feeling it's written
by someone who should really write novels.'[6] Equally, his own analysis

of *In Celebration*, which, with a distinguished cast led by Alan Bates, ran for sixty-seven performances at the Court, identifies one character, Steven, as the kind of part which makes huge demands on an actor because of the way it is written. The character, played originally by Brian Cox:[7]

has to sit in silence for virtually the whole play, not because the author doesn't think he's important, but because he hasn't got anything to say, or if he has, he can't express it. Someone who'd been an actor or brought up in a theatrical tradition would never have written a character like that. . . . Now I know more about the theatre, I would never dare to write parts like that again, making that kind of demand on an actor . . .

If the first two plays of Storey's to be produced demonstrate their literary pedigree, the third, *The Contractor*, made demands of a quite different kind, and involved the construction of a large tent, the laying down of a dance floor, the raising of coloured awnings, the dressing of the tent, and then the removal of all of it, on the Court's stage. It marked a development in the way Storey perceived theatre work:[8]

I wanted to write something that was not dramatic in the conventional sense. I wanted to do a play without any dramatic gesture where the reality of what people are is the drama rather than the irreconcilable conflicts. . . . I just thought the visual texture of the play should be complementary to the emotional texture.

The mechanics involved in getting the play on were complex and formidable. Only at the first public preview did the tent roof stay in place, and the play's running time then came down from three hours, twenty minutes to something over two hours.[9] *The Contractor* began a process of minuting life as ordinarily lived, as opposed to the devising of theatrical confrontation, and it led directly to the writing of *Home*.[10] Initially, *Home* was not thought of as a main bill play:[11]

When *Home* came into the theatre . . . I remember it being said to me that we could do it in the Theatre Upstairs, that it was not really a play for downstairs. And I think I only read about ten or fifteen pages and I said that of course it was a play which should be done downstairs, but it must be cast marvellously. And I sent the play to Gielgud.

It was cast marvellously and marked the first performances by John Gielgud and Ralph Richardson for the English Stage Company.[12] They were fortunate in the rest of the casting, which was Warren Clarke, Dandy Nichols and Mona Washbourne. The presence of Gielgud and Richardson ensured that the play would receive great attention and it played for forty performances to a box-office of 94 per cent, before moving to the West End, and thence to Broadway. It was, quite simply, one of the greatest successes of this period of the Court's life.[13]

Just as the early plays came from watching *Arnold Middleton* on stage, so *The Changing Room* was born from watching *The Contractor* during its West End run:[14]

> Suddenly this notion of people coming into the set and changing the set somehow as they play – the play arrived. Somehow their characters change as a response to the change of the set and then they take it all down and go away. The image of people coming into a room, which was changed by them, and they in turn were changed . . . was curious and I thought of a changing room. Then suddenly – the changing room. . . . That image came and I think I must have written it almost straightaway, over four or five days, I think it was.

The room itself was immediately established as the main character in the play, but the image was also related for Storey to the business of acting, the collaborative activity itself:[15]

> The play was very much prompted by watching the actors [in *The Contractor*]. I found it fascinating to watch twelve people who had really nothing in common apart from the fact that they were actors, being unified by work, by an activity which absorbed them completely for part of the day. When it was over, they broke up and went away . . .

The play also is a result of the work done with Anderson up to that point. Its specific antecedent is *The Contractor*, whose 'physical momentum' is combined with the 'emotional momentum' of *Home*.[16] For Storey, it represented 'a kind of quintessence of all those experiences, of what we'd done together on the previous plays . . .'[17]

The setting of the play, a Rugby League changing room, takes Storey back to his earlier experiences. At the age of nineteen, he signed a fourteen-year contract with Leeds, and played for two years with Leeds 'A' team, before buying himself out.[18] At the same time, Storey was studying at the Slade School of Fine Art. In 1963, he spoke of this section of his life.[19] The game itself he characterized as an 'extremely hard game, fierce and grinding, and almost a natural extension of the experience that a man undergoes in digging coal underground. It requires not so much tremendous physical strength as a very peculiar, innate stamina which has as much to do with a man's mental attitudes as it has with his actual physique.' The game reflected, and was an expression of, the society which promoted it. The world of the industrial West Riding 'was an acutely physical one, a world of machines and labour and commerce, and one in which the artist, the man whose work had no apparent use or purpose, was not merely an outsider but a hindrance and a nuisance'. Storey describes the landscape within which *The Changing Room* was, eight years later, to be set as 'intensely and even obsessively puritan', distrusting the isolated and solitary man, 'believing not in the separation of the individual but in his absorption within society'. It was out of the dichotomy between the worlds of the north and south, the isolated and the communal figure, the physical and the spiritual, that *This Sporting Life* began its initial stages, whose central figure, Machin, was 'a creature produced it seemed by the very physique of the north itself'. Having made him, Storey 'within the terms of the materialistic society which I felt had bred him watched him, a physical dynamo, career down his crude path to destruction'.

Home emerged from the image of the white table at the end of *The Contractor*. *The Changing Room* begins with bringing on one figure, Harry, and Storey 'waited to see what would happen. . . .'[20] What happens is that over the course of Act one, all the thirteen players, plus two reserves, gradually straggle in to get ready for a match. They are joined by the trainer and his assistant, the referee (briefly), a masseur, the chairman and the club secretary. Harry, the cleaner of the room, is already present. By the end of Act one, twenty-two figures have occupied the stage. Act two takes place initially in the match interval. After the game resumes, Kendal, a second row forward, is brought in with a broken nose and then taken to hospital. The final Act of the play takes place after the game. The players emerge from the communal bath and gradually go, leaving the room to Harry.

The first act of the play is in effect a transformation scene. Within the gradual movement of a number of disparate figures from individuals to a team ready to play, and united by the job in hand, are a complex series of smaller transformations, which are triggered with each entrance of one or more figures. The nature of the context – the room – is subject to the variable pressures exerted upon it as the room is gradually filled. It exists as an image in the minds of the members of the team. It then fuses into a single image once the team takes precedence over its respective components. In this sense, the room is an alien habitat for whoever enters it and becomes familiar once the creation of the team is complete. Further, if the room changes in response to entrances, it is also true that the figure or figures who come on affect those already there. The metaphor of a particular kind of society is always implicit.

Initially, the room itself is allowed to be seen empty. Apart from the music from the tannoy, there is quiet. The room is not particularly welcoming, and primitive in its comforts. It is functional. Harry, the room's cleaner, is seen cleaning up in a desultory way until the first member of the team, Patsy, a wing threequarter, enters. He is described in the stage directions as 'narcissistic' and most of his initial actions bear this out, as he examines his kit, combs his hair and generally admires himself.[21] The method, announced with Patsy, of developing the play, is deliberately oblique. Patsy, here and throughout the play, says little, but a clear sense of him is established by his actions: not simply the self-regarding ones, but his tendency to treat Harry as a servant in asking for towels and a coat-hanger. Patsy's sense of the room and its other occupants effectively lays down a marker for the way in which the audience is invited to view the unfolding of the play. After conducting a desultory conversation with Harry, largely to do with Harry's being convinced of the imminence of a communist take-over of the world, the two figures are joined by Fielding, who is in his middle thirties and plays prop forward. He is a large, easygoing figure, whose entrance is hardly noticed by Patsy. But Fielding establishes a physical presence quickly and locates himself as someone whose needs are simple and basic. All he wants is a 'sup of ale . . .', to which Patsy sarcastically adds, 'Ten fags . . .', and Fielding, quite impervious, completes the routine: 'That's all I need.' The gap between the two figures is completed. Fielding complains in a resigned fashion about living in the country, 'wife's idea', as opposed to his idea of the good life: 'everything you could bloody want: pit, boozer, bloody dogs. As for now . . . trees, hedges, miles o' bloody grass. . . .' There's something irresistibly comic about the slightly indignant tone of Fielding, as he from time to time shows his sense of displacement by taking a rise out of other team mates. There is, however, a large difference in tone between Fielding's grumbling and Patsy's complaints or implied criticisms.

Shortly after this, Morley (the lock forward) and Kendal (a second row forward) enter. While Morley goes straight to the lavatory, Kendal, 'A worn, somewhat faded man', shows off with pride an electric tool set, which he will attempt to show to anyone who looks interested throughout the act. Patsy, apart from the odd remark to join in the general banter, spends much of his time trying to call attention to himself, in particular to a damaged shoulder. When the masseur, Luke, enters, Patsy is the first one to demand attention. The four players on stage are then joined by Fenchurch (the other wing), Jagger (a centre) and Trevor (full back). Fenchurch is 'neatly groomed . . . small, almost dainty'; Jagger is described as 'rather officious, cocky'; and Trevor is a schoolmaster. As Trevor comes on, the point is established that, at this stage, there is an obvious social range being presented. Figures who might not otherwise mix are being brought together to form the team. The general business of preparing for the match halts for some figures as Walsh, the other prop forward, enters in a dark suit, buttonhole and smoking a cigar. Walsh is identified by the immediate reaction as one of the jokers in the team, and he duly reacts to the effect he has created. Little escapes Walsh, as he aims his lines, apparently innocently, at Trevor having a wife with a degree, what he describes as Kendal's do-it-yourself kit, and asks if Patsy's jersey has been warmed for him. Walsh's energy is a consequence of his having a need to be in the changing room and in the team. It is important as reassurance and his confidence comes from being part of a group. He's not at all downcast as Sandford, the assistant trainer, tells him off for smoking and solemnly marks his cigar with a pencil before allowing Sandford to confiscate it. At this point, most of the players are in the early stages of changing. Walsh, on the other hand, has not begun, while Fenchurch and Jagger are reading the racing pages. The way this is shown is drawn from Storey's observation of his own playing days:[22]

> The players do come in for about the length of an act when they start kitting up for a match. It's actual length. . . . Some players like to get into their kit, like an actor into his costume, and have an hour of picking their nose, thirty minutes of walking up and down, becoming the part they are going to play when they go out, whereas other players have to get in in the last five minutes. They've still got their bloody overcoats on, and suddenly, whoosh, it is all on, and they're ready . . . it's a very similar thing to acting. They're both changing rooms.

The team is gradually completed as the other centre, Stringer, and the scrum-half, Copley, come in, followed soon after by Atkinson (second row) and Clegg (hooker), together with the two reserves, Spencer and Moore. Only the captain, Cliff Owens, is now absent. Owens changes upstairs and the sense of hierarchy in the club is established by this and by the fact that Sandford as a figure of authority is quickly displaced by the arrival of Crosby, the chief trainer. By the time the referee, Tallon, enters to inspect the team, most of the players are ready as Crosby begins the team talk and the final run-up to play.

The creation of the team over the course of the act comes not from the dialogue but from the physical activity which is continuous. All the action proceeds at different levels within the framework of preparation. Gradually, a team forms, with each player proceeding at a pace which offers statements about the character involved. They all move in different ways. Around them wanders the figure of Harry. He has in total about seven lines in the whole act, but he is never still, and what he does demonstrates how the act builds up.

After his first appearance to sweep up, he begins a series of well rehearsed actions. The towels are brought in, jerseys and shorts are laid out for each player. Then a pile of jockstraps is distributed. After that, the boots arrive and take several journeys. The last of the boots is followed by shoulder pads, after which come the tie-ups for the stockings. During this, Harry tidies the place, constantly annoyed by the mess of the invasion. Tracksuits come next and buckets and water bottles. One of his last actions is to bring in the resin board and two rugby balls, after which, the main work completed, he attends to the fire. It is an independent routine and, apart from the early chat with Patsy and Fielding, it is almost entirely silent. When he does speak, it is because someone is getting at him. As with Harry, the actions involved more often than not exist independently of the lines which are spoken. The lines exist as an extension of the physical activity. Frequently, what is said does not specifically relate to what is done. The variety shown comes not from the fact that different things are being done, but that the same things are being done at different times. As a consequence, all of the actions form a kind of commentary on other actions. How people do something expresses inevitably a good deal about them, since a comparative analysis is happening as a continuous process.

Gradually, as the uniform goes on, the room and the players begin to feel the change: 'A slight air of expectation has begun to filter through the room.' Players begin to perform actions simultaneously, if only small, detailed actions – rubbing limbs, shaking fingers and flexing. The noise of a growing crowd infiltrates the room and the pressure develops. Some react by being silent, some joke, others show their nerves by disappearing to the lavatory. Crosby then goes into the sequence immediately prior to the match. On the floor of the changing room, the scrum packs down against Crosby and the two reserves, rehearses two set pieces, and the team is suddenly in existence. At this point, the club chairman and secretary arrive and the players come into a formal half-circle to hear his encouragement. The owner of the club solemnly produces platitudes about playing fair and the best team winning. At Thornton's exit, the team lines up in numerical order, exit to be greeted by the crowd, and the changing room is left to Harry. The transformation sequence is completed.

Act two takes the play on to a point towards the end of the first half of the game. The empty and dark changing room is entered by the chairman and club secretary, retreating from the freezing weather. While his players are working, Thornton sends Mackendrick off to find a drink, while he settles himself in front of the fire. As Mackendrick exits, Harry returns and a conversation, if one-sided, develops briefly between owner and cleaner. Thornton's manner is affable and commanding. He patronizes Harry's sense that the old days were better – 'Knew your place before. Now, there's everybody doing summat. . . . And nobody doing owt' – but agrees with, as he is bound to do, Harry's implied meaning of an old hierarchical system. At the same time, he is boss and likes it, as when he merely raises a hand to listen to the crowd, and Harry obediently falls silent. Nowhere does Thornton suggest that he knows anything about the people under him. When Mackendrick on his return derides the dreadful conditions of the past, Thornton is genuinely surprised: 'I never knew you had strong feelings, Mac.' The sense of a figure owning but not bothering to understand becomes very strong. He is, after all, not watching the match, but having news of it relayed to him via Mackendrick. As half time arrives, Thornton leaves. He returns later in the interval in order to suggest that he has been watching the game, congratulating Morley on his try, which was scored while the chairman was sitting in front of the fire: 'Not often we see a run like that. . . .'

As the tired players gradually revive during the interval, Crosby gees them up for the second half. They go back on and, briefly, Luke stays behind to talk to Harry. He establishes what he already knows, that Thornton has not been watching the match, and that Harry himself has never seen a match. Harry's job is to run the changing room. Thornton's job is to own the club. As Harry says: 'It's his place. . . . He can do what he likes. . . . He can sit in here the whole afternoon if he bloody likes.' Vividly, Thornton's sense of possession is created by Luke's saying that he has seen Thornton, late at night, sitting alone in the stand. For Harry, the world consists of owners and owned and his insistence that that is the way it should be demonstrates by its vehemence that he stands as a victim of the system he appears to endorse. Once Luke has gone, Harry reverts to his routine, running the bath and laying out the towels, as the tannoy relays the progress of the game. He is interrupted as the injured Kendal is brought in. In his concussed state, he worries about his new tool-kit. The bleeding, bewildered figure is presented as being too old for his position, getting injured because he is slowing up. Beyond that, a figure ground down by other factors is summed up by Luke: 'Tool-kit. . . . Bloody shelves. . . . Bloody wife. . . . Been round half the teams i' the bloody league . . . one time or another.' Kendal's history of not being quite hard enough to survive is made clear as he dazedly talks of beginning his playing days when he was fifteen. After nearly fifteen years of the game, he is shown as totally at the mercy of the conditions which grind him down. The act ends with the tannoy describing the progress of the game, as one of its players is led off to hospital.

With the game over, the final act reverses the processes of the first, as the players clean themselves up and gradually disperse. A different kind of energy is apparent with the work done, characterized by horseplay in the bath and a good deal of exuberant joking. Not for all: as in Act one, Patsy is ahead of the others. He is already out of the bath and drying himself, with the same meticulous care as when he prepared himself for the match. The only other figure to be nearly ready is Spencer, the reserve, who did not play. Around these two, Harry and Crosby begin to sort out the debris. Inevitably, the centre of all the row in the bath is Walsh and a two way dialogue is conducted between the changing room and the bath (offstage up left) from which jets of water intermittently emerge. The men gradually come in to dry themselves, being attended to by Luke for cuts and bruises. Eventually, only Walsh is left in the bath. The men dress. Patsy, the first to complete dressing, reacts quickly when autograph books are sent in. The virtually silent Stringer angrily demands showers for after the match and complains about the lack of hygiene in a communal bath. The business of characterizing the figures still continues until the end of the play, as details identify them a little further. As Thornton enters to distribute his congratulations, the room is now full of the players, except Walsh. By the time Walsh enters, most of the players are dressed. Patsy has already gone. Walsh, the life and soul of the team, as he believes, dresses, but unlike most of the other players, keeps his towel decorously round his waist. And the horse he has backed wins. He is a figure who is difficult to subdue, even if he is more complex than most of the others ever suspect.

The aftermath of the game gradually peters out, as the players leave, and the team is dismantled. Finally, Crosby and Owens reduce the play to a two-handed dialogue. As they go, Harry begins sweeping, the room falls silent, and changes back.

Casting an entire Rugby League team for the play presented, as Anderson put it, 'a Herculean challenge'.[23] Anderson and Storey, when casting, were clear that 'the actors should not only be correct in relation to class and to background, but also to the position on the field that they were supposed to be playing, so that it could look like a genuine team'.[24] Storey's view was that 'the main problem was trying to get the temperament to coincide with the physique. It came down to that in all the casting sessions that we had. Occasionally, you'd get someone who was physically right, but who was temperamentally wrong . . . the temperament, I suppose, was included in the class, as it turned out, because we found some Cockney actors who fitted into a Northern temperament.'[25] A further problem was that the play was not composed of lengthy speeches. Characters have, on the whole, lines here and there, so that building a company became more a matter of the chemistry between actors. The consequence of these prior conditions was group casting sessions. The process took about three months and the total number of actors seen came close to 600. Storey recalls that actors were seen in batches of between twelve and twenty: 'they used to be queuing just outside the door.'[26] Peter Schofield, who was eventually to play Bryan Atkinson, came from Lancashire, and had spent many years in repertory at Preston, Southport and York. He was called to audition through his agent:[27]

> On arrival at the Royal Court, Lindsay walked a large group of us round to the Irish Club and we went into an intensive group reading, with parts being swapped around. . . . I was lucky enough to be selected from the one audition, whilst others were called back one or more times. One had no idea which part one was being considered

for, but I suppose the idea was the reverse of the usual one. Lindsay needed to see various people and then allocate the roles afterwards.

Don McKillop, another Lancashire actor, was summoned by his agent from a holiday in Cornwall. At the Court, he met Anderson and Gillian Diamond, the play's Casting Director 'and we talked a bit about the background to the play, and a bit about my background. In the afternoon . . . we did a kind of rehearsal audition, playing various parts with different people.'[28] McKillop was eventually cast as the masseur, Luke.

Brian Lawson, also from Lancashire, found the experience of his audition to be slightly different:[29]

> My first meeting with Lindsay was in one of the Court offices, and the only other person present was Gillian Diamond. . . . They were both very easy and natural with me, charming but not consciously so. They played no games with me. . . . I read a bit from the play for them. . . . A week later, I was called to a casting session. And ten days after that, to another one. And these were really different from anything I'd previously known. They happened in a large rehearsal room . . . and present at them were Lindsay, an assistant director, various stage staff members, and a complete cast for the play. . . . We spent the entire morning there, and what we did was read the whole of the second half of the play. Seemingly arbitrarily, roles were assigned, and Lindsay invited us to get up on our feet and 'move' the play, *ad-lib* as we thought fit. We did. . . . After a coffee break we read the same section of the play again, with different roles assigned to different actors. Except for me. I read Tallon the referee both times, as I also did at the second casting session I was called to. Tallon was the only part I ever read. . . . Lindsay must have known what he wanted from the word go . . .

Casting Brian Lawson was one of the easier decisions: 'He obviously couldn't be a player, but there was something about him that lent itself to that part and no other. . . .'[30] Two other actors were cast who were already known to Anderson. Warren Clarke had understudied in *The Contractor*, and played in *Home*, 'so Warren had been part of the team in a way'.[31] And Jim Norton had also appeared in *The Contractor*. Despite an indifferent audition, Anderson over a drink offered him the role of Patsy and Storey recalls that he was 'very diffident and felt he couldn't do it'.[32] Some actors were cast as part of the company almost immediately. Such a figure was Alun Armstrong (Billy Spencer). At one session, 'he had actually one word, which was "Aye". The moment he opened his mouth, I remember looking at Gillian, and it was instinctive. You just knew immediately that was it. . . .'[33]

The major casting problem was that of Walsh. Towards the end of the sessions, advertisements were placed in *The Stage* and in the *Evening Standard*. The latter (2 September 1971) asked for 'One bulky, coarse, extrovert and loud-mouthed, working-class male actor, aged between 35 and 40, who speaks with a North Country accent.' Though couched in jokey terms, the advertisement did produce Peter Childs, who played Fenchurch. But Walsh was still a problem:[34]

> Walsh was the part we actually couldn't cast within days of
> rehearsals. . . . We kept getting people who were big and Northern,
> but they were all soft. We went through a formidable list of
> people. . . . What was missing in all the others was weight of
> temperament.

Virtually at the last minute, the part went to Edward Judd: 'Eddie was a real lifesaver. Right at the end with that part missing from the jigsaw, and then out of the blue this figure came in. . . .'[35]

The method of rehearsal for the play is well described by Storey in connection with an earlier play, *In Celebration*. Invited to the opening rehearsals, the writer watched the events 'with an increasing sense of boredom':[36]

> Nothing appeared to happen except the endless arrangement of cups
> and saucers, the laying down and taking up of coats and bags, the
> movement from point A to point B by way of point C, to be
> reconstituted as a move to point C by way of point B. The expected
> discussion of interpretation, significance and effect, of emotion,
> temperament and motivation . . . never occurred. . . . It was only
> at one of the previews that the significance of what I was watching
> became apparent. . . . The 'mechanics' I'd been watching over the
> previous four weeks were nothing less than the visual equivalent of
> those same 'mechanics' which had absorbed me in the writing of
> the play . . . the 'mechanics' of the rehearsals were suddenly revealed
> to be the medium through which experience, not in an abstract sense,
> but in all its particularities, could be discovered.

The working method perceived by Storey intensified with the physical demands of *The Contractor* and found a kind of apotheosis in *The Changing Room*. Elsewhere, Storey defines Anderson's characteristic direction as 'empirical': 'Lindsay's tendency with actors and with writers is to let them have their head, if what happens is real, then he accepts it, and if it's not, he'll say so, rather than determine beforehand what's required. . . .'[37] Inevitably, such a way of directing makes demands on everyone:[38]

> I do remember the first day. It was awful. Just sort of feeling helpless,
> and they were all sitting around expecting one to sort it out . . . the
> play is rather like a ballet and the only way you can start working is
> to get the people on the stage and start juggling. The movements

are not generally dictated by the lines, although you have to put people in the right relationship in order for the lines to work, and there were various things that you could use, such as getting the stuff put round . . .

The mechanical demands of the play ensured that from the beginning, the actors had playing kit, without which the processes could not be blocked. Equally, the business of undressing to change into the kit was insisted on very early, despite the coyness of some actors:[39]

On the second day of rehearsal we were all rather surprised to find little piles of rugger kit. . . . We were then asked to undress and change into the gear. Since we had a female stage manager, there was a good deal of coyness and haste about this, but it was to become a daily practice, and the value became apparent later on. By dress rehearsal we were nonchalantly wandering about the stage having forgotten our nakedness weeks ago. . . . Most of us had not played rugby or had this experience of casual communal nudity.

That few of the actors had played rugby was remedied when Anderson took the company late on in the rehearsals to the Bank of England sports ground, where they did play under the eye of Bev Risman, a celebrated player and then Technical Adviser to the Rugby League. Before going out to play, Anderson ran Act one in the changing room. After that, the game and then the rest of the play, including the communal bath. As Peter Childs recalls, 'A very rough, enthusiastic, unskilled, and mercifully fairly short game was played and then we were gasping for breath, Lindsay threw us into the Act two dialogue. . . . This was to stick in the mind so forcefully that every time we played this scene in the theatre, there was very little phoney, "puffed-out, exhausted" acting. We could all remember exactly what it felt like. . . .'[40]

The authenticity of the presentation extended to Anderson's taping a soundtrack of the crowd at Wigan's ground, and of the noise of a changing room at Leigh. This was complemented by Jocelyn Herbert's set for the play, of which Brian Lawson remarked that 'It wasn't a set at all; it was a changing room. Even the loos on stage were useable. That set gave me the feel of a real changing room, much more than the "real" changing room we'd all been to.'[41] It is a singular compliment to Herbert's work that an actor such as Don McKillop remarks simply that it was 'Great. It looked authentic – what more can you say?'[42]

The Changing Room opened on 9 November 1971. Anderson remembers 'walking past the front of the Court, I think it was two or three days before it opened, and David said to me, "Do you think it can work? Is there enough there?" Because one did feel that since it was choreography, it's like a ballet, is there enough for people to bother about? As it turned out, there was. . . .'[43] The play ran for thirty-nine performances and, having achieved box-office figures of 89 per cent, transferred to the Globe Theatre on 15 December. For many of the actors, their first appearance in the West End was short-lived. In spite of the critical acclaim for the play, a mixture of power cuts and the refusal of the Globe management to alter its price seating plan, cut the run short. Michael Codron, the co-presenter of the play in the West End, reported to a Management committee meeting of 15 February that business at the Globe had dropped and that he was attempting, in the usual way, to obtain reductions from the royalty earners and the theatre itself, so that the play could be 'nursed' until business picked up. By the week ending 1 March, the receipts at the Globe had dropped below the get-out figure, and it was decided that the play would close on 18 March. The brief appearance in the West End produced a net loss overall of £867. What happened to *The Changing Room* when it transferred is a telling example of the arbitrariness to which even a great success is subject. Those who took part in it, however, recall it as important to them as actors. Brian Lawson characterizes the response of the actors to the production:[44]

We performed without make-up, and whilst at first I felt naked without it, I got over that, and it was doubtless one of the contributing factors in not feeling that we were acting at all. I was not giving a performance. I just was. So it was easy – in the sense of being 'full of ease'. I came into the theatre each evening, I changed my clothes, I trundled myself on to the stage, opened my mouth and the words came out. Naturally, and as if for the first time.

7 · From April 1970 to July 1972

The accounts of the financial year ended 4 April 1970 showed the Company to be in some difficulty. The net deficit amounted to £12,754. It was reported that 'the liquid reserves of the Company have effectively been exhausted by the net loss for the year'. This in spite of the fact that the box-office had averaged 57.6 per cent and seats sold amounted to 64.9 per cent. Though the cost of productions was under budget by £3,300, the addition of two Artistic Directors cost £4,100, publicity was over budget by some £1,400 and payments to visiting companies exceeded the allocation for payment to artists by £2,400. What may appear minor in scale does, when added in to the overall costs, prove significant. The telephone bill, for example, rose by over 50 per cent in the last nine months of the year. The report somewhat drily suggests that 'the only reason that can be offered is increased activity in the theatre, with three Artistic Directors'. The next three months, however, showed an improvement. In the main bill, *Widowers' Houses*, followed by the visiting Café La Mama, and David Storey's new play, *Home*, produced figures which averaged 58.3 per cent box office. *Three Months Gone* at the Duchess Theatre, was producing a small profit for the Court, but *The Contractor* at the Fortune Theatre was still recovering its production costs. Overall costs were under budget but the two main factors in the recovery were first, the contributions to costs made by outside managements to *Widowers' Houses* (Michael White and Memorial); to *The Contractor* (Michael Codron); and to *Three Months Gone*, which ran to 5 September. Second, the seat prices at the Court rose with the production of *Home*. The capacity take rose, therefore, from £379.14.0d. to £443.15.0d. By 4 July, the position financially was better than anticipated by £6,900.

The press announcement of the Court's plans for the immediate future was received with greater enthusiasm than was usually the case. Newspapers for 29 April noted plays by Storey and Hampton, as well as the Café La Mama, but paid most attention to the fact that the casts included distinguished figures such as Gielgud, Richardson and McCowen. The

Daily Telegraph felt that after the Court's 'great successes with *Uncle Vanya* and *Widowers' Houses*, these plans should establish 1970 as the theatre's best year for a very long time'. The inclusion of actors of such a calibre at the Royal Court drew the inevitable comments. Maggie Smith, attacking the 'mumbling about a "tyranny" of stars at the National Theatre', remarked 'The Royal Court is jammed with stars at the moment.'[1] At the same time, the Arts Council, in a report published in 1970, defined the purpose of the Court as different from the National and Royal Shakespeare Theatres in 'identity, scale and purpose. . . . It is avowedly a theatre of experiment.' Thus the Arts Council felt justified in advocating 'a higher rate of support than the average. . . . We consider that the subsidy they receive should be regarded not only as support for the work at the Royal Court but as a subsidy also to widen the spectrum of new talent for the benefit of the whole English theatre. . . . It is a dynamo of change and experiment.'[2] The report also drew attention to the fact that 'the particular quality of the subsidized theatres in London is particularly dependent upon the personality of the individual in charge . . .'.[3] It is an obvious but important comment and, in the case of the Court, the potential difficulty of two or three individuals in charge is reflected in the pamphlet published by the Company to mark the fourteenth anniversary of its founding. *Royal Court 1970* reviews four years' work and contains articles by both Gaskill and Anderson. For Gaskill, the central questions are: 'How many new plays have we done? How many writers have we discovered? How many of our writers have gone on writing for the theatre?' The list includes Storey, Bond, Hampton, Hopkins, Seabrook and O'Neill, Rosen, Antrobus, Cregan, Howarth, Orton, Norman, Soyinka, Wesker and Wood. Gaskill also notes how the conditions have changed but not a great deal. New writing now appears from Glasgow and Nottingham, from Hampstead and Edinburgh, but, with the exception of Stoke, he insists that the Court can still claim to stand alone in supporting its writers 'in the face of adverse criticism or financial loss'. At the centre of Gaskill's piece is the story of the battles with the censor and the fight to establish Edward Bond. The overall tone is clearly one of feeling that there is much to do. An audience for new work on a large scale still did not exist and, even if in the provinces weekly repertory has ceased, it is still the case that, with honourable exceptions, theatres outside London are generally unreceptive to the changes created by the Court. Until and unless other theatres take up the cause, 'writers will still leave the theatre for films and television – however much they may feel that the theatre is the touchstone of their quality'. The essay is a personal one and carries the marks of four years' struggle. Lindsay Anderson's contribution to the pamphlet takes the larger view and sets the four years in the context of the Court tradition, which he tries to define. He lays stress on the Court's 'naturalistic bias and its emphasis on the social perspective', but argues that to present the tradition purely in terms of social drama would be a distortion. The original aim in 1956 was that of a writer's theatre:

not on principle committed to any single school of writing, presentation or political thought. . . . It is no accident that Osborne was the first great Royal Court discovery, and has in a sense remained its archetypal figure ever since: the leading figure in a whole movement of writers working in a style characterized in ethic by a kind of non-schematic progressive conscience, and in its treatment of character by a passionate concern, sometimes fierce, sometimes tender, for the individual human being.

Anderson's broader sense allows him, rightly, to show that the Court, as well as other, more politically committed writers, produced 'humanistic talents as various as Wesker and Arden, Storey, Howarth and Hampton'. The difference between the two artistic directors is one of emphasis, rather than radical disagreement. Yet Gaskill's four years to 1970 were characterized by, at heart, an intensely political debate. The central figures in these two essays are Bond and Osborne respectively. If Osborne was for Anderson the archetypal figure, there is little doubt that for Gaskill, Bond had replaced Osborne as the pivotal figure in the argument from 1965. Though the Court contained both figures, it appears that for Anderson the Court should as a *sine qua non* define itself by the extent to which the Company insisted on both figures as a key to its style. For Gaskill, what was represented by Bond *was* the Court under his leadership. If this seems an over-simplified account, the pattern of work done at the Court over the next two years does demonstrate the priorities of the three artistic directors. The seasons which they put on reflect their sense of direction, and their interpretation of the Court tradition. Anderson, reflecting later on these years, insisted that Devine and Richardson 'had no favourable disposition towards writing just because it was "new"'. The placing of 'new' in inverted commas indicates his hostility towards the novel or the faddish, rather than to good new writing and his record of production at the Court clearly bears that out.[4] Gaskill's view is not dissimilar: 'I think the whole idea of the Court, certainly George's idea of the Court, mine too, was that you could do modern work, which would be capable of being seen against any major play on a larger stage. . . .'[5] Again, talking of Devine, Anderson defines Devine's commitment 'above all to the service of the theatre – the theatrical experience; not the theatre as a "vehicle" for ideas, which is in itself a form of philistinism, though rarely recognized as such; and not the theatre as a laboratory for aesthetic experiments'. In the same piece, Anderson insists that to talk of the Court as a socialist theatre 'was largely nonsense. It was not even a very intellectual theatre. The tone was far more humanist than intellectual. Liberal, if you like, in its strong rather than its soppy sense. And this commitment inspired all the choices, and was the basis of the style.'[6] Though Anderson is here referring to the early years of the Court, it is a view he maintained in his second period at the Court. Gaskill puts it slightly differently and differs a little:[7]

I remember in the early days, there was a very strong fellow feeling between Ann Jellicoe, Keith Johnstone, N. F. Simpson and, although he was not a Court writer, Harold Pinter, who were very close to each other, and they'd all had bad notices, they'd all suffered under the critics. They felt there was a certain similarity in their work . . . as far as one could define what they believed, it was that the theatre was only to demonstrate things and never to use discussion or talk. It was, if you like, an anti-Shavian feeling. You could use dialogue to express relationships but never to discuss ideas on the stage and they were very clear about that . . . a kind of anti-rationalist, anti-wit tradition . . . but I can't say that I would ever have been totally committed to it myself as a theory of theatre.

Effectively, the difference in emphasis (which is perhaps finally a difference in ideology) was between taking the Court further on in its development, and maintaining its position as the home of liberal theatre (in Anderson's sense of the word). Lord Harewood draws this distinction:[8]

I think that Bill wanted to build a new empire, a new kind of theatre on the foundations which George gave and I think Lindsay wanted to continue the same theatre. I think in the end . . . that Bill was right. I don't think you can ever just go on. Either we were wrong as a board not supporting him enough, which I slightly felt . . . or he was not quite right in how he stacked and played all the cards. . . . Lindsay and Tony Page put us back on a line that had been a winning line, which we'd abandoned and which we needed to get on to again, maybe to get back to the pure line again . . .

By this stage, in 1970, the different, and for some, opposing strands of Court work were separating. The creation of the Theatre Upstairs, as a response to what was happening elsewhere in the theatre, began on occasions to be the repository for work which was felt not quite right for the main stage. In other words, the Theatre Upstairs partly absorbed the function of the Sunday night performances, but lost for the most part the direct life line to the main bill:[9]

The Sunday nights had died. They were a really important part of the work of that theatre and they were replaced by the Theatre Upstairs. As soon as you have two theatres like that in the same building, you do syphon off something and you do start to say well, it's all right for the Theatre Upstairs, whereas in the early days at the

Court, anything that was of any quality at all had to be shown in the main house.

What was being developed in the Theatre Upstairs was to be replicated throughout the theatre at large, but it also established the concept of alternative theatre, which then to a large extent became contained within its separate environment. Quite apart from the inherent difficulty of transferring an Upstairs show to the main stage (a problem which the Sunday nights did not face), it was also the case in the early stages of Upstairs that the kind of theatre on show was rather different from the main fare. Nicholas Wright considers it to have been a style alien to the Court's experience, to do with environmental theatre, expressionist, non-social realist, non-verbal (often), a reaction to American influences and the work of the then *avant-garde*. Oscar Lewenstein sums this up well:[10]

The Theatre Upstairs was the first of what has become a whole host of those sort of theatres, so Bill's instinct must have been in accordance with the feelings of the time. . . . Bill was much more sympathetic, as I was I think to the sort of fringe activities than perhaps Lindsay or Anthony Page would have been. God knows what George Devine would have thought of them.

Anderson was hostile to Upstairs for two reasons: that it destroyed the Sunday nights, 'and to be honest I'm not sure even now that the tradition wasn't a better one'; and, second, that Upstairs 'was always to me fringe and I've never approved of the alternative society . . . a bit of a self-glorifying ghetto'.[11] Though Gaskill took part in the programme upstairs, and remained committed to its development, neither Page nor Anderson directed Upstairs. Even so, the progress of Upstairs was successfully buttressed by the advent not only of differing kinds of groups, but also by performances in 1970 of writers such as Beckett, Brenton, Hare, Heathcote Williams, Jellicoe, Barry Hines, Howard Barker and Ionesco. In this sense, it was as much a writer's theatre as the main house.[12] The main stage was occupied by a mixture of established Court writers (Howarth, Storey, Hampton), all of whose plays in the season transferred; by imports (two from Nottingham, one from the USA); by one revival (*Uncle Vanya*); by Heathcote Williams's *AC/DC*; Mike Weller's *Cancer*; and by the *Come Together* festival in the autumn.

In another area, that of the Schools scheme, the Court's work persisted, though without gaining the priority which Devine and Gaskill had originally intended to give it. Jane Howell had inaugurated an ambitious attempt to involve schools in production in 1969 when in May she had written to 2,500 London schools to set out plans for a fortnight's work on the theme of revolution, which would culminate in a Sunday night performance on 27 July. Eleven schools finally took part. On a grant of £400 the play evolved, was presented, and transferred to the Roundhouse

for a week in August. *The Times* for 28 July judged it 'a splendid vindi-
cation of the Royal Court's Schools Scheme', although the *Guardian* (2
August) reported disquiet in educational circles at the show's theme. Jane
Howell was assisted on *Revolution* by Pam Brighton, who took over the
schools work when Howell left at the beginning of 1970. Pam Brighton's
account of her appointment rests on her belief that she happened to be
there, working as Howell's assistant and consequently was given a trial
run by Page and Anderson, at a time when Gaskill was away: 'So I think
I kept quite quiet for the first couple of months . . . when Bill came
back, he came back with a lot of energy and he sent me off round the
country. I can remember going to Bolton, looking at all these Theatre in
Education companies . . . and the first big thing I did was [*The*] *Sport of
My Mad Mother*.'[13] Jellicoe's play, originally seen at the Court in February
1958, opened for ten days in June 1970:[14]

> and as it was closing, Bill said, 'That's very good. A lot of the things
> you've done on that have been very interesting. Now.. . . do another
> couple of weeks' rehearsal and do it again.' And it was wonderful.
> Bill always used to come into dress rehearsals and then he'd take
> you back to his office just for half an hour and sit you down and tell
> you what you'd done right and done wrong. That actual teaching
> situation I don't think exists any more in the theatre.

Gaskill had reported the success of the play to the Management committee
on 20 May. There had been open rehearsals, a Saturday morning group,
and there were plans for a summer project. This became *Songs My Mother
Taught Me* in August as a Sunday night, co-directed by Brighton and
Howell, with some forty teenagers. The constant problem was that this
kind of work was regarded by some as peripheral. It was also under-
funded. The grant at that stage was only £3,000, of which £1,000 was
for the director's salary. However, the work continued to develop and
began to be linked more to the Theatre Upstairs and, in November,
Howard Barker's *No One was Saved* was shown Upstairs as part of the
Schools scheme, the rehearsals of which were attended by schoolchildren.

Gaskill's sense of the changes taking place in the theatre at large
remained with him on his return to the Court in 1970. He indicated to a
Management committee of 20 May his desire to hold a festival of new
work in both theatres later in the year. By 15 July Gaskill had toured
parts of the country and seen a number of local festivals, each of which
had been funded by the New Activities committee of the Arts Council.
The budget discussions of 15 July, both for the alterations to the theatre
and for running and production costs, were centred on keeping the
projected loss for the festival down to £4,000. Beyond the festival, Gaskill
proposed (on 31 July) a winter season of four plays with Peter Gill. A
company of about fifteen actors would be engaged to do *The Duchess of*

Malfi and *Mann ist Mann*. Gill also wanted to add a satirical revue, while Gaskill was hoping for a new play from Edward Bond. The pattern aimed at was a group of actors contracted to play the small season, as had been the case with the D. H. Lawrence trilogy. It was at this time that there were moves, principally by Gaskill, to appoint Gill as a long-term Associate Director, perhaps in an attempt to balance the artistic direction more equally. With *Three Months Gone*, *Home* and *The Contractor* running in the West End (and *The Philanthropist* shortly to join them), the Court financially looked stronger than it had for some time. However, on 4 August, the day after *The Philanthropist* opened, Neville Blond died, aged 74. The obituaries came from diverse sources; from the theatre, from industry and from medicine. All spoke of his energy, commitment and toughness. Devine in his retirement speech suggested that a fundamental part of success involved finding a good chairman, and there is little doubt that, for the most part, the English Stage Company would have been the poorer without Blond.[15]

The Council met on 1 September 1970 to decide upon a new chairman. After tributes had been paid to Blond, Lord Harewood took the chair. After the names of Elaine Blond, John Montgomerie, Michael Codron and Tony Garnett had been proposed as new members of Council – of the four, only Garnett declined – the meeting proceeded to discuss the filling of the chair. Lord Harewood had already asked Greville Poke if he would be prepared to move from secretary of the Company to chairman. Poke declined on the grounds that the difference of opinion between him and the Artistic Directors over the 'Spurling' affair had been so great that he would not enjoy the full confidence of the Artistic Directors. Lewenstein and Fox were asked to make statements and, whilst they both felt that they would serve, Robin Fox proposed Lord Harewood as chairman of Council, with a separate chairman of the Management committee. Harewood declined on the grounds that he had insufficient time to devote himself to the job. Fox and Lewenstein left, the Council took the opinions of Gaskill, Gill, Anderson and Page, after which they left, and discussions ensued. In the event, Council was unable to choose between the two. Harewood again resisted further involvement in a suggestion from Peggy Ashcroft that he become chairman with Fox and Lewenstein as vice-chairmen. Helen Montagu relayed a message from Fox and Lewenstein that they would be prepared to act as co-chairmen. It is clear from the discussion that there was not an obvious candidate for, although Council eventually appointed Fox and Lewenstein as co-chairman, it felt that the Company needed a figure such as Neville Blond had been, with 'an outside, independent line' to bring to bear upon the problems. The appointment, therefore, was for a maximum of two years, during which time efforts would be made to find an independent figure.

Almost as a footnote, the position of vice-chairman, held by Alfred Esdaile, was abolished, given that there were now two figures in charge. Lewenstein continued to chair the Artistic committee, and Fox undertook to chair the Management committee, with each acting as the other's deputy.

By the time the *Come Together* festival opened (21 October), the Company accounts showed a surplus of £21,000. Box-office takings, budgeted at 55 per cent, had averaged 65 per cent; transfers had produced to date £10,800. 1970 was in this respect one of the best ever years at the Court. Yet the underlying currents were still visible. Not everyone welcomed the wholesale importation of the largely *avant-garde* into the Court. For a brief period, the whole theatre was colonized:[16]

> That was a typical kind of division in the theatre, because Lindsay
> was absolutely against it. That was a real kind of attempt to push
> something, not something of my own work but my response to what
> was happening in the theatre at large, something that we mustn't
> miss out on. . . . I thought it was very extraordinary, an amazing
> three weeks. But it didn't actually feed anything into the theatre. I
> don't think it left much trace in the work that followed. It immediately
> reverted to being what it had been.

As the festival began, Gaskill outlined in *The Times* for 21 October his reasons for its happening. The idea was to show the best of the experimental work at the Royal Court, 'partly to give it the recognition it deserves; partly to see it in the context of a Writer's Theatre and partly in the hope that there may be cross-fertilization between the different kinds of work shown and for future work in the theatre generally'. According to the article, the early invitations were to groups such as The Freehold, The People Show and The Other Company. The festival then grew with the addition of painters and sculptors. The Theatre Upstairs would contribute *AC/DC*, and Brenton's *Christie in Love* and *Beckett 3*. Added to this were pop groups such as Lifetime and Fotheringay, while the Gentle Fire announced the first performance of a piece by Stockhausen. In the event, over twenty kinds of groups participated. Further additions included Brighton Combination, Pip Simmons, The Alberts, Theatre Machine and Ken Campbell, while Peter Cheeseman's Stoke company represented 'the theatre outside London'. The Court was quite radically changed for the festival. The stage was raised and extended; the stalls were stripped out. Tiered seating was placed on the stage itself. The effect, wrote Gaskill, would be something akin to Elizabethan theatre, with a large popular audience standing around, 'and a more comfortable elite sitting above it'. It was a direct and imaginative response to the fact that most of the groups invited produced work well outside the framework and implications of the proscenium arch. And, interestingly,

Gaskill resisted the temptation to take the festival to a more obvious setting, such as the Roundhouse and remarks, surely with a sardonic air: 'The Royal Court is a stubborn, old and beautiful building which resists change.' The *Sunday Telegraph* for 18 October could not resist commenting that the Court, 'dismayed by its run of commercial successes . . . was about to run an Underground festival so that the theatre could be empty and lose money again'.

It was an extraordinary event, aggressively presented in its publicity: 'The Royal Court is committed to new work and has a long history of discovering and defending new writers, but this is the first time that we have presented the new music and performances that have their basis in sculpture and the visual arts, rather than theatre as we know it.' It should also be noted that if the Court had not battled with the censor, a good deal of what was shown in the festival would never have been allowed. At the same time, equally important for Gaskill was a judgment as to how the new work related to the more established work. Thus the publicity advertising *Beckett 3* states baldly that 'No Festival representing a state of change in the theatre could be complete without the revolutionary simplicity of this great dramatist.'[17] Predictably, many reviews concentrated upon what was regarded as bizarre and outlandish (true in some cases), but the chief reaction is that of the astonishment felt by many at work which hitherto had not existed in the physical context of a theatre. Its home was more that of an arts laboratory than a traditional theatre building. The chief excitement was generated by the range of the work, rather than by any sense of homogeneity. Where the Victoria, Stoke presented Peter Terson's documentary account of the 1861 Whitby lifeboat disaster, Theatre Machine under Keith Johnstone represented totally improvised work in comedy and the use of masks, which had first begun in the Court Studio in the early 1960s. Ken Campbell offered a cabaret of 'pub humour, dirty jokes and songs', while Naftali Yavin's The Other Company took groups of fifteen at a time on an environmental journey. Brighton Combination presented a politically oriented account of the National Assistance Board ('The NAB Show'),[18] and Pip Simmons showed a musical version of Chaucer's 'The Pardoner's Tale'. The People Show managed successfully to upset nearly everyone with part of their work being conducted in a telephone booth in Sloane Square; inside, Nancy Meckler's Freehold gave their version of *Antigone* under the influence of the Living Theatre, Café La Mama and Grotowski. CAST (Cartoon Archetypal Slogan Theatre), one of the earliest of the experimental groups, offered *Auntie Maud is the Happening Thing*, a survey of working-class conditions over forty years. Three pieces which enabled certain critics to deride most of the work came from Stuart Brisley, *A Celebration for Due Process*; Carlyle Reedy; and Peter Dockley with *Foul-*

fowl. Brisley's happening concluded with his vomiting from a height of twelve feet, which did nothing to endear him to reviewers or to most of the audience.[19] Carlyle Reedy devised a mysterious dream event, while Dockley (who had worked at the Theatre Upstairs in December 1969) created a sequence involving chicken feathers, actors painted blue and carpet foam. The Court itself, apart from Beckett and Brenton, produced *AC/DC*, with which the festival was planned to open. However, Pat Hartley, who created the role of Sadie when the play opened for the first time Upstairs in May 1970, was refused a work permit. She was replaced by Sheila Scott-Wilkinson and its performance in the festival was put back until 31 October. On its first appearance in May, the play, which had been rewritten a number of times since 1966, created something of a sensation. Nicholas Wright, who directed it, notes that 'it had a weird first night. *Time Out* gave it a wonderful review and the play got a sort of identity as the first seventies play'.[20] Williams's account of it to Nicholas Wright perhaps indicates why the play went through so many versions:[21]

The play is better than anything else I've written. I'd like to see it done. It's also intractable in this sense: its terms of reference are not usual. The normal turnover of tensions in plays seem to revolve round territory, property, aggression, sex etc. Here those elements exist: but there is also another element: psychic territory. Mind transplant. The idea that someone can steal your preoccupations before you've got to them yourself. Synchronicity: the acausal connection between events. E.S.P. Terrorism. Telepathy. All things which I believe to be behaviourally operational. The idea that there are other systems of transmission and reception apart from word and gesture is going to be hard to convey . . . in the meanwhile, the main part in the play has changed sex. What was Hurst is now *Sadie*, American, black, big and tough. . . .

Reviews of *AC/DC*, as with the festival, ranged from the hostile to the mystified to the enthusiastic. For some, the play characterized a new direction. The *International Herald Tribune* for 14 November called it 'the first play to explore fully and explain a generation's shift in sensibility'.[22] Equally, the festival was dismissed in some quarters as irrelevant. Yet, as one writer suggested, 'only a year later it was possible to look back on the *Come Together* festival and realize that the new groups had created a new working context in which talents like Brenton and Simmons could mature in a decisive and original manner'.[23]

Gaskill reported to the Executive committee of the Theatre Upstairs on 10 November that he was very pleased with the festival. Though financially 'it had been a disaster' (31 per cent box-office, but 76.0 per cent seats sold at a reduced price), West End profits had been used to offset the costs, then estimated at about £13,000. The Artistic committee of 26 November proceeded to discuss the choice of two plays to complete the Gill/Gaskill season after *Mann ist Mann* and the possibilities for Anthony Page's season, which would run from the end of June to December. In the first category were plays by Sam Shepard, Dennis Cannan, Antrobus, Orton, Beckett, and Seabrook and O'Neill. Also possible was a dramatized version of Heathcote Williams's book, *The Speakers*. The idea came originally from Peter Gill.[24] The Page season also listed Shepard and Cannan, added Tennessee Williams and the new Storey play, *The Changing Room*. Other writers mentioned were Athol Fugard, Barker, Weller and an Orton three-play season. Seven writers were under commission. These deliberations were reported to the Council at its meeting on 2 December, when Gaskill was able to report a very successful year. *Three Months Gone* stayed for six months in the West End; *Home* transferred for thirteen weeks and then opened on Broadway; *The Contractor*, after thirty-six weeks at the Fortune Theatre, was to go to the USA early in 1971. *The Philanthropist*, which ended Hampton's two years at Resident Dramatist, was still running at the Mayfair (it actually ran for three years) and was likewise due to go to the USA. After the Artistic Directors had been congratulated, Nicholas Wright reported on an equally successful year Upstairs. With very few exceptions, every performance had sold out. After the expressions of pleasure had died down, there was a row about the value of *Come Together*, initiated by Tony Richardson who questioned whether it had all been worthwhile and who clearly felt that some of the productions were not 'worthy of the high standards of the English Stage Company'. The minutes blandly record that 'A long debate followed and varying views were expressed.' On another matter, Jocelyn Herbert queried the current value of the Artistic committee, thus referring to the point made by Lindsay Anderson on his return to the Court in 1969. Council was advised that Lord Harewood intended to resign as the chairman of the committee and that, for some time, Lewenstein had acted in his place.[25] Harewood maintained his connection with the Company, however, in agreeing to become President of the Council. The matter of the future of the Artistic committee was referred to that body to decide. Council also heard that the directors had not yet signed new contracts, but that when they did, Gaskill would be responsible as Artistic Director to Council. The other three would be his Associates, who would from time to time assume responsibility for certain periods or seasons. The underlying difficulty of this particular quartet of directors had not been solved by the beginning of 1971. Blacksell at a Management committee of 5 January obliquely referred to it when he urged a periodic review of general thinking about policy should take place every two years. He asked for Council to meet more frequently for this purpose.

Blacksell's point was taken up on 16 January when the Artistic committee met to discuss its future. The full committee had not met since July 1969. Since that time a sub-committee of the four directors, chaired by Lewenstein, had replaced the main group, and this obviously was the basis of Jocelyn Herbert's query as to the purpose of its existence at the December Council. It was decided that the original committee be disbanded and the current sub-committee be extended. Jocelyn Herbert was immediately co-opted, and there was also the possibility that the Resident Dramatist (now David Hare) and the Literary Manager (Jonathan Hales) should be members. In effect, the new arrangement was the one proposed by Anderson on 7 July 1969 and reflected his sense that the Artistic committee had been reduced to impotence (see chapter 5). The 15 January meeting also agreed to urge Council members to see all the plays presented and that they be given free seats for previews, first nights or subsequent performances.[26]

The first main bill production of 1971, Peter Gill's *The Duchess of Malfi*, threatened to revive the row over critics. It was accorded a generally hostile critical reception and took only 39.5 per cent at the box-office. Gill, who became ill after the production, wrote a letter complaining about the treatment accorded to his production by the critics and their general attitude to classical revivals at the Court. In discussions at a Management committee of 3 February, there was a suggestion that the Arts Council should renew its offer, made in 1969, of a seminar on press criticism and Lewenstein proposed to contact Lord Goodman about it.[27] However, the committee at its 20 January meeting was annoyed to find that the original idea of a season of four plays with the same company, as proposed by Gill and Gaskill, had fallen apart. Helen Montagu reported that the budget for *Mann ist Mann* would be exceeded because only two of the *Malfi* actors were actually being used for the Brecht play. Lewenstein was angry at the lack of consultation and said if he had known he would not have approved the high budget for *Malfi* or allowed the extra rehearsal periods. Since the artists had been contracted and rehearsals had begun for the Brecht, he was powerless, but clearly disturbed that the very same matter which had arisen over *Early Morning* had recurred. On the following day, the Company suffered the loss of Robin Fox, who died on 21 January. Fox had been a most effective bridge between the Artistic Directors and the Company administration. At the Council of 26 March which formally recorded the death of its co-chairman, Gaskill, among many others, paid tribute to Robin Fox:

I think the qualities that I thank Robin for most and do thank him
for now was his loyalty not only to me but his very own clear idea
of what our organization was and meant. He was extraordinary in
helping me and the Company to make decisions. These qualities

have seen me personally and the work of the Company through tricky situations.

He spoke feelingly and truthfully. Fox, like Lord Harewood, as a great friend of Neville Blond's, had frequently acted as pacifier and buffer between the late chairman and his Artistic Director. With Fox gone, Lewenstein took on sole responsibility as chairman from January.

After attempting for many years to obtain the rights from the Brecht estate, *Mann ist Mann* finally opened on 1 March. It was the first main bill Brecht production since *Happy End* in March 1965, and Gaskill's first Brecht for the Court. As a companion piece, Bill Bryden devised a show around a short Brecht sketch, *The Baby Elephant*, which opened Upstairs on 9 February. *Mann ist Mann* averaged 40 per cent at the box-office and was not considered by Gaskill to be amongst his best work.[28] It was during March that Nicholas Wright resigned as the director of the Theatre Upstairs and was succeeded by Roger Croucher, initially for six months from April 1971. Gill's illness after directing *The Duchess of Malfi* left a gap after *Mann ist Mann* and Roger Williams was asked to direct Dennis Cannan's *One At Night*, which had figured on the list of possibilities for both the Gill/Gaskill and the Page season. The proposed new play by Edward Bond, which was experiencing casting difficulties in the title role of Lear, was put back, and eventually David Hare's *Slag*, then on Broadway, was the choice for the fourth play. As *Mann ist Mann* continued downstairs in the main bill, E. A. Whitehead's first play, *The Foursome*, opened Upstairs on 17 March and provided the first direct transfer from Upstairs when it went to the Fortune Theatre in May. It was a success story of the kind experienced by Christopher Hampton with *When Did You Last See My Mother?* transferring from a Sunday production in June 1966. The 1970 George Devine Awards reflected the new writers in going to Heathcote Williams and Whitehead.

The new financial year opened with *One At Night*, which received a hostile critical reception by and large, played to only 28.2 per cent at the box-office, and provoked discussions in committee as to whether it should close after four weeks, but it was decided that savings would be negligible. At the same time, the Court celebrated its fifteenth birthday. The fifteen years were assessed by Nicholas de Jongh, whose feeling it was that the house writers of the Court were maintaining the theatre's reputation:[29]

In the past 15 months the Court has entered another great phase – great in the sense that the dramatists it has cultivated or discovered are simultaneously at a period of fecundity. John Osborne's adrenalin has flowed again and a play from him, and others from Edward Bond and David Storey, are scheduled for production this year. The Theatre Upstairs, which seemed to have started its career to provide a new experience in exemplary disasters, has developed into a fine place for writers whose reputation is not secure or even conceived.

De Jongh's assessment is accurate and his description of the function of Upstairs demonstrates the extent to which policy had developed. In earlier years it would have been the case that writers who had yet to establish or create a reputation, if thought good enough, would have been placed within the possibilities which included a main bill presentation. By 1971, Upstairs had assumed that function, and, given the difficulty of transferring downstairs, had therefore to establish themselves in a quite different kind of auditorium. A production within the context of Upstairs could by definition not teach a new writer anything about the context of downstairs. Thus the pattern of separation evolved and while it is not true that dramatists did not get into the main bill, it is true that it became more difficult. The main stage throughout 1971 was held by Osborne, Bond and Storey between August and the end of the year. Gaskill clearly did not subscribe to the policy which still thought of the West End as worth the effort:[30]

> I cannot myself see much future for the West End theatre, or the
> Broadway theatre. Obviously it will go on. We keep saying it's dying
> and it doesn't die. It is rapidly becoming a tourist attraction, and may
> survive like the Monarchy. . . . But we have to hope that what we
> call Theatre will continue to have some vitality and bear some
> relationship to life, and to change in society. And that may not just
> come through the writer.

The bridge between traditional and experimental theatre was not happening in the way Gaskill originally envisaged it via *Come Together*. Experimental theatre was in evidence at the Court but Upstairs, and to some extent by visiting groups. Between June and September 1971, the Traverse, Edinburgh, and its offshoot, the Traverse Workshop, produced four shows. Pip Simmons appeared in September, and Portable Theatre, working with the Traverse, showed *Lay By* as a Sunday night production.

The final show of the Gill/Gaskill season was David Hare's *Slag*, a new version of the production which had originally opened at the Hampstead Theatre Club on 6 April 1971, and which then went to Broadway. It was thought of as a transferable production before it opened. The Management committee was told on 7 April that the obstacle to this was whether Lynn Redgrave would be available if the show transferred. Despite the uncertainty, it was decided to go ahead at the Court, even if a transfer proved impossible. At the same meeting, it was announced that Osborne's *West of Suez* had arrived, with a request from the author that it be done as soon as possible. There were, however, existing commitments to a proposed production of Duras's *Suzanne Andler* and to plays by Bond and Storey. Osborne was to be offered dates in the winter season. By 27

April, Osborne had threatened to withdraw the play from the Court and to open it in the West End with the Court involved in the production if it wished. Page, whom Osborne wanted as director, had meanwhile decided he did not want to direct *Suzanne Andler* in the main bill. An offer to put the play on Upstairs was refused both by Eileen Atkins, who was to have played in it, and the commercial management involved, and the play was withdrawn. This paved the way for the suggestion that Osborne's play be put on after the scheduled production with Peggy Ashcroft of Duras's *The Lovers of Viorne* (first seen in September 1969 at the Court with Madeleine Renaud). The proposal was dependent upon Bond's allowing his *Lear* to be put back by two weeks. However, Page, though happy to direct *West of Suez* at the Court, felt that he could not undertake its presentation in the West End, in view of his commitments as Artistic Director. In fact, the play eventually transferred to the Cambridge Theatre on 6 October, and *Slag*, which opened on 24 May, did not, since Lynn Redgrave was available only for a six-week transfer, which, financially, proved unattractive. *Slag* played to 82 per cent box-office, and was the first main bill production by Max Stafford-Clark, who in 1980 became Artistic Director of the Court. Not a Court director, Stafford-Clark gives a graphic account of an early stage of the production:[31]

> Lindsay, Tony Page and Bill were all present at the first production meeting at which the poster was discussed. It was decided that this should feature a pair of female breasts. Now, on the post-*Hair*, pre-feminist fringe, a pair of tits was a pair of tits, and as such adorned many a fringe production. No Pip Simmons show was complete without several. This was not so at the Court, where they were perceived as an aesthetic feature of the production, which must be discussed in exhaustive detail. After 40 minutes' discussion on breasts, involving some of the keenest minds currently working in British theatre, Lindsay's suggestion of a pair of ceramic tits was agreed upon . . . although I make the point frivolously, this was the first lesson I learned from the Court: that the 'standard' of the 'work' was the important criterion and that this led to the meticulous examination of every detail of the production.

While one aspect of the educational system was being shown in the main bill, a very different account opened Upstairs on 24 June, when Pam Brighton revived Barry Reckord's *Skyvers* for the Schools scheme. Reckord's play had first appeared as a Sunday night in April 1963. Brighton had originally wanted to do Wesker's *Chicken Soup with Barley*, but the author would allow it only if it appeared downstairs.[32] The production of *Skyvers* occasioned an Extraordinary meeting of the Management committee on 2 June. Pam Brighton had written to schools informing them that the play had been 'slightly up-dated' and suggested that the production was more suitable for children of thirteen and above. Lewenstein had seen the production and, supported by Poke and Codron, said that the show contained improvisation and that numerous swear words had been inserted. The changes went way beyond the definition of 'slightly up-dated'. After discussion, Helen Montagu was told to ring schools to make clear the nature of the script changes, and the committee resolved that an advisory group be set up to advise Pam Brighton in future. Great care should in future be taken to give accurate information about schools productions. It is something of an irony that the few occasions on which the schools work occupied the centre of a meeting were invariably to do with complaints. Brighton, supported by Gaskill, weathered the rebuke and the production transferred to the Roundhouse on 8 September.

By July, it had been agreed by the Artistic committee that Anthony Page should continue to run the theatre until Whitehead's new play, *Alpha Beta*, opened in January 1972, at which time Gaskill would reassume control. The theatre would be dark for one month after the conclusion of David Storey's new play, *The Changing Room*, so that air conditioning could be installed. The future programme would open with *Alpha Beta*, include Charles Wood's *Veterans*, if Gielgud agreed to be in it, and Osborne's version of *Hedda Gabler*. Other possibilities for downstairs included work by Hare, Wesker, Howarth and Edna O'Brien, while Upstairs might house Matura's *As Time Goes By*, Harald Mueller's *Big Wolf*, and Ken Campbell. The Artistic committee also discussed the growing possibility of a new theatre in Hammersmith, which was being talked of as a new theatre for the Company or a second, experimental theatre. By 24 September, the committee revised its plans. The plays by Whitehead, Wood, Mueller and Osborne were now definite. The Hare play was rejected. Wesker's play (*The Old Ones*) had been accepted by the National Theatre. Howarth's play, and O'Brien's, were put back. A new Antrobus play had arrived, and Peter Gill wanted to revive Bond's *The Pope's Wedding*. The difficulty of putting together a programme is well illustrated by these accounts, but the flexibility thereby made available seems important. The Antrobus play, *Crete and Sergeant Pepper*, late on the scene in these discussions, nevertheless did find its way into the programme in May 1972, because Peter Gill took it up and directed it. There were rumbles of discontent about the programme both inside and outside the Court. Though *West of Suez* opened on 17 August and played to 92 per cent, one reviewer noted that 'When Sir Ralph Richardson makes his entrance . . . the audience claps for several respectful moments. It seems all too fitting – the knowing star in a well-made hit by our leading playwright. Who mentioned anger? Who whispers now of a theatre of dissent?'[33] On the same main stage on 26 September, the multi-authored

Lay By played on Sunday. According to David Hare, it was remarkable that it was done at all. Howard Brenton, Brian Clark, Trevor Griffiths, Stephen Poliakoff, Hugh Stoddart, Snoo Wilson and Hare, who came together at an Arts Council conference run by Pam Brighton, combined to produce a deliberately shocking story about pornography and its violence. When it was written, Gaskill felt it should be done Upstairs for a week and worked on by a group such as Stafford-Clark's but it met considerable opposition. This Hare attributes to the new overall policy of the Artistic Directors. Some of them[34]

> developed an attitude to new work which made the championship of
> new scripts so arduous and humiliating that it's a wonder people
> stuck their necks out at all. No, they did not want plays from Howard
> Brenton (one artistic director said he should be taken out and buried
> in a hole in a field); yes, they had promised unconditionally and
> irrevocably that as an act of faith in the seven writers involved . . . *Lay
> By* could be scheduled for a Sunday night performance, but now they
> had decided to *read* it and it was no longer a good idea . . .

The discontent as to the use of the Court's resources was not to go away and surfaced early in the new year. However, even at this stage, the priorities of differing factions were apparent. The programme for *West of Suez* carried a declaration, written by Anderson, as to the central function of the Court:

> Sometimes the very catholicity of the theatre's policy may seem to
> blur its image. But empiricism, based on certain values, can be a
> vital principle. A sixteenth season that offers new plays by Osborne,
> Bond and Storey; that sees Christopher Hampton continuing to break
> records in a West End theatre; that will present second plays by
> David Hare and E. A. Whitehead, and Athol Fugard's third – such
> a season will provide its own definition of personality, of function.
> The Royal Court will continue to be the home, we trust and affirm, of
> humanist theatre.

A month later, Edward Bond's *Lear* received its first performance, directed by Gaskill.[35] Accompanying the programme was a leaflet by Bond, 'The Writer's Theatre', in which he asked what the Court's function was to be:

> if I had to depend on Shaftesbury Avenue or Broadway (or off-
> Broadway, or off-off-Broadway, the progression tells its own story)
> I would go mad. . . . I'm clear about what the Royal Court means to
> me, but what does it mean to the society in which I write . . . how
> much, and how well – as writers and audience – do we use the Royal
> Court?

For younger writers, the division was a political one: 'A direct confrontation finally occurred between those who wanted the Court to be a socialist theatre, and those who wanted it to be a humanist theatre and, no question, the humanists won.'[36] On another level, the fact was that many of the established writers were producing plays. Stafford-Clark's view in 1981 was that:[37]

A whole generation of writers was not wooed by the Court ironically enough because it was so strong it didn't need them. It had Lindsay Anderson doing a David Storey play, Bill Gaskill doing an Edward Bond, Anthony Page doing an Osborne and, with the help of a modern classic like Beckett, it virtually had a year's programme. There was no room for anyone else. Indeed Howard Brenton's vivid image is that the battlements of the Court were littered with the corpses of rejected writers.

If Upstairs was still promoting a small number of new writers such as Alexander Buzo and Hugo Claus, the main bill was showing, and very successfully, Storey's fifth play for the Court, *The Changing Room*, which played to 89 per cent (see chapter 6).

Early in December, the anxieties of a number of Court staff regarding the artistic policy showed in a petition (dated 8 December), signed by twenty-three people. The petition expressed 'a growing concern at the number of Royal Court productions which appear in many respects to be designed for the West End. We feel that several unhealthy factors have appeared, and we wish to register our protest and concern.' The statement goes on to argue against the Court as a try-out theatre, against the idea that plays were failures if they did not transfer, that planning of productions should not be in terms of transfer, and that the Court should 'seriously re-examine its attitude towards its work'. A meeting of the staff was arranged for 27 January 1972, prior to the Council meeting on the same day. At the Council, Lewenstein reported that the meeting had been 'fairly short with an exchange of views about policy'. It was short largely because Anderson, according to Greville Poke,[38]

really lashed out at the staff over this petition and told them exactly what he thought of them and of the petition and of the seasons that they had been running and the whole thing collapsed.

The petition was part of a larger problem to do with the theatre's policy and administration, for at the same Council, the decision was taken to appoint a new Artistic Director.

The contracts of all the Artistic Directors were due to expire in July 1972 and Lord Harewood, chairing this section of the Council meeting, explained that it was now necessary to decide before the end of January whether the contracts were to be renewed or other arrangements made. Greville Poke indicated that discussions had been taking place over the last few months as to the future. He informed Council that Lewenstein's name had been suggested for the post of Artistic Director. After

Lewenstein had made a statement to the Council as to his proposals for the future, similar statements were made in turn by Anderson, Page, Gill and Gaskill. After the directors and Lewenstein had withdrawn, Council heard the views of those present and those of Council members unable to attend (reported by Poke), together with a written statement from Gaskill. This statement, dated 24 January 1972, reviewed the current situation and proposed, *inter alia*, the formation of a small semi-permanent acting group based Upstairs but with a capacity to tour outside London; the expansion of the Schools programme; fixed experimental seasons in the main bill; the use of a larger house, such as the Old Vic, for long runs of large-scale work, whilst retaining the Court as an experimental centre; the training of young directors who would be administratively capable of managing different aspects of the Court's work; and invitations to foreign experimental groups. Council, at the end of its discussions, invited Lewenstein to assume artistic control for three years beginning 27 July 1972.

In this decision, Council was virtually rubber stamping a *fait accompli*, for the idea of Lewenstein's taking over had been growing over the previous few months, from a point at which Gaskill had begun to say that he would not continue. Gaskill's account seems characteristically honest:[39]

> It's foolish of me, but you do cling to jobs when they've been as wonderful as that one and I think even then I thought I could start all over again. . . . I started to have new ideas about forming companies, touring companies, based on the Theatre Upstairs, but I couldn't have gone on by myself, and I certainly couldn't have continued with Lindsay and Anthony. Then the whole idea of Oscar taking over seemed to many people to be a very reasonable idea, that you should have a kind of administrative figure with three artistic directors. We had long meetings about that. I wasn't in favour of it and I think at the last minute I said I'll sell myself but by then it was too late, because everyone had bought the other idea . . .

Greville Poke said that the Council

> thought Bill was going and . . . that Oscar would become the new Artistic Director. Then Bill suddenly put in an application to say that he'd changed his mind. . . . It was then decided that the only way of settling that particular problem was to interview them both. When he came in and told us that he wanted to go back to the repertoire system, you can imagine the effect on the Council, taking us all the way back to the word go. In fact, Oscar gave a much better interview to the Council. We were much more convinced and we felt much more secure in Oscar's policy for the Court, which really wasn't very different . . .

According to Poke, it was Gaskill's vacillation in the months leading up to the Council meeting which prompted Lewenstein's appointment. It 'had caused the Council to lose faith and by that time the idea of Oscar had started to grow in their minds as somebody they could rely upon more than Bill'.[40] Most people involved inevitably took sides. The Council was clearly intent on securing and continuing the run of success of recent seasons and reacted strongly against Gaskill's entirely typical suggestions of innovation and experiment, which certainly would not have made for financial security. Pam Brighton's version is that Gaskill lost a battle between two different kinds of Royal Court, 'the kind . . . that wanted to retain it as very much a try-out theatre and felt that Bill was so lacking in any kind of commercial nous, and dangerous in that he would support ideas that were equally lacking in commercial nous – those were the factors in play'.[41] What actually was happening was that the two strands of Court work, new writing buttressed by revivals and the occasional transfer, were separating both practically and ideologically. This separation had been threatening from the inception of the Court but came actually into being during Gaskill's time. It was made visible to some extent by the creation of Upstairs. No one, obviously, saw this as a consequence, but it became one. To some extent, the advent of Upstairs, together with the sharp increase in costs towards the end of the 1960s pressured the Court into continuing the more purely experimental and innovatory work within a smaller scale. The main stage was cleared to some degree in order for the more obviously commercial work to occupy it and guarantee the theatre's existence. Gaskill's proposals, which reflect quite closely his original manifesto of 1965, put experimental and studio work at the heart of the enterprise. By definition, the concept required a larger subsidy and a commitment to a certain kind of future. His supporters saw that as renewing the theatre's vitality and prestige. His opponents saw the demise of the Court. For good or ill, the opponents won.[42] Lewenstein reported to the Management committee of 1 March that Anderson and Page were prepared to remain as Associates. Peter Gill was uncertain. Gaskill declined the offer. The current Artistic committee would handle policy until 31 July, after which the committee would consist of Lewenstein, Anderson, Page and Jocelyn Herbert, together with Gill if he wished.

The year 1972 opened with Whitehead's *Alpha Beta*, a two-hander starring Rachel Roberts and Albert Finney (who, by the end of March had accepted an invitation to become an Associate Director). The play did very good business (88 per cent) and transferred on 16 March to the Apollo Theatre.[43] Meanwhile, the Theatre Upstairs celebrated its third birthday in February. Sixty-one productions had been seen by February including, from 4 February, John Arden's *Live Like Pigs* for the Schools programme. In committee, there were plans for expansion. The Artistic committee heard from Lewenstein on 2 February about three possibilities. Hammersmith Council was very receptive to the idea of the Court's using a second auditorium when a new theatre was built there. The Old Vic had expressed an interest in the Court's occupying that famous theatre when the National Theatre moved to its new building. And the Roundhouse might be available for periods of six months in a given year. These matters were to occupy the Company in one way or another well into 1973. The Arts Council had expressed some backing for the Old Vic scheme, although by 3 February, it was telling the Court that an anticipated gap between budget and subsidy for 1972–3, if not forthcoming from transfers, would have to be made up by some 'profit making activities'. The exploration of other theatres as a means of extending the Court's range and thereby increasing its revenue was primarily Lewenstein's idea, backed by some Council members. By the time Council met on 3 March, there was a need to choose between Hammersmith and the Old Vic. The decision was made in favour of the latter, not least because the Arts Council made it clear that extra subsidy would more likely be available for the Vic than for Hammersmith. The Roundhouse project remained but mainly because that did not involve the Court in management and administration of another house. As the financial year closed, Council agreed to pursue the Old Vic negotiations as vigorously as possible.[44]

Alpha Beta was followed in the main bill by Charles Wood's *Veterans*, with John Gielgud. It was, according to Gordon Jackson, who played in it, 'Written for – and about – John Gielgud. He was marvellous in it. . . . At the time he was afraid of *Veterans*. Quite a lot of four letter words in it, that shocked his followers.'[45] It provided the Court with another big financial success (86 per cent) and the box-office figure for the financial year produced 68.8 per cent. There was an overall surplus for the year of £12,640, of which £8,609 had been allocated to special maintenance projects, leaving a net surplus to carry forward of £4,031.

Gaskill's last production as Artistic Director was the British première of Harald Mueller's *Big Wolf*. Written in 1968 and first performed in Munich in 1971, it had been seen at the Court in 1971, when Pam Brighton directed an amateur performance Upstairs on a Saturday morning. Gaskill decided to bring the play into the main bill and though officially the production was co-directed by Gaskill and Brighton, Brighton dropped out after about a week. The young actors in the show were drawn from Brighton's production of *Skyvers* (June 1971) and she found that co-directing simply did not work. The production played to only 15.7 per cent at the box-office. Instead of directing *Big Wolf*, Brighton developed a show about the current housing situation. It came out of workshops: 'Bill had always had a very strong policy of workshops. I organized a workshop for about two weeks and out of it came the idea of doing a show about housing that would not only play the Theatre Upstairs but go out and do pubs and schools.'[46] The play, *Show Me the Way to go Home*, opened on 16 May and occasioned a letter of complaint about alleged anti-semitic elements. It was promised that in the unlikely event of a revival, the complaint would be very carefully considered. Peter Gill's last main bill production under Gaskill's tenure was John Antrobus's *Crete and Sergeant Pepper* (Gill's next main bill appearance was not until November 1973, when he directed Lawrence's *The Merry Go Round*.). In the programme, Gill placed a piece on 'The Royal Court and its Actors', in which he describes the consequence of not having a permanent company:

> The necessary care in finding the right actor for the part in a new play (often involving young or unknown actors being cast in leading parts) gives the actor at the Court a special value, without the dangers inherent in permanent companies, of a part being found for an actor rather than a play being put on for the public.

Good acting at the Court, according to Gill 'is more an informing value than a style. It can be described perhaps as a feeling for observed reality and a belief that while the actor is uniquely himself, he must still meet all the demands of a particular writer. People come to the Court to see new plays, but the actual contact with another human being remains the theatre's touchstone.'

Virtually Gaskill's last action as Artistic Director was to give details at a press conference of the Neville Blond Fund on 8 June. The fund was to be used primarily for the commissioning of new plays and for future productions. The fund had been launched in 1971 and Gaskill announced that, so far, thirteen writers had received commissions, including Antrobus, Cannan, Wilson John Haire, Matura, Snoo Wilson and Stephen Poliakoff. Five days later, the Artistic committee was told that an earlier Gaskill commission given to Howard Brenton, who succeeded Whitehead as Resident Dramatist, had produced a play called *Magnificence*. The play, sponsored by the Neville Blond fund, eventually appeared in the main bill in June 1973 (see chapter 8). Brenton's salary as Resident Dramatist also came from the fund.

William Gaskill vacated his post as Artistic Director of the Royal Court at the end of July 1972. The formal goodbyes were said at Council on 6 June. Greville Poke said that the Company owed him 'an immense debt of gratitude for the wonderful work he has done' and noted that Gaskill had been part of the Court for close on fourteen years. Lewenstein's view was that Gaskill had 'sown many seeds for the English Stage Company' and Isador Caplan wryly observed, as the Company's legal adviser, that 'the last few years have been very exciting, and very difficult at times for me!' In reply Gaskill tried to identify the particular blend which constituted the work at the Court:

> It has been a wonderful seven years. I think that what I am most pleased about is that I do think there was a tradition – and still is – which, I think, to some extent I have been responsible for. So many people involved in many different ways with the theatre had worked for George, with me, Anthony and Lindsay and will now work with Oscar. I think, as always, that the Court is not a theatre which can exist as a traditional theatre or live off its past glories. After 16 years it is very difficult not to be aware of the splendour. It has always been very important to look to the future and the new writers. I think George once said when he retired that the Court must keep its eyes on the horizon. It is amazing after 16 years to still be placed at the head of the British theatre, and still people think of it as an experimental theatre. And we still mean so much to young writers, who would still rather have their plays done at the Court than anywhere else. . . . We stand between experimental and traditional theatre – the important thing is to always look ahead.

It is no more than coincidence that the plays running as he departed were by Osborne in the main bill (an adaptation of *Hedda Gabler*) and by N. F. Simpson in the Theatre Upstairs (*Was He Anyone?*).

As is often the case when a central theatrical figure leaves, some of his appointees also go, shortly afterwards. At the Court these included the Casting Director, Gillian Diamond; the General Manager, Helen Montagu; the Chief Electrician, Andy Phillips (who in the event remained for another year as Lighting Designer); and the director of the Schools programme, Pam Brighton. Roger Croucher took a year off from running Upstairs and was replaced by Nicholas Wright. Gaskill returned in 1973 to direct Edward Bond's *The Sea*. Thereafter he did not work at the Court until 1976 as co-director of a visiting show by Joint Stock Theatre Company. After Peter Gill directed *The Merry Go Round* in 1973 he did nothing else until Bond's *The Fool* in 1975. Lindsay Anderson directed two more David Storey Plays (*The Farm*, 1973, and *Life Class*, 1974). He also in 1974 did a Sunday night revival of *In Celebration*. Joe Orton's *What the Butler Saw* in 1975 was his final production of the decade for the Court. Anthony Page's work for the Court during this period ended with a Beckett double-bill in 1973 (one of which was revived in 1975) and Storey's *Cromwell* (1973).

8 · Howard Brenton's *Magnificence*

In July 1968, Gaskill had told his Artistic committee that the Court should respond to new work which was beginning to emerge. He said: 'We cannot ignore certain kinds of freer, more experimental work which is now being shown. We must let in this new element. At one time we were aware of Brecht and Ionesco and to cut off the Court from this type of play would be a very crucial decision.' Part of Gaskill's belief that it would be disastrous for the Court's development if the new writers and new theatrical forms were not housed in Sloane Square was satisfied by the range of experimental work which began to appear Upstairs, but the main stage productions still reflected for some time the continuing work of the established writers. *Magnificence* was the first play by a younger writer associated with fringe theatre to find its way on to the main bill when it opened for a three-week run on 28 June 1973.

The events leading to the production, however, reflect the genuine and disparate feelings of the senior directors at the Court during the period. Up to 1973, Brenton had had seven of his pieces produced at the Court, of which two were Sunday night performances and five Upstairs. His first play to be shown there was *It's My Criminal* in August 1966, as part of a double bill. Its reception was poor. Nevertheless, he was supported by Gaskill:[1]

> Gaskill had been very kind to me . . . he'd done a dreadful play I
> wrote on a Sunday night . . . and he then got me a job backstage.
> I found myself with the stagehands, simply because I had no money.
> I was sleeping on a floor in Notting Hill and walking to the theatre
> each day to come to rehearsals for *It's My Criminal* and Gaskill found
> that out. He then by a nudge got me a job in an office. It was all
> Gaskill. He was extremely careful with me, a dramatist who was very
> much at odds with some of the things he was doing . . .

An association with the Court after a Sunday night production would, ordinarily, have resulted in Brenton's becoming part of the group of writers who developed in this way. However, Brenton after 1966 took a different direction, and wrote for a number of groups and a series of smaller theatres, amongst which were Brighton Combination, the University of Bradford, Portable Theatre, the Open Space and the Oval House. His development as a writer was therefore not to do with the Court. Indeed, four of the works shown at the Court up to 1973 were in productions by outside companies.[2] It was the work done outside the Court which led to a renewed association by 1969 because 'The Royal Court had seen my plays and contacted me. And although I'm not in the tradition of the Court – I'm not what you would call a humanist writer, not of the mainstream of the Court at all – they've always been good to me.'[3]

As a consequence of the renewed contact, Brenton wrote *Revenge*, which opened in September 1969 Upstairs:[4]

When I had *Revenge* on, it was rather well received and I went to Bill and we went to the Antelope pub and I asked him if he'd put it on downstairs and he said, 'No, but I will commission you to write another play'. . . . When he formally commissioned me, he took me out to lunch with Edward [Bond], which was the first time I'd met him. Edward was delivering the second version of *Lear*, and I remember that very vividly. It was a very Gaskill occasion. . . . I felt completely tongue-tied. It's typical of Bill to have a new writer he was commissioning, as he was receiving a play from Bond. It's Gaskill's sense of humour, I think.

The commission was given in 1971 under the auspices of the newly-established Neville Blond Fund. The play, or rather the first version, was delivered early in June 1972, but it had taken a long time to write. Brenton recalls that at the time when his play, *A Sky Blue Life*, was receiving lunchtime performances at the Open Space in November 1971, Jonathan Hales, the Literary Manager at the Court said ' "For God's sake, hurry up and get the play in". I thought that must mean that Bill was not going to be in the job much longer and I can remember feeling very frustrated.'[5] By the time the play was delivered, Brenton had become Resident Dramatist at the Court, but there then ensued a long struggle to get the play performed, which was to take over a year.

Council was informed on 6 June that 'We have just received an interesting play commissioned from Howard Brenton.' The Artistic committee was told seven days later that both Page and Lewenstein had read the play and 'Both thought it should definitely be done Upstairs if it was finally decided it was not strong enough for Downstairs. Albert Finney was reading it and would then pass it on to David Storey.' A week later, the same committee discussed the play. Anderson had not read it, 'but it was generally thought that it should be seriously considered for a three-week run in the main theatre though this could be lengthened if it had an exceptionally strong cast. Anthony Page agreed to discuss the play with Howard Brenton and talk to Oscar Lewenstein after that when a final decision could be made.' By August 1972 the play's fate had not been decided and it was not listed firmly in the future programme. Instead, Page reported to the committee that he had talked briefly to Brenton and that Brenton 'was proposing to do substantial re-writes. The Committee decided to defer decisions on this play until the re-writes were done.' Behind this particular case of *Magnificence*, there was a more general problem. There were a large number of plays waiting to be done but the money was in short supply: 'It was felt that the losses sustained by the theatre this year made it particularly necessary to bear financial considerations in mind for the last quarter of the year.'

Brenton initially wanted Page to direct his play: 'I admired him very much. I liked the *Hedda Gabler* that he did [June 1972]. I thought that was really superb.' He also wanted one of the senior Court directors 'to actually come to water and do some of my work, but I think a number of writers felt that and in a way they never did. We found our own directors.'[6] One of the senior directors was clear about the play. For Lindsay Anderson, *Magnificence* was a play 'which I never liked and of course disgraced myself with the young *avant-garde* by making it quite clear that I didn't like it and I've been regarded as a reactionary ever since. . . . I said to Anthony Page, "if you like *Magnificence* so much, why don't you direct it?", which of course he wasn't prepared to do . . . but I was very aware that we needed that breadth of opinion in the Court.'[7] Brenton recalls that Anderson 'let it be known in no uncertain terms that he disliked the play, but that's fair enough, really.'[8] And Max Stafford-Clark, who directed the play eventually, remembers Anderson in the interval of the first preview, saying, ' "You don't really think this is a good play, do you?" He positively disliked the play and his attitude certainly was extremely contagious. . . .'[9] At least, Anderson spoke his mind for all to hear. Elsewhere in the theatre, it was difficult to tell what would happen to the play. Matters came to a head around Christmas of 1972:[10]

> I fought for the play a lot. . . . Oscar offered me a Sunday night . . .
> but he promised to beef up the decor a bit, and I had the presence
> of mind to turn that down. They then said they would do it Upstairs
> and I also said no, I didn't want that. So the play was a kind of
> football and I talked to Tony Page several times, but never felt he
> was really going to come to water about it . . .

Meanwhile, the rewrites were under way. The play went through three versions in a rather public fashion:[11]

> My trouble with the play was that I was still half an apprentice writer
> and the first version was clearly far too short. I then rewrote a fat

version of it, where I made a number of mistakes, like I had Alice appear in the first act, come through the window into the squat scene, and I over wrote the end. I then realized I had to work again on that, which I gradually did bit by bit and I was perhaps being something of an innocent in that I would show bits of writing to anyone that was around . . . re-writing in a rather quasi-public way.

The objections to the play, whether on the grounds of its politics or its quality were allowed to gain ground basically because there was no one director lobbying sufficiently strongly for its production. Many productions depended on the energy with which an individual within the Court pursued the campaign. *Magnificence* for most of this period did not have a powerful voice arguing for it.[12] At one point, the play was going to be farmed out to the Young Vic, with an option on it for this purpose until the end of March 1973. The Court production came about because in the event elements of the proposed new season had to be postponed. There were two productions planned of plays by David Storey, which were to follow Bond's play, *The Sea*. Anderson was unable to direct because of film commitments and the plays were therefore put back. In the gap thereby created for June and July, the Management committee of 27 February 1973 proposed *Magnificence* and *The Removalists* by David Williamson. Each would have a three-week run (with three weeks' rehearsal), and a production budget of £4,000 each, thus being costed *in toto* for the average budget of one main bill production. An Australian impresario was to be the Court's partner for Williamson's play, while *Magnificence* would be sponsored by the Neville Blond Fund. In the same meeting, Lewenstein asked for two more resident directors. These were Pam Brighton and Max Stafford-Clark. When the production dates were finally set, Brenton asked for Stafford-Clark as director, whose last production at the Court had been Brenton's *Hitler Dances* for the Traverse Workshop and who had directed David Hare's *Slag* in the main bill at the Court in May 1971. Brenton's impression was that 'what we ended up with was a kind of runt version of what was going to be a grand new play season, a burst of new work and all that happened finally was my play and David Williamson's play. It tends to happen in theatres.'[13]

What also happened was that *Magnificence* was done as a cheap production. The Management committee was informed on 6 April that the restricted budget left very small amounts for the scenery and fit up, 'but the Committee felt that we should attempt to do this'. The effect was that the play's set was built in a rather shoddy way. The stage management disliked the play 'partly because the set had been constructed cheaply and there were no eye-holes in the battens, so they loathed it because the set was rubbish, which meant that the play was rubbish . . .'.[14] Equally, Lewenstein was clearly nervous about the play's content. A few days before it opened, he was reluctant to inform the contributors to the Neville Blond Fund that the Fund had commissioned the play and recommended to the Management committee that the play should go on before informing the contributors.

Magnificence is written in eight scenes. Part of the impact of the play derives from the driving honesty of the writer to bring together a broad series of ideas which have difficulty on occasions in coalescing, but which in their portrayal show a struggle to come to terms with central issues affecting Brenton's own generation: the effect and failure of the revolutionary events in France in May 1968; the failure of the concept of an alternative culture; the despair of a certain kind of revolutionary figure; the need for sustained and systematic political organization; the inadequacy of isolated gesture, even though romantically stirring; above all, the imperative of finding a way to proceed. All this, and a public theatre in London to try it in for the first time. The brief Brenton set himself was daunting. Part of the play is a further exploration of ideas set out in a short film script, written by Brenton, directed by Tony Bicat, and first shown in London during 1972. The film, amongst other things, tells the story of three young people who kidnap an eminent politician, then torture and murder him. As the police close in, the three figures destroy themselves. The film, *Skin Flicker*, seemed to Brenton unsatisfactory, primarily because the figures involved were not shown as analysing their activity. No sense of discovery was involved, no process. A film basically about the Red Army Faction demonstrated activity after conclusions had been reached. *Magnificence* attempts a more complex account of what is learnt by experience.[15]

The play tells the story of a group of five young people who occupy a derelict house as a squat. The room they settle in is empty apart from a mound of old newspapers in one corner. They write slogans and their names on the wall, unfurl a banner on which is written 'We are the writing on your wall' and sort out the food stores.[16] In between settling in, the group argues about the next step. After drawing attention to the plight of the homeless and the empty decaying houses in London, Veronica asks: 'And what happens now?' The reply is: 'We occupy the place.' Will, who makes the answer, sprays the slogan, 'Anarchy Farm' on the wall and 'That about sums it up.' Implicit in the first scene is the anger which fuels the decision to occupy, but no sense of what then happens. As if to query this lack, the scene ends with an old man suddenly emerging from the pile of newspapers. He says nothing and shambles off to the lavatory. In the next scene, the play goes to the street outside the house to a freelance bailiff, Slaughter, and a young constable. Slaughter has an eviction order, is ready to act and proposes to go in at first light. The two figures discuss in a laconic way theories of evolution, the beast in man, the rising standard of education in the police force, and Slaughter's self-pitying account of how nobody loves him, especially since having been the subject of a television documentary. The ex-policeman, Slaughter, poses a cynical view of the world, hates all politicians and has 'murder in my heart'. His contempt for ordinary procedures parallels the chanting group in the house and, though the scene is comic and whimsical, it is also seriously aimed as the policeman warns him not to step outside the law. Back in the squat in scene three, amidst the turds hurled in through the window, Mary deals with Veronica's blackheads, the room is in chaos, and the realities of the occupation are very apparent. Mary, six months pregnant, does her exercises. The old man sits and watches. The doubts grow, principally from Veronica and Jed. Finally, Slaughter and his men break in, and in a scuffle, Slaughter kicks Mary. In a tableau to close the scene, Jed tells what happened. Mary lost her baby. Jed got nine months in prison for retaliating and in prison became a drug addict. As the scene ends, Jed carries the play forward to the day of his release: 'Honed down. Pure. Angry.'

The first and most of the third scene are written as naturalism. It's clear that Brenton knew both the theatre he was writing for and its characteristic audience. He remembers someone at the interval saying, 'Oh! It's another Jimmy Porter, isn't it? . . . a sordid room.'[17] The design for scenes one and three was a box set at an angle. Three flats were flown in, with a window back centre, the door to the room at stage left and the lavatory door stage right. The flats were a dirty yellow and the floor was made of planks. Outside the room, the back wall of the theatre, the surround and the proscenium arch were painted a dark chocolate, so that 'you had this tiny little naturalistic stage within a stage, which is then dismantled and thrown away, so there was a complete change of direction in the play. You begin with what I'd looked on as naturalistic writing . . . and the play then changes tack and there's a deliberate collision of two sorts of styles.'[18] The different styles of the play, which become very apparent from scene four onwards, begin to emerge before that. The Slaughter–constable encounter in scene two was conducted downstage of a front cloth:[19]

> The cloth was a cartoonish representation of the front of a house at
> night and that was because you had two rather music hall-like
> characters standing in front of it . . . one of the principles that we
> decided on was to follow the style of the scene you are playing and
> the play will ring true. Don't worry about over-image . . . the comic
> scene between the bailiff and the ex-copper is broadly written and it
> will prosper if you present it in front of a strange cloth which has a
> quasi-comic design on it. The other scenes will prosper as long as

they are kept real – if you really think how dirty you can get by
staying too long inside that little room . . .

Equally, the change in the style of the play is signalled by Jed's speech
to the audience which closes scene three. The stage directions indicate a
'freeze in a tableau. The lights change. Dark shadows from bright lights
low across the tableau. An effect of sudden negativing, an x-ray . . . .
Jed speaks aside to the audience.' The effect of this is to cut powerfully
across the preceding naturalism, and springs from Brenton's conviction
that modern writing had lost certain skills:[20]

I do think that there is a certain battle to be fought about the styles
which are acceptable within one play. Coherence within a play is
not a matter of choosing to write in one style. That's just sameness,
superficial neatness. Actual coherence means using many different
styles, moulding them, a deliberate process of selection, in order to
express that *whole* in a play. Shakespeare did this all the time . . .

Because Brenton attempted to establish different worlds in the play, it
followed that different styles could be the means of achieving the contrast.
The 'arsenal of the playwright' should include stylistic variety and 'I
wanted with *Magnificence* to claim that freedom.'[21]

The rest of the play asks for a bare stage and the audience is presented
in scene four with brilliant light filtered through flown-in tree greenery.
The setting is a Cambridge college garden in early morning: 'You present
this greenery, hanging over a dark stage and you play some weird,
beautiful music, and on the first night there was an "oh!" from the
audience because the play had changed tack.'[22] From the squat to the
apparent serenity of a different world, from naïve would-be changers of
the world to the encounter of Babs, an old-style Tory minister, who is
dying amidst beautiful surroundings. Babs has summoned a current Tory
cabinet minister, Alice, to spend the day with him. They discuss, in tone
of effortless civility, political matters and life in Cambridge while, at the
same time, delivering a series of asides to the audience as commentary
on the action. The scene is sour and comic and satiric. The difference
between them is expressed by Babs as he nears his death. He categorizes
Alice as one of a new breed of politician:

You are a fascist. Oh, I don't mean jackboots and Gotterdammerungs.
You are a peculiarly modern, peculiarly English kind of fascist.
Without regalia. Blithe, simple-minded and vicious. I hate you. You
scare me sick. Mao had better come quick, for I think there's a
danger, a very real and terrible danger, that *you* may inherit the earth.

The description of English fascism offered by Babs becomes the basis of
Jed's later conviction that only violent action can possibly disrupt such
perversion. The scene takes the play far away from naturalism, most
particularly when, during the scene, the two men exit, to re-enter after

a pause in a punt for the rest of the scene. On a bare stage, the effect is powerful. It provides what the play's director called 'a gracious metaphor . . . the immediate and simple and economic transformation of the stage'.[23] If the deliberate effect of scene four is romantic, scene five deals with the day of Jed's release from prison. It is the beginning of Jed's domination of the play, as he looks for revenge. The scene contains extraordinary effects. Jed, in his damaged state from prison and drugs, ignores those who have come to meet him for a startling appearance by Lenin. As the stage 'floods with red, awash with banners and songs', Lenin at the back of the stage goes through heroic postures, sweeps downstage shouting slogans through a gale created by a wind machine.[24] In the face of Lenin's grand assertions, Jed offers a 'Morsel of contempt' as a contribution; a 'Little bit of hate'. What it will be is not disclosed here. In scene six, Jed goes to see Will, who has moved from statements of anarchy to a mindless and soporific existence on drugs. His despair is powerful and pathetic: ' 'Cos his dreams are very fragile, Jed. Delicate. Precious. And his brain wall's thin, and liable to rupture, as a result of all the changes. . . .' Where Jed has become committed to action, Will has softened into helplessness, still with the tokens of change about him, badges and Che Guevara tee-shirts. What provoked the squat has fragmented into, on the one hand, a vicious hatred and, on the other, a refuge in dreams. But Jed needs Will and slaps him into consciousness. Opposing methodologies meet in scene seven, where Cliff, for the first time in the play, articulates a way other than Jed's intention to 'Disrupt the spectacle. The obscene parade. . . .' Cliff's way is to organize and politicize, to form a mass movement, but Jed is impervious to reasoned argument and he speaks the epigraph from Brecht which prefaces the play:

> Sink into the mire
> Embrace the butcher
> But change the world

The freedom afforded by the stylistic change from the earlier naturalistic scenes in the play allowed Brenton to modify the stage conditions according to needs. The writing in *Magnificence*:[25]

> sometimes gets closer to the psychology or the internal landscape of a character, particularly with Jed. You feel that the whole stage has got to follow him. Rather than say the stage is a neutral world, the stage has to comment because the writing is hotter. When you see all those characters in the second half who were in that naturalistic room during the squat, they are now in really a rather damaged and psychotic state and actually you stage them on a grey looking area and they're in a room [scene seven]. There's mention of a cup of

tea, but there are no props, no table and chair, no doors, because you just want to examine the state they are in. It's got personal.

The final scene of the play is in the garden of Alice's country home. Jed, dragging the nervously chattering Will with him, captures Alice and puts a hood on him to which are attached sticks of dynamite. When the dynamite fails to go off, Alice 'draws on great reserves to save the situation – his class privileges, his army training and his politics'.[26] Alice, once the hood is removed, talks the situation into his control and recognizes Jed as a situationist. He learnt the term at a summer school run by the Special Branch. Jed, at bay from Alice's analysis of him, tries to explain to Alice and himself:

> . . . I am deeply in contempt of your English mind. There is BLAME
> THERE. That wrinkled stuff with the picture of English Life in its
> pink, rotten meat. In your head. And the nasty tubes to your eyes
> that drip Englishness over everything you see. The cool, glycerine
> humanity of your tears that smarms our ANGER. I am deeply in
> contempt of your FUCKING HUMANITY. The goo, the sticky
> mess of your English humanity that gums up our ears to your lies,
> our eyes to your crimes. . . . I dunno, I dunno, what can a. . . .
> What can a . . . Do? To get it real. And get it real to you . . .

As Alice suggests drinks on the lawn, Jed, defeated, throws the hood to the floor, the dynamite explodes and they both die. The last image is of Cliff. He delivers a coda:

> Jed. The waste. I can't forgive you that.
> (A pause.)
> The waste of your anger. Not the murder, murder is common enough.
> Not the violence, violence is everyday. What I can't forgive you Jed,
> my dear, dead friend, is the waste.

The ending of the play was rewritten a number of times. Over the three versions, the bomb exploded in version one, not in the second version, and finally did in the third draft:[27]

> And then I had this terrible feeling of sourness, almost of obscurity,
> and so I put in this sort of Jacobean epilogue, which I don't know
> was ever really satisactory. It announces the play as a tragedy and
> that the subject was waste. It's a bit like Enid Blyton writing, where
> she says, 'Dear children, the clowns came into the ring at the circus,
> and they were very funny, and the children laughed'. It doesn't
> actually deliver the jokes . . . it's a bit of a cheat, really, but I think
> it was necessary. I remember discussing that with Oscar.

Stafford-Clark points out a practical problem with the play's ending with an explosion:[28]

> To end a play on an effect seems quite a callow decision . . . if the
> explosion was too loud, people did say, 'Oh God!' or whatever and

their concentration on the play at the end was absolutely dislocated
by the explosion . . . it's not as if you have a three page scene after
the explosion and the audience settles down and begins to listen again.
You have a few lines . . .

In fact, the epilogue attempts to rescue the play from Jed, and to allow
more weight to the views of Cliff. On the one hand, the play is a kind
of requiem for people like Jed; on the other, it attempts an analysis of
what is wrong with Jed's position. Brenton set out to write a play 'about
a group of people who really went for the world':[29]

As I proceeded I began to realize that this was impossible. Jed's
attitude leads to acts of terrorism which are futile. So what began
to emerge was a kind of tragedy, a tragedy not of pride or of fate but
of waste . . . I wrote the play for people like Jed. . . . A lot of my
generation feel like Jed in the play – there's a feeling of rage around,
of impotence, a sense that one has to make a mark on the world . . .

What Brenton elsewhere defined as 'a huge personal element' in the play,
that 'it was written about people exactly my age whose minds bear similar
shapes to mine and my friends',[30] involved him in a sequence where the
means of countering Jed's despair is reduced almost to silence. Cliff's
attitude is meant as the realistic alternative. Three years after the play
was performed, Brenton's view of this part of the play was that the need
to show Jed marred the structure of the play:[31]

the person who's carrying the wisdom of the play is the boy, Cliff.
His knowledge of what's going on and what to do about it and his
sense of the tragedy involved is very strong, but he disappears from
the play. He doesn't occupy a central scene. The central scene is
between the bomber and the guy whose libertarian ideals have
decayed. There were ideas in the play which were just not getting
a voice and in fact these were the ideas I believed in. So I wrote an
epilogue. I had this man come forward and say exactly what I felt about
it. It's a very puny ending. . . . There are precious things about Jed
– his ferocity and his conviction and his allegiances are admirable.
A tragedy is involved because he takes a wrong direction, as one could
oneself so easily. . . . I do endorse the romantic element [in Jed]. I
don't endorse what he did with it.

The opportunity to work on the main stage at the Court was exploited
by Brenton in a number of ways. If the play describes the situation of a
generation not until then given much space in the Court's main bill, it
also inevitably pursues ways and means which provided a counter to some
of the staging solutions created during the 1960s. Quite apart from the
fact that choosing the name of Cliff is a glance at Cliff in *Look Back in
Anger* – 'It was deliberate. I chose the name deliberately, a deliberate
kind of echo, more personal'[32] – and that the use of Jed as a name may

be an attempt to explain more carefully a comparable figure in Osborne's *West of Suez*, Brenton met head on the dominant production style of the Court at that time, as he judged it to be.

An example of this may be found in the lighting of shows at the Court and Brenton's response to it. The lighting systems current at the Court from the mid-1960s are explained by Gaskill:[33]

We devised the system of lighting at the Court, mainly the work of Andy Phillips, which was initially based on what we called a Brechtian lighting. You have to remember that the main thing about Brechtian lighting was that they used open white, they don't use colour. If you check open white, it becomes softer and warmer and if you don't want it to become warmer you have to use a particular colour – a grey blue – and it cools the whole thing without appearing to colour the stage at all, so that the eye on it remains very cool. Andy's way of lighting is to use a great number of lights but to use a lot of them on check, so the whole stage is covered and rather evenly covered. There is no part of the stage that is unlit. There is no dramatic highlighting, no chiaroscuro at all, but the effect is not non-atmospheric . . . the theory behind it is that if you want to look at something in a detached and objective way you mustn't guide or prejudice the spectator by saying that this is more important than that or this is brighter than that. You have to look at the whole stage space because everything in that space is important. That's the kind of political philosophy behind it and I believe in it absolutely.

Though Gaskill is careful to insist that 'What I'm theorizing about now is not something I ever theorized about with Andy. It was just something which evolved and was very strongly felt against other ways of lighting in the theatre', what he describes held full sway at the Court when he was Artistic Director. Brenton's play was felt by the writer to demand a different solution:[34]

I was aware with *Magnificence* that we had a kind of epic-shaped play on our hands. Because of the fierce nature of the writing and also an attempt to use theatricality as an argument in itself, a neutral space was not going to work for us . . . that is, the kind of stage evolved by Bill Gaskill and the designers he has worked with, which is a very cool neutral area which says 'stage' and really doesn't change – the actors go on and change it. That degree of coolness doesn't really follow the nature of the writing. You need the stage to be expressive on your behalf. So what we did with William Dudley, the designer, was to reverse the light. We reversed the usual colouring of the epic stage currency, and blackened the stage. We're not talking about realism, we're talking about a hot, expressive nature.

Speaking of his play, *Weapons of Happiness* (1976), Brenton instances the necessity of using many lighting forms in order to follow the mind of a character, much as he does with Jed: 'if we're going to get to that mind, we've got to blank out things around *us*, so it's legitimate to change the lighting, damp down other people around him, put a follow spot on him – things which are meant to be anathema to the way solutions were found for plays in the sixties'.[35] Just as Gaskill and Phillips reacted to lighting design current in the early 1960s, so Brenton argued for solutions to fit his kind of writing in the early 1970s. The box of light became a box of darkness. Out of that, 'we light what we need, which ends up with what could loosely be called an expressionist lighting and staging'.[36]

Brenton's own judgment of his play is characteristically honest. The play worked:[37]

> But I think parts of it were not formal, big-theatre writing. A lot of it – particularly the third part of the play, really would have worked better in the round, whereas the beginning of the play would work better in the proscenium arch, with, perhaps, a greater formality than we had at the Court. Perhaps the difficulty in the play is immaturity. The trouble was, it was half-and-half, you see. It was still, in a sense, half a fringe play and half a big, formal theatre play. And you can't help that, you're just growing up.

Over the twenty performances, *Magnificence* achieved only 26 per cent of capacity, with 36 per cent of seats sold. The total loss for the run was £12,500 against the Arts Council grant of £7,500. Stafford-Clark's judgment of the production was:[38]

> The reputation of the play and the perception of it as a kind of turning point, the first time that kind of work has been welcomed on to a main stage, was out of all proportion to what it cost and the number of people who saw it. At the time those of us who were involved were aware that it was a significant step.

As a consequence of seeing *Magnificence* on 11 July, Peter Hall commissioned a play from Brenton.[39] In July 1976, *Weapons of Happiness*, the first new play to be presented at the National Theatre, opened in the Lyttelton auditorium.

Abbreviations

Browne   Terry Browne, *Playwrights' Theatre. The English Stage Company at the Royal Court*, London, Pitman, 1975

Findlater Richard Findlater (ed.), *At the Royal Court. 25 Years of the English Stage Company*, Ambergate, Amber Lane Press, 1981

Wardle   Irving Wardle, *The Theatres of George Devine*, London, Cape, 1978

Notes

Introduction

1 Peter Thomson, *Shakespeare's Theatre*, 1983, 'Introduction', p. xiii.
2 John Elsom and Nicholas Tomalin, *The History of the National Theatre*, London, Cape, 1978, p. 315.
3 R. B. Marriott, *The Stage*, 26 May 1977.

Chapter 1   Prologue: William Gaskill's first season, October 1965 to March 1966

1 Ronald Duncan, *How to Make Enemies*, London, Hart-Davis, 1968, p. 385. Duncan's central complaint was to do with the loss of power of the Artistic committee, which originally and uniquely in theatre companies controlled the choice of plays. The original group, consisting of Lord Harewood, Duncan himself and Oscar Lewenstein, effectively set policy in a way which no Artistic Director could tolerate. Devine's gradual assumption of budgetary and artistic autonomy by 1959 was a step of great importance in the development of the company (see *Wardle*, pp. 213ff.). Duncan was not alone in this view. Greville Poke, as secretary of the Company, complained to J. E. Blacksell, one of the founder members, about the choice of plays. Referring to a meeting of the Artistic committee of 31 October 1958, he says that the committee is in an untenable position: 'What does it mean? If it means that we members of the Artistic Committee have got to support George if he makes a snap decision to put on a dreadful play like *Live Like Pigs* then I am not playing . . .' (Letter to Blacksell, 7 November 1958). The relationship between the Artistic committee and the Artistic Director remained a problem throughout this period. Lindsay Anderson made much the same point on his return to the Court in 1969 (see chapter 5). Duncan continued to complain about Court policy. Writing to Blacksell on 12 November 1965, he objected to Gaskill's policy: 'I indicated that although Gaskill and his kind think people should be committed when they write

plays, they are irritated if the same people are in any way committed in other kinds of opinion.'

2 Details of one such attempt are in *Browne*, pp. 42–3.

3 *Browne*, pp. 43–4, details the proposed joint venture between the Company, Oscar Lewenstein Productions and Laurence Olivier Productions, to take the Metropolitan Theatre, Edgware Road, in 1960. The scheme collapsed when it was discovered that the theatre stood in the path of a proposed new road. Again in 1973, a proposal for the English Stage Company to lease the Old Vic Theatre was defeated. Oscar Lewenstein, then Artistic Director, was the chief proponent of this scheme but notes that 'Everybody's very sentimental about the Royal Court' and that there was 'a fear that taking another theatre would weaken the Royal Court' (Interview with the writer, 14 December 1983).

4 'Vital Theatre', *Encore*, vol. 6 no. 2, March–April 1959, pp. 24–5.

5 *Evening Standard*, 21 June 1960.

6 Devine, *op. cit.*, n. 4, p. 24.

7 Details of the work of the Writers' Group are given in Keith Johnstone, *Impro. Improvisation and the Theatre*, London, Faber, 1979.

8 'The Right to Fail', *The Twentieth Century*, vol. 169, February 1961, p. 130.

9 'Court Account', *Guardian*, 2 April 1962.

10 An account of Devine's pre-Court career is available in Irving Wardle, *The Theatres of George Devine*, London, Cape, 1978.

11 'Memorandum on the Royal Court Theatre Studio', dated August 1964; see also *Ten Years at the Royal Court, 1956/66*, published by the English Stage Company, 1966.

12 Arts Council of Great Britain, *17th Report*, 1961–2, p. 35.

13 Devine interviewed by Michael Mende and Karen Tottrup, *Trial Run, the Royal Court Magazine for Schools*, Spring 1963.

14 'Drama and the Left', *Encore*, vol. 6 no. 2, March–April 1959, pp. 8–10.

15 *Daily Telegraph*, 21 May 1962.

16 Interview with the writer, 11 September 1984. Though Devine attempted to pre-empt discussion over the appointment, there were other suggestions, and what is implicit in the suggestions is the struggle between differing views of what the Court should be. Blacksell argued the case for someone like Robert Helpmann who would think of drama 'in terms of the concentration of experience inside a stylized, controlled environment. This involves the heightening of the emotions by movement and sound, as well as apt use of language' (Letter to Lord Harewood, 10 December 1964). Harewood had already effectively dismissed the suggestion in answer to a previous letter as adding 'unnecessary complications to the already difficult business of finding an artistic director, and indeed make it almost impossible for anyone to accept!' (Harewood to Blacksell, 7 December 1964). Undeterred, Blacksell wrote to Duncan on 18 January 1965, wondering if Robert Shaw might eventually take over. On the same day, he wrote to Harewood suggesting he take over, and then to Greville Poke, making a similar suggestion if Harewood should decline. In effect, Blacksell was looking to

restate the Company's original aims. He issued a policy statement in January 1965, in which he said that Devine should be consulted and his advice sought 'in the appointment of his successor, but he should not be the Kingmaker. We, the Directors . . . must appoint somebody who will carry out the original Artistic Policy laid down so carefully at the beginning of the venture.'

17 *Findlater*, p. 66.

18 *Browne*, p. 48.
   The lunch took place on 6 January. Speculation as to his successor ranged from Lindsay Anderson to Kenneth Tynan, from John Dexter to William Gaskill to Peter Brook (*Yorkshire Post*, 7 January 1965; *Observer*, 10 January 1965).

19 *Findlater*, p. 61.

20 *Browne*, p. 49.

21 William Gaskill's career up to 1965 is detailed by Gaskill himself in *Findlater*, pp. 57–61. After attending Hertford College, Oxford, where he went from Shipley, Yorkshire, he worked for a time in weekly repertory (Mansfield, Redcar, Swindon), for Granada television, and then joined the Royal Court in 1957. Between 1957 and 1965 when he became Artistic Director at the age of thirty-four, he directed ten plays at the Court (including work by Simpson, Osborne, Howarth and Arden). This period also included work at Stratford (*Richard III*, *Cymbeline* and *The Caucasian Chalk Circle* at the Aldwych Theatre), at York (the *Mystery Plays*) and at the National Theatre as an Associate Director (*The Recruiting Officer*, *Philoctetes*, *The Dutch Courtesan* and *Mother Courage*). He also directed (in 1965) Arden's *Armstrong's Last Goodnight* at Chichester.

22 This complicated subject is well dealt with by Martin Esslin, 'Brecht and the English Theatre', *Tulane Drama Review*, vol. 11 no. 2, Winter 1966, pp. 63–70. See also Richard Findlater, 'No Time for Tragedy?', *The Twentieth Century*, vol. 161, January 1957, pp. 56–66; Peter Daubeny, *My World of Theatre*, London, Cape 1971, pp. 258–63; and Kenneth Tynan, 'Decade in Retrospect: 1959', *Tynan Right and Left*, London, Longman, 1967, pp. 11–15.

23 *Plays and Players*, June 1965, on the occasion of Gaskill's own production at the Old Vic.

24 Tom Milne, 'And the time of the great taking over: an interview with William Gaskill', *Encore*, vol. 9 no. 4, July–August 1962, pp. 10–24. This is an excellent account of Gaskill's early working methods in rehearsal. Three years later, Gaskill refers to the difficulty of translating Brecht so as to give English actors a good script to work with (*Encore*, September–October 1965, p. 23).

25 *Encore*, vol. 9 no. 4, p. 22.

26 Interview with the writer, 13 December 1983. It was Olivier who described the process of getting Gaskill to the National as 'the wooing of Billy Gaskill' (Logan Gourlay, *Olivier*, London, Weidenfeld & Nicolson, 1973, p. 167).

27 *Ibid.* pp. 167–80 contain an interview with Gaskill in which he analyses the

early position of the National and the conflict between himself and Tynan's views. Some idea of Gaskill at work at the National is contained in Kenneth Tynan's account of Gaskill's rehearsing *The Recruiting Officer* in *The Sound of Two Hands Clapping*, London, Cape, 1975, pp. 119–26.

28 Interview with the writer, 18 September 1984.

29 Harewood, *op. cit.*, n. 16.

30 Interview with the writer, 14 December 1983. Lewenstein is perfectly correct regarding directors wanting permanent companies. After describing the failure of his first attempt, Devine made it clear that he would try again ('The Royal Court Theatre: Phase One', in Harold Hobson (ed.), *International Theatre Annual*, vol. 2, 1957, pp. 152–61).

31 Tom Milne, 'Taking Stock at the Court', in Charles Marowitz, Tom Milne and Owen Hale (eds), *New Theatre Voices of the Fifties and Sixties: Selections from Encore Magazine 1956–1963*, London, Methuen, 1965 (re-issued 1981), pp. 62–7.

32 Gaskill, *op. cit.*, n. 26.

33 *Ibid.*

34 *Findlater*, p. 61.

35 Gaskill, *op. cit.*, n. 26. Unlike Cuthbertson, Johnstone had been involved, either as writer, director or assistant, on eleven Court productions, beginning in June 1958. Gaskill, Cuthbertson and Johnstone discussed their plans publicly together in *Plays and Players*, November 1965.

36 *Ibid.*

37 At the Court, Howell had already directed a production of Jellicoe's *The Sport of My Mad Mother* (brought from the Bristol Old Vic Theatre School in May 1960) and assisted on *Kelly's Eye* by Henry Livings in June 1963. She was made an Associate Director in May 1967.

38 Gaskill, *op. cit.*, n. 26. Helen Montagu's account of these early stages can be found in the *Guardian*, 6 July 1978.

39 By 1965, Gill had acted as assistant on three main bill productions, written *The Sleepers' Den* (given as a Sunday night production, February 1965) and had directed *A Collier's Friday Night* (Sunday night, August 1965). This last was to lead to the celebrated Lawrence trilogy in 1968.

40 Interview with the writer, 29 March 1977.

41 Ann Jellicoe had received four main bill and one Sunday night production up to 1965. Two of the main bill shows had been translations (of *Rosmersholm* and *The Seagull*). N. F. Simpson had received five productions (four main bill, one Sunday night), four of which had been directed by Gaskill. John Arden had received three main bill and one Sunday night production. Edward Bond's *The Pope's Wedding* had appeared on Sunday, 9 December 1962. Nowhere is Gaskill's strong sense of loyalty to Court writers more apparent than in his choice of these four dramatists to begin his new regime.

42 Letter to the writer, 17 January 1984.

43 *Plays and Players*, September 1978. Shepherd had already auditioned for the

new company in the summer of 1965: 'I failed. They thought I was
interesting, but crazy' (*Findlater*, p. 105). After that, he wrote his letter.

44 Letter to the writer, 23 November 1983.

45 Interview with the writer, 7 January 1984.

46 Interview with the writer, 12 December 1983.

47 Greville Poke is clear that the early years of the Company saw a strong
attempt to rid the theatre of the club ethos, generated by Clement Freud's
club upstairs and the fact that the licensee, Alfred Esdaile, had done a
number of 'club' productions in the early 1950s, largely to circumvent
stringent fire regulations: 'We were then madly trying to kill the idea that
you had to become a member of the Royal Court club to get into the
theatre' (Poke, *op. cit.*, n. 28).

48 This was not new. Devine had proposed estimates on a five-year basis in
October 1964, which would add a 5 per cent increase to all items annually
(*Browne*, p. 54). The Court constantly attempted to establish itself on other
than a seasonal basis. It has never been possible.

49 Sheridan Morley, *Theatre World*, November 1965. It is characteristic and
inevitable that comparative judgments would automatically come into play
at this stage. Jellicoe, equally characteristically, attacked the prejudice and
power of critics, particularly as regards new work: 'I felt very strongly on the
first night of *Shelley*, that everybody was sitting there waiting for another
The Knack, waiting for the story line to proceed by means of action and
all this sort of thing. Whereas what I am doing now is something quite new,
for me at least' (*Plays and Players*, February 1966). See also her *Some
Unconscious Influences in the Theatre* (the Judith Wilson lecture, delivered in
the University of Cambridge, 10 March 1967), Cambridge, Cambridge
University Press, 1967; and 'Covering the Ground', in Susan Todd (ed.),
Women and Theatre. Calling the Shots, London, Faber, 1984, p. 89.

50 Figures for this and all other productions are in *Findlater*, Appendix 2.

51 Williams, *op. cit.*, n. 44.

52 Gallagher, *op. cit.*, n. 42.

53 Jellicoe, Simpson and Bond were all interviewed about their plays in the
season in *Plays and Players*, November 1965.

54 *Jury: A Magazine of Film and Theatre*, 29 November–13 December 1965.

55 Bernard Gallagher recalls the intervention of the Chamberlain in this
production:

> Private Attercliffe, talking of the excessively easygoing landlady of the
> inn, had to say something about her opening her arms 'and let 'em all
> come in'. Colonel whoever-it-was found this very suggestive and ordered
> that the line be altered to 'let 'em all come'.

This gem, spoken with conspicuous relish by Sebastian Shaw, became a
most wonderfully dirty line and gave the cast all the more enjoyment because
we knew it had been written by the censor (Gallagher *op. cit.*, n. 42).
Gallagher felt of the production that:

> On the whole . . . it didn't work, despite having a good cast who did their
> best. Possibly we felt ourselves to be in the shadow of the original

production . . . which many of us had seen and admired. Rehearsals were uneasy; I didn't feel Jane Howell had much confidence in herself at the time. . . . All this may simply be a reflection of the fact that I was never comfortable in my own part as the Pugnacious Collier, though I still don't know why. (*ibid.*)

56 Greville Poke cites this as one difference between Devine and Gaskill:
Neville Blond in the earlier days with George, had insisted that every member of the Council come to every first night . . . and what's more, we were expected to turn up in dinner jackets. . . . I saw his point. The first night of a play that opens cold in a London theatre is not the happiest of occasions and things can go wrong. He wanted, naturally, the Council to see the play once it had settled in (Poke, *op. cit.*, n. 28).

Gaskill also suggested that the practice of giving actresses flowers on first nights looked rather silly in a repertory system (Management committee, 3 December 1965).

57 Gaskill, *op. cit.*, n. 26.

58 Anderson's account of Devine is in *Tribune*, 28 January 1966; Gaskill's feelings are contained in the title of his article in *Plays and Players*, March 1966: 'Man for the Future'. A memorial meeting at the Court was held on 18 February by Devine's friends. It was at this meeting that the George Devine Award Fund was announced as a practical tribute to an eminently practical man.

59 *Wardle*, pp. 269–70. Cregan's first play, *Miniatures*, had received a Sunday night performance on 2 May 1965. According to David Cregan,
Transcending 'was written very quickly as a curtain raiser to the longer piece, *The Dancers*. It was a fast moving piece, based on a very gloomy R. D. Laing sort of situation. Jane [Howell, the director] couldn't see that it was as funny as it was and had rehearsed it very studiously. The Sunday night production of it, and of *The Dancers*, was postponed because she couldn't get it right, and eventually, on the final Sunday itself, after a long dress rehearsal, she handed it over to Bill to sort out. . . . I don't know what he did with it . . . but anyway, the audience laughed on the first line and never stopped laughing thereafter. He seemed delighted with this. He loved that feeling of fireworks, provided it took him with it . . .' (Letter to the writer, 6 December 1983).

60 Gaskill, *op. cit.*, n. 26. Simpson's admiration for Gaskill's tenacity remains:
Commitment of any kind, but especially in the theatre, is commonly shot through with pomposity and humbug and sheer fatuousness. Ignorance is a great help too. Gaskill is freer of all these than anyone I know, and as committed. . . . It was at an earlier period, from about 1957 to the very early sixties, that I learnt most from him, and came to respect his judgement and objectivity and unostentatious willingness to stick his neck out for other reasons than to draw attention to it (Letter to the writer, 6 December 1983).

61 Gallagher, *op. cit.*, n. 42.

62 Hughes, *op. cit.*, n. 46.

Chapter 2   Edward Bond's *Saved*

1 John Barber, *Daily Telegraph*, 21 December 1984 and Martin Esslin, *Plays*, February 1985.

2 Herbert Kretzmer, *Daily Express*, 4 November 1965; J. W. Lambert, *Sunday Times*, 7 November 1965; Kenneth Hurren, *What's On in London*, 12 November 1965.

3 They included Ronald Bryden, *New Statesman*, 12 November 1965; Alan Brien, *Sunday Telegraph*, 7 November 1965; R. B. Marriott, *The Stage*, 11 November 1965; and, notably, Penelope Gilliatt, *Observer*, 7 and 14 November 1965. A selection of reviews and comments may be found in the writer's *Bond On File*, London, Methuen, 1985.

4 Letter to Richard Scharine, 19 March 1971.

5 Johnstone, Letter to Richard Scharine, March 1971.

6 Quoted in Malcolm Hay and Philip Roberts, *Bond: A Study of his Plays*, London, Methuen, 1980, pp. 40–1.

7 *Findlater*, p. 85.

8 *Plays and Players*, February 1983.

9 *Ibid.*

10 Interview with Malcolm Hay and Philip Roberts, 22 March 1977.

11 Interview with Malcolm Hay, 31 August 1977.

12 Interview with Malcolm Hay, 19 July 1977.

13 Interview with Malcolm Hay and Philip Roberts, 15 September 1978.

14 *Findlater*, p. 83.

15 Jocelyn Herbert, *op. cit.*, pp. 84–5. Jack Shepherd speaks feelingly of the demands made in this context upon actors, especially young ones:
    > it does require an enormous talent and experience to do it. Otherwise, people look incompetent. So over that period of time a lot of people at the Royal Court did look incompetent, myself included. . . . One didn't have professional experience to withstand that kind of exposure. You couldn't act your way out of it, you couldn't energize your way out of it . . . with people who'd been in the business two or three years, it is almost cruel (Interview with Malcolm Hay, 31 August 1977).

16 Bond, *Plays: One*, London, Methuen, 1977, p. 227.

17 *Ibid.*, p. 20. All subsequent references to the play are to this edition.

18 Interviews with Malcolm Hay and Philip Roberts, 22 March 1977, and 15 July 1977.

19 Interview with the writer, 29 March 1977.

20 Gaskill, *op. cit.*, n. 18 (15 July 1977).

21 Gunter, *op. cit.*, n. 19.

22 Letter to Max Stafford-Clark and Danny Boyle (directors of *The Pope's Wedding* and *Saved* respectively, Royal Court 1984–5), 5 November 1984.

23 Bond, *Theatre Quarterly*, vol. 2 no. 5, January–March 1972, p. 11.

24 Gaskill, *op. cit.*, n. 10.

25 *Ibid.*

26 *Ibid.*

27 Letter to Tony Coult, 28 July 1977.
28 For a longer analysis of *Saved* and for its relationship with Bond's other
plays, see Malcolm Hay and Philip Roberts, *Bond: A Study of his Plays*,
London, Methuen, 1980. For a detailed bibliography of productions of and
articles about *Saved*, see the same writers' *Edward Bond: A Companion to
the Plays*, London, Theatre Quarterly Publications, 1978. For Bond's views
about this and other plays, see Philip Roberts, *Bond on File*, London,
Methuen, 1985.
29 *Gambit*, vol. 5, no. 17, pp. 40–1.
30 Interview with the writer, 7 January 1984.
31 Interview with Malcolm Hay and Philip Roberts, 26 July 1977.
32 Butler, *op. cit.*, n. 30.
33 Richard Wherrett, programme note for Bond's *The Sea*, Nimrod Theatre,
Australia, May 1979.
34 Murray Mindlin, *Forum World Features*, week of 27 November 1965.
35 *The Times*, 3 April 1966.
36 *Daily Telegraph*, 2 April 1966.
37 *Daily Telegraph*, 4 April 1966.
38 Interview with the writer, 18 September 1984.
39 Details of these productions are contained in Malcolm Hay and Philip
Roberts, *Edward Bond: A Companion to the Plays*, London, Theatre
Quarterly Publications, 1978. A good account of the censor's activities in
connection with the Court is in *Browne*, pp. 56–71.

Chapter 3 From April 1966 to March 1968

1 Amongst those students buying tickets was Pam Brighton, then at the
London School of Economics, who in the summer of 1968, joined the
Court as Jane Howell's assistant on the Schools Scheme. At that early stage,
she 'used to go to the Court. . . . I thought it was the most exciting theatre
in London . . . It was incredibly cheap to go there as a student. An amazingly
cheap night out . . .' (Interview with the writer, 13 December 1983).
2 By 19 April, the Artistic committee had modified this aim. Though the
award was originally for ' "a person of the theatre", it was felt that a
dramatist should be looked for primarily'.
3 *The Times*, 6 April 1966.
4 *Ibid.*
5 *Ibid.* A number of assessments both of the Court's work and of the English
theatre generally were written at this stage. The Court produced its own
account, *Ten Years at The Royal Court 1956/66*, with contributions by both
Blond and Gaskill; and the *Tulane Drama Review*, vol. 11 no. 2, Winter
1966, carried Gordon Rogoff's 'Richard's Himself Again: Journey to an
Actors' Theatre' (pp. 29–40); John Russell Taylor's 'Ten Years of the English
Stage Company' (pp. 120–31), where he suggests that the company 'now

carries the heavy liability of its own recent past' (p. 129); and Charles Marowitz's 'State of Play' (pp. 203–6).

6 Gaskill, Letter to Richard Scharine, 19 March 1971.

7 Hampton's play was directed by Robert Kidd, making his professional debut. He was to direct all of Hampton's plays for the next ten years. Kidd was an Assistant Director at the Court in 1966 and in 1975 was appointed joint Artistic Director with Nicholas Wright.

8 Williams's biggest success, given eventually on a Sunday night on 14 May 1970 and transferring to the main bill on 11 November, was *AC/DC*. From 1966, the play went through a long series of rewritings.

9 *Observer*, 24 April 1966.

10 Orton's piece was generally well received. Brenton's play was savaged: 'If there is no better play than this among the English Stage Society's rejects, then heaven help the English stage' (*Morning Star*, 23 August 1966).

11 Letter to the writer, 6 December 1983.

12 *Daily Express*, 30 July 1966. David Nathan in the *Sun* (16 September 1966) felt that 'the rather personal way she pronounces English . . . will make her Lady Macbeth . . . more than usually interesting'.

13 *Guardian*, 16 September 1966.

14 Letter to the writer, 28 November 1983.

15 Letter to the writer, 6 December 1983.

16 Though the production with the original leading actors was envisaged as running for up to five or six weeks, Roëves and Engel knew they would be taking over a few days after the opening (*Guardian*, 26 October 1966).

17 *Wardle*, pp. 165–6. Lindsay Anderson had approached *Julius Caesar* at the Court in November 1964 in a similarly radical way and 'having been generally bored by Shakespeare on the stage, I want to find out for myself if his writing has really become as unmeaning as it often seems' (John Ripley, *Julius Caesar on stage in England and America, 1599–1973*, Cambridge, Cambridge University Press, 1980, p. 263).

18 *Findlater*, p. 96.

19 Jackson, *op. cit.*, n. 14.

20 Roëves, *op. cit.*, n. 15.

21 *Daily Express*, 22 October 1966. Guinness made other comments, on the need for a longer rehearsal period among other things, in Ronald Hayman, *Playback 2*, London, Davis-Poynter, 1973, pp. 41–2. Simone Signoret gives a graphic and unsentimental account of the production in her autobiography, *Nostalgia Isn't What It Used To Be*, London, Panther Books, 1979, pp. 370–6.

22 Not every critic was against the production. Among those who liked the work were the *Times Educational Supplement* (25 November), Harold Hobson in the *Sunday Times* (23 October), and R. B. Marriott, *Stage*, 27 October.

23 *Ten Years At The Royal Court 1956/66*, p. 30.

24 As printed in the *Evening Standard*, 25 October 1966.

25 *Observer*, 30 October 1966, while Gaskill was in Tunisia.

26 As reported in the *Daily Sketch* and *Daily Mail* for 31 October.

27 *Evening News*, 31 October. Esdaile and Gaskill crossed swords again soon after, over *Early Morning*. Esdaile was the licensee of the theatre as well as vice-chairman, but he was in many ways rather remote from the Company's affairs. Greville Poke, who knew him from the inception of the Company, said of him that eventually he just 'faded out . . . he was the most extraordinary man. He hardly ever missed a first night. . . . He constantly criticized everything that was going on. He was rather a pain in the neck in a way . . . he didn't like anything practically that went on . . . yet he always went there . . .' (Interview with the writer, 18 September 1984).

28 Interview with the writer, 13 December 1983.

29 Interview with the writer, 18 September 1984.

30 *Ibid.*

31 Interview with the writer, 11 September 1984.

32 *Observer*, 6 November 1966.

33 Another play by Soyinka, *The Trials of Brother Jero*, had opened at Hampstead in June 1966, where both Gaskill and O'Donovan had seen and liked it. Because of O'Donovan's illness, Gaskill took over as director of *The Lion and the Jewel*.

34 Gill's account of the play is contained in *Plays and Players*, January 1967. It bears an interesting resemblance to the ideas propounded by Gaskill in his work on Restoration plays earlier at the National.

35 Gaskill wrote to Neville Blond on 6 January 1967 before Blond was due to give his annual lunch for the critics, urging him if possible to mention the schools project, 'as it is perhaps the most important new development of our work'. In the same letter, he is concerned at attending the lunch, in view of the recent row, 'but if it is in any sense going to help the company then we [he and O'Donovan] should be glad to be there, and if we are not there it would certainly appear as if we are sulking, or are being treated as bad boys by the Management Committee. I do think you will have to face the fact that your Artistic Director and his associates have always resented, und will always resent, the notices they get and are never going to be fond of the critics'.

36 Gaskill subsequently paid tribute to Gill (who came to be regarded as his natural successor):

> It's rare for the Court to have periods where it's known for a long time in advance what it's going to do. I think it's survived because it's lived in that way . . . it could take something exciting if it arrived . . . it's risky because you may have fallow patches in which you haven't got anything and then you're very dependent on the ideas of individual directors who are your associates, like the Lawrence plays which were absolutely Peter Gill's idea, which then became very important in the work of the theatre (Gaskill, *op. cit.*, n. 28).

This 1967 Lawrence production was also notable as the first show costumed by Deirdre Clancy, who was to become one of the best designers to work at the Court.

37 *Browne*, p. 82.

38 See, for example, *Drama*, Winter 1967, p. 43.

39 David Storey interviewed in *Plays and Players*, September 1967. Lindsay Anderson had been invited by Gaskill to direct the play, but had other commitments.

40 Shepherd gives an account of his role in the play in *Plays and Players*, *op. cit.*, n. 39.

41 Letter to the writer, November 1983. Howarth gives an interesting account of his work in the *Guardian*, 28 August 1970. O'Donovan's contract had expired by June 1967. It was not renewed.

42 The play was originally intended for the Empire Pool, Wembley, but when rejected, was directed by Jane Howell 'with about two hundred kids'. Jellicoe's account of the play and its influence upon her later successes in community theatre is in 'Covering the Ground', Susan Todd (ed.), *Women and Theatre. Calling the Shots*, London, Faber, 1984, pp. 82–96.

43 Gaskill, *op. cit.*, n. 28. Jocelyn Herbert gives an account of the evolution of the workshops (*Findlater*, pp. 83–4) and suggests that the reason was that 'few new plays were done which demanded much in the way of scenery and costumes, and that they were therefore no longer financially viable'. See also 'In the Workshop', *Plays and Players*, October 1967.

44 *Findlater*, p. 101. Gaskill was aware of the developments in the USA. He notes in an internal document for autumn 1967 on the Court's Studio that 'In the United States, where the unemployment rate among actors is higher than in England, there is a great deal more studio work which has resulted in the exciting off-Broadway development of recent years – particularly the Open Theatre . . . ' (p. 2).

45 See Malcolm Hay and Philip Roberts, *Bond: A Study of his Plays*, London, Methuen, 1980, chapters 2 and 3; *Browne*, pp. 56–71.

46 Gaskill, *op. cit.*, n. 28. There were others who were very unhappy with it. Poke wrote to Blond on 25 January 1968 about his and Blacksell's response:

> I think it would be true to say that one or two other members of the Artistic Committee also asked Bill to explain why he was so desperately keen to do this play, because those who questioned him were not convinced as a result of their reading that it was such a marvellous play. . . . In giving his reply I was not convinced by Bill that it was a great play, but I was convinced of his very strong desire to do it, and it was because of that that I voted in favour of its presentation.

Gaskill replied shortly to Blacksell on 29 January that 'Our whole battle is concerned with whether we should fight to do the play we want to do, or tamely concede defeat to all the people who want to stop us.'

47 In the accounts to 30 March 1968, it is shown that the costs incurred when *Early Morning* was scheduled for the main bill amounted to £680. This was written off. The Sunday night production of 31 March (which actually fell into the year 1968–9), was underwritten by the Company to the extent

by which costs exceeded £600 (the average costs of two Sunday night productions which would be paid for by the English Stage Society). The total cost for the eventual performance came to £2,112 which left the Court a total of £1,512 to find. It is also worth noting that Gaskill's action in going ahead before the budget had been presented was not a unique event. Greville Poke recalls that it 'was always happening. Even in George's time, when he was pretty punctilious about those sort of things, a play would occasionally go into production without the Management Committee having seen a budget. Tony Richardson would launch a play, get it going, cast it and we'd then see the budget. Then we would scream like anything . . .' (Poke, *op. cit.*, n. 29).

48 Harewood, *op. cit.*, n. 31.

49 Gaskill, *op. cit.*, n. 28.

Chapter 4   D. H. Lawrence's *The Daughter-in-Law*

1 Interview with the writer, 3 April 1985.

2 *Ibid*.

3 Interview with the writer, 7 January 1984.

4 Letter to the writer, 26 April 1984.

5 Gill, *op. cit.*, n. 1.

6 *Ibid*.

7 See *Wardle*, p. 277, for some of these details.

8 The existence of *The Daughter-in-Law* came as a surprise to most Lawrence scholars. The manuscript was left by Lawrence in the keeping of Frieda's sister, Else Jaffe, when he left Germany in September 1913. Else finally sent the manuscript, together with others, to Frieda in London in 1933. The play was copyrighted in May 1934. Three copies of the play were typed up in May 1933. A set of carbons found their way to the University of California, Berkeley. It was from the carbons that the Heinemann text was taken. The circumstances surrounding these events, together with an account of a version of the play, described as 'An Unrevised Play by D. H. Lawrence Completed by Walter Greenwood', and performed in 1936 under the title of *My Son's My Son*, may be found in Keith Sagar, 'D. H. Lawrence: Dramatist', *The D. H. Lawrence Review*, vol. 4 no. 1 (1971), pp. 154–81; Sylvia Sklar, '*The Daughter-in-Law* and *My Son's My Son*', Sagar, *op. cit.*, vol. 9 no. 2 (1976), pp. 254–65; and Sagar, 'The Strange History of *The Daughter-in-Law*', *op. cit.*, vol. 11 no. 2 (1978), pp. 175–84.

9 Gill, *op. cit.*, n. 1.

10 *Ibid*.

11 The Lawrence play was actually used as an exercise to propose the closing of the Court's workshop. See Chapter 3, p. 61.

12 *Evening Standard*, 1 February 1967.

13 Gill, *op. cit.*, n. 1.

14 *Observer Magazine*, 12 February 1984. The effect on Gunter was strong: 'I was really taken aback at the conditions they were working in and that was one of the reasons I suppose that we put such detail into the whole atmosphere of the set, because one was very disturbed at what one had seen up north' ('Desert Island Discs', BBC Radio 4, 29 July 1983).

15 *Plays and Players*, October 1982.

16 Gill, *op. cit.*, n. 1.

17 *Ibid.*

18 *Ibid.*

19 *Ibid.*

20 Anne Dyson, Manchester born, was already familiar with the plays when the production of *The Daughter-in-Law* was announced. She had wanted to play when young in *The Widowing of Mrs. Holroyd*. She told her agent that she wanted to play Mrs Gascoigne, and, after 'struggling with the dialect until four in the morning', went to audition (Interview with the writer, 10 October 1979).

21 *The Daughter-in-Law* appears to have been Lawrence's sixth full length play. The approximate dating is *A Collier's Friday Night* in 1909; *The Merry Go Round* and *The Widowing of Mrs. Holroyd* in 1910; *The Married Man* and *The Fight for Barbara* in 1912; *The Daughter-in-Law* in 1913; *Touch and Go* in 1918; and *David* in 1925. Since some of these were revised, especially *The Widowing of Mrs. Holroyd* for its 1914 publication, the dating demonstrates only that six of Lawrence's eight plays occupy the years between 1909 and 1913. The great novel, *Sons and Lovers*, was begun in 1910 (see Keith Sagar, *D. H. Lawrence: A Calendar of his Works*, Manchester University Press, 1979, *passim*).

22 James T. Boulton (ed.), *The Letters of D. H. Lawrence*, Volume One, September 1901–May 1913, Cambridge, Cambridge University Press, 1979, pp. 500–1. The difficulties of getting his work on the stage may be seen by reference to the letters. During Lawrence's life, only *The Widowing of Mrs. Holroyd* and *David* were produced, the former in 1920 and 1926; the latter in 1927. Lawrence wrote to Edward Garnett on 1 February 1913 about the prevailing theatrical conditions in England:

> I believe that, just as an audience was found in Russia for Tchekhov, so an audience might be found in England for some of my stuff, if there were a man to whip 'em in. It's the producer that is lacking, not the audience. I'm sure we are sick of the rather bony, bloodless drama we get nowadays – it is time for a reaction against Shaw and Galsworthy and Barker and Irishy (except Synge) people – the rule and measure mathematical folk. . . . I don't want to write like Galsworthy nor Ibsen, nor Strindberg nor any of them, *not* even if I could. We have to hate our immediate predecessor, to get free from their authority (Boulton, *op. cit.*, p. 509).

23 *D. H. Lawrence: Three Plays*, with an Introduction by Raymond Williams, Harmondsworth, Penguin Books, 1969, p. 87. Subsequent references to the text of the play are from this edition.

24 Boulton, *op. cit.*, n. 22, p. 199.

25 For another account of the play, see Sylvia Sklar, *The Plays of D. H. Lawrence*, London, Vision Press, 1975. Lawrence himself, in an essay written later on, characterizes the difference between the colliers and their wives, in 'Nottingham and the Mining Country', 1929, published in *The New Adelphi* for June–August 1930, and reprinted in the *Selected Essays*, Harmondsworth, Penguin Books, [1950], 1978, pp. 114–22. An extract from this essay was included in the programme for both the 1967 and 1968 productions, as was a glossary of some mining terms. The relationship of the play to the story, 'Fanny and Annie' (written May 1919) is well known, and the latter may be found in *England, My England*, Harmondsworth, Penguin Books, [1960], 1983, pp. 175–90.

26 Gill, *op. cit.*, n. 1.

27 Dyson, *op. cit.*, n. 20.

28 Letter to the writer, 1 May 1984.

29 Dyson, *op. cit.*, n. 20.

30 Gill, *op. cit.*, n. 1.

31 Dyson, *op. cit.*, n. 20.

32 Gill, *op. cit.*, n. 1.

33 *Ibid.*

34 Dyson, *op. cit.*, n. 20. Judy Parfitt's account of the scene is in *Plays and Players*, June 1968. Barry Hanson kept a log of the rehearsals, which was published in *Plays and Players*, April 1968.

35 Gill, *op. cit.*, n. 1.

36 Parfitt, *op. cit.*, n. 34. Gill received a note from Gaskill while in hospital:
He sent a note saying, 'I want to move the cup. Is that all right?' I sent a note back saying, 'Look for some reason I'm completely stuck on the love scene [Act 2]. I don't seem to be able to do it.' And when I saw it – they'd let me out because I said I'd discharge myself – Bill had directed that scene so beautifully, very flowing, and full of sentiment (Gill, *op. cit.*, n. 1).

37 The notes exist in a typescript in the Press Office at the Royal Court.

38 Dyson, *op. cit.*, n. 20.

39 Gill, *op. cit.*, n. 1.

Chapter 5   From April 1968 to March 1970

1 *Evening Standard*, 2 April 1968. *Freethinker*, 19 April 1968.

2 Interview with Malcolm Hay and Philip Roberts, 26 July 1977.

3 Interview with Malcolm Hay, 18 November 1977.

4 Greville Poke, quoted in *The Stage*, 10 April 1968.

5 Interview with the writer, 18 September 1984. Gaskill found that news of the private performance 'was being leaked all the time. We think it was being leaked by the box office, who were absolutely treacherous . . . when

you know the police are actually waiting for you to do something, you suddenly become aware that there are spies within the theatre. It gets very unpleasant' (Interview with the writer, 13 December 1983).

6 *Daily Telegraph*, 9 April 1968.

7 Interview with the writer, 13 December 1983.

8 The censor, moribund by now, flickered into life to demand cuts in Bond's next play, *Narrow Road to the Deep North*, before it opened at the Belgrade Theatre, Coventry, in June 1968. It is said that the cuts were eventually agreed to and then ignored in the production.

9 Gaskill, *op. cit.*, n. 7.

10 Gaskill pressed the idea of a studio whenever he could. For example, the Court was asked to submit to Sub-Committee B of the House of Commons Estimates Committee any evidence regarding the work of the Arts Council in relation to subsidized theatre. The memorandum to be sent was submitted to a Management committee meeting of 25 July. In the document (p. 3), Gaskill urged the need for a studio to be shared by the Court, the National Theatre and the Royal Shakespeare Company, since 'the continuing health of the British Theatre may depend on it'. The 'Minutes of Evidence', ordered by the House of Commons to be printed on 24 June 1968, contain interesting figures of actors' salaries at the time. Poke told the committee that the minimum fee for a walking-on part or an understudy was £18 a week. The minimum for a speaking part was £20. For a 'star', the fee could go up to £50 and £45 for a 'non-star'. In rehearsal, the fee was £12 per week. In comparison, the minimum at the National Theatre was £15; at the Royal Shakespeare it was £14, with both theatres going to a maximum of £80 (Minutes 2280–3, p. 308).

11 *Plays and Players*, July 1968.

12 Interviewed by Brendan Hennessy in J. F. McCrindle (ed.), *Behind the Scenes: Theatre and Film Interviews from the Transatlantic Review*, London, Pitman, 1971, pp. 44–50.

13 Gaskill, *op. cit.*, n. 7. Irving Wardle wrote a thoughtful article at the time about the problems of young directors in *New Society*, 29 August 1968.

14 Nicholas Wright, interviewed by Malcolm Hay, 18 December 1979. Thirteen productions of the kind described by Wright went on in the club during the spring and summer of 1968. They are listed in a pamphlet, *Royal Court 1970*, issued by the theatre, and range from Sam Shepard's *Red Cross* to Keith Johnstone's *Moby Dick*, to Mike Leigh's *Down Here and Up There*, to John Arden's *Squire Jonathan*.

15 Letter to the writer, 1 May 1984. As well as these late shows, Gaskill, according to Pam Brighton, by now Jane Howell's assistant, had a steady policy of organizing workshops whenever time allowed (Interview with the writer, 13 December 1983). Some of them are described by David Cregan:

He was always a wonderful teacher of masks, and a splendid director of comedy . . . and we did mask work, we involved ourselves in a 'happening' in Sloane Street, we even played a kind of cowboys and indians game in which I set fire to a tent he was sitting in . . . He involved himself in a public performance of a *bunraku* kind, himself being a puppet (Letter to the writer, 6 December 1983).

16 Wright, *op. cit.*, n. 14.

17 *Plays and Players*, March 1969.

18 *The Stage*, 13 February 1969.

19 *Plays and Players*, September 1968.

20 *Plays and Players*, March 1969.

21 Letter to the writer, 11 May 1984.

22 *Daily Mail*, 26 April 1969.

23 Gaskill, *op. cit.*, n. 7. Jane Howell elsewhere speaks of the lack of a sense of direction, the 'absolute state of flux' which she felt existed at the Court and in the theatre generally during this time (*Plays and Players*, October 1968).

24 Gaskill, *op. cit.*, n. 5.

25 Interview with the writer, 14 December 1983.

26 Poke, *op. cit.*, n. 5.

27 Anderson, *op. cit.*, n. 21. J. E. Blacksell's (a founder member of the Company) view was that 'Gaskill's decision to seek to direct elsewhere was brought about by a clash of personalities with the Chairman. Page and Anderson were invited because of Anderson's skill in direction and Page's considerable contacts with a number of theatrical people' (Letter to the writer, 3 November 1984). Anderson was officially invited to return on 16 July, when Robin Fox sent him a contract for the period 30 June 1969 to 28 March 1970. In an accompanying letter, Fox states that 'The Company very much hopes that a way can be found, acceptable to you, Mr. Page and Mr. Gaskill, by which you will have both a continuing voice in the Artistic policies of the Company, and also periods of time of sole or joint Artistic Direction of the theatre so as to allow Mr. Page and Mr. Gaskill freedom to engage in work outside the Royal Court, as well as yourself.'

28 Interview with the writer, 5 December 1984. Up to 1985, Anderson had directed ten plays at the Court (seven of them in the main bill) and returned, as has been seen, to direct David Storey's *In Celebration*, April 1969. Page had directed seven plays for the Court up to 1965 (six main bill) and returned in 1968 to direct three plays by Osborne (*Time Present, The Hotel in Amsterdam* and a revival of *Look Back in Anger*). Anderson's own account of his early association with the Court is in *Findlater*, pp. 143–8.

29 Gaskill, *op. cit.*, n. 7.

30 Lewenstein, *op. cit.*, n. 25.

31 *Findlater*, pp. 139–40.

32 *New Statesman*, 16 January 1970. Norman's account of the evolution of the play itself, which began life late in 1966, and went to the Royal Shakespeare Company and the National Theatre before Anderson took it, is in *Why Fings Went West*, London, Lemon Tree Press, 1975.

33 The 'childish business' was, however, continued by Lawson who renewed his attack in *The Spectator* for 13 December, alleging that Blond's letter to *The Times* of 6 December was written by Anderson, and suggesting that

Blond should make way for a younger man. The letter was written by the Artistic Directors, in consultation with Harewood, Peggy Ashcroft and Robin Fox. It was then signed by Blond.

34 *Plays and Players*, December 1969. On another occasion, Anderson remarked that 'There are very few organizations that actually will put up with somebody who is generally as abrasive or self-indulgent as I am apt to be' (*Guardian*, 4 May 1977).

35 I am obliged for this information on the 12 January meeting to Donald Howarth. There is no record of the meeting in the Court's archives.

36 *Daily Telegraph*, 10 January 1970.

37 Donald Howarth's play had been commissioned by Gaskill and, five months after its submission, was rejected. However, Anderson and Page liked the play (which transferred to the Duchess Theatre in March 1970): 'Bill, over a beer in the Antelope (a pub at the back of the theatre) told me he'd been "quite wrong" about the play, when he'd read it and rejected it. . . . If he hadn't gone to Germany, the play wouldn't have had a Court production and the chance to succeed that goes with that' (Letter to the writer, November 1983).

Chapter 6 David Storey's *The Changing Room*

1 David Storey interviewed by Ronald Hayman, *Playback 1*, London, Davis-Poynter, 1973, pp. 7–20.

2 *Plays and Players*, September 1967.

3 *Ibid.*

4 Hayman, *op. cit.*, n. 1.

5 *Ibid.* Anderson's interest in Storey's work shows in a programme note he contributed to *The Restoration of Arnold Middleton*, in which he stated that Storey's unique quality 'seems to me a sort of elemental poetry, a passionate reaching-out, and ambition of concept that carries him beyond neatness, completeness, civilized equilibrium. He seeks to penetrate the soul; yet he never forgets the relevance of the social world in which souls meet, conflict and struggle. He labours, often desperately, to balance the ambiguities of our nature, our situation: male and female, tenderness and violence, isolation and love. . . .'

6 Hayman, *op. cit.*, n. 1.

7 *Ibid.* Though *Arnold Middleton* had transferred successfully, *In Celebration* stayed at the Court. Storey at one stage thought the play might transfer if a West End theatre became available but at the same time 'I am not sure how successfully it would move' (*Evening Standard*, 20 May 1969). Anderson maintains the play did not transfer, simply because the West End theatre managers did not want it (Interview with the writer, 29 April 1985).

8 *The Times*, 4 April 1970.

9 Storey's account of this, and other aspects of his work, is in *Findlater*, pp. 110–15.

10 After its run at the Court, *The Contractor* at one stage was not going to transfer. Anderson recalls a meeting at the Court, at which Michael Codron was to announce that the play would not transfer because he could not find a suitable theatre. Anderson suggested the Fortune Theatre, which was available, but which was thought to be too small to take the play: 'Codron went to Devine's former office, and telephoned. He came down to say that they were interested and it ran for nine months' (Interview with Lindsay Anderson and David Storey, 29 April 1985). Since *The Contractor* did not go on at the Fortune until April 1970, it was revived, rather than transferred.

11 Anderson, interview with the writer, 5 December 1984.

12 The first meeting of writer, director and the two eminent actors is chronicled by Storey in *Findlater*, pp. 113–14.

13 Storey analyses *Home* in Hayman, *op. cit.*, n. 1, pp. 16–17.

14 Interview with David Storey and Lindsay Anderson, 29 April 1985.

15 *New York Times*, 20 April 1973.

16 *Findlater*, p. 115.

17 Storey, *op. cit.*, n. 14.

18 Storey's brother played for Wakefield Trinity. One of Anderson's earliest pieces of film work was called *Wakefield Express*, made in 1953. Anderson showed Storey the film when they were working on the film of *This Sporting Life*. In a sequence set on the Wakefield Trinity ground, David Storey pointed out his brother.

19 The radio talk given by Storey was printed in *The Listener*, 1 August 1963. It was called 'Journey through a Tunnel'.

20 Storey, *op. cit.*, n. 15.

21 This, and subsequent references to the text are taken from the edition published by Penguin Books, 1973.

22 Storey, *op. cit.*, n. 14.

23 Letter to the writer, 13 December 1984.

24 Anderson, *op. cit.*, n. 14.

25 Storey, *op. cit.*

26 *Ibid.*

27 Letter to the writer, 20 February 1985.

28 Letter to the writer, 6 February 1985.

29 Letter to the writer, 5 February 1985.

30 Storey, *op. cit.*, n. 14.

31 Anderson, *op. cit.*

32 Storey, *op. cit.*

33 Anderson, *op. cit.*

34 Storey, *op. cit.*

35 *Ibid.*

36 *Findlater*, pp. 111–13.

37 Hayman, *op. cit.*, n. 1, p. 9.

38 Anderson, *op. cit.*, n. 14. Storey retails one account of Anderson's introducing the use of liniment (the smell of which eventually filled the theatre) as one mechanical device: 'You [Anderson] invented the liniment

for Michael Elphick and you said, "Well, just rub yourself with some liniment", and Michael said, "I've rubbed myself twice already with the fucking stuff!", and you said, "Well, rub yourself again" ' (*ibid.*).

39 Peter Childs, letter to the writer, 5 March 1985.
40 *Ibid.* Brian Lawson, as Tallon, was made to referee the game: 'I didn't know the rules, or very much at all of what the game is about. "Doesn't matter", said Bev, "You're the Boss. If you see something you don't like, blow your whistle" ' (Anderson, *op. cit.*, n. 29).
41 Lawson, *op. cit.*, n. 29.
42 McKillop, *op. cit.*, n. 28.
43 Anderson, *op. cit.*, n. 14.
44 Lawson, *op. cit.*, n. 29.

Chapter 7   From April 1970 to July 1972

1 *Observer*, 5 April 1970.
2 *The Theatre Today in England and Wales: The Arts Council of Great Britain*, 1970, pp. 31–2.
3 *Ibid.*, section 212, note (c), p. 71.
4 *Findlater*, p. 143; of the ten plays directed by Anderson between 1957 and 1964, only one (*Julius Caesar*) was not a modern play. Between 1969 and 1974, he directed seven main bill productions, all of them plays by David Storey.
5 Interview with the writer, 13 December 1983.
6 Findlater, *op. cit.*, n. 4, pp. 146, 145.
7 Gaskill, *op. cit.*, n. 5.
8 Interview with the writer, 11 September 1984. Anderson puts it in the following way:

it implies more consciousness and deliberation than life often provides. . . . It wasn't an attempt to pick up where George Devine left off. It was just agreeing with him. We felt roughly what George had felt, so that our instinct was towards that. Neither Anthony nor myself were studio type avant-gardists in the way that Bill and Peter Gill were, so it was natural for us to think of theatre differently. . . . After George and Tony [Richardson] there were two very distinct kinds of tradition at the Court . . . (Interview with the writer, 5 December 1984).

9 Gaskill, *op. cit.*, n. 5.
10 Interview with the writer, 14 December 1983.
11 Interview with the writer, 5 December 1984. It is, however, characteristic of Anderson that he later reviewed his attitude. In a letter to Council of 30 May 1975, at a time when the Theatre Upstairs was closed, he notes that it was 'not a part of the Royal Court's activities with which I have ever been closely associated – or perhaps even as sympathetic as I should have been. But there is no denying that its achievements over the last three or four

years have been quite outstanding, and have added immeasurably to the reputation of the theatre.'

12 Clive Goodwin gives a lucid picture of the work done Upstairs and of how it developed in *Plays and Players*, August 1975.

13 Interview with the writer, 13 December 1983. The production occasioned a letter from the Arts Council complaining about obscene language in the play.

14 *Ibid.*

15 *Browne*, p. 91. See the obituaries published in *The Times*, *Guardian* and *Daily Telegraph* for 6 August; *The Stage* for 12 August; and the *Jewish Chronicle* for 14 August. J. E. Blacksell added to the obituary in *The Times* on 11 August a note on the importance of Blond's friendship with Joe Hodgkinson of the Arts Council which, without Blond, 'would have been a much more tedious and problematic relationship'. This occasioned a letter from Hodgkinson to Blacksell of 12 August, in which he pictures Blond at the first ever meeting of the Court's Council: 'Neville was going round his chums at the table, and dunning them for what he thought they could stump up to start it off. And suddenly he fixed those relentless eyes on me. "And what the hell can we put the Arts Council down for?" Then came the growl and scowl at my very unsatsifactory answer! And so began a lasting, warm and jealously treasured friendship with one of the kindest men I have ever known.' He was to be badly missed in the following years. Lord Harewood wrote to Lindsay Anderson on 21 February 1974 to say that 'we all very badly miss Neville, who had dynamism, even when he was old and sometimes got it wrong, and could make people feel that a corporate venture was in hand and that he himself would not let anyone down. Nor did he, as far as I can remember, in spite of ghastly rows at Council meetings with Bill and people like that. . . .' Anderson himself, writing to Lord Cudlipp on 27 March 1975, said that Blond 'more or less "adopted" the whole enterprise, and took a fatherly, not to say proprietorial attitude towards it. . . . Neville Blond was a rather extraordinary fellow. He didn't know much about art, but he had a very good intuition about people, and he also cared very much about the status and the success of the English Stage Company. . . . He also provided rather a salutary reminder that everything had to be paid for.'

16 Gaskill, *op. cit.*, n. 5. On the other hand, Anderson seems not to have objected to a project if the support for it was strongly argued:

I think I originally suggested *Come Together*. I remember saying to Bill, why don't you bring it to the Court, why don't we have it here? Do it. . . . I didn't see very much of it quite honestly. It's not my scene. It's terribly shameful to have to admit it but they've never meant anything to me (Interview with the writer, 5 December 1984).

17 Elsewhere, Gaskill insists that '*The People Show* or The Living Theatre must at some point be able to relate to what Beckett is – which wouldn't be true of, say, Chekhov. Beckett is the great archetypal figure in modern theatre . . .' (*Plays and Players*, May 1970).

18 The publicity handout for Brighton Combination notes that after three years based in Brighton, the group was touring:

We are looking for larger premises. And for more money. Our overdraft hit £1000 for the umpteenth time this week. We're fed up. After carting this bleeding scaffolding over the roofs thank you and good night. We acknowledge support from the Arts Council (bless their socks).

19 According to Gaskill, Lewenstein was the only one who liked Brisley's piece. Lewenstein 'would nearly always come down on the side of experiment and was the only person who was enthralled by it and in that way Oscar's great. He would always come up trumps. There's a bit of Glasgow Unity still in him' (Gaskill *op. cit.*, n. 5).

20 Interview with Malcolm Hay, 18 December 1979. Gaskill had actively encouraged the play's development. Williams, in a letter to the writer (December 1983), says: 'Bill Gaskill sent me a telegram: "Very excited about AC/DC. It will almost certainly be banned by the Lord Chamberlain". He was instrumental in transferring it from the Theatre Upstairs to the Theatre Downstairs.' It was the first production to transfer in this way and opened on 11 November.

21 Williams, letter to Wright, no date.

22 The play is analysed by Katharine Worth in *Revolutions in Modern English Drama*, London, Bell, 1973, pp. 160–7. Useful accounts of the festival may be found in *Plays and Players*, December 1970; *Browne*, pp. 93–4; and Peter Ansorge, *Disrupting the Spectacle*, London, Pitman, 1975, pp. 38–9. This last also discusses *AC/DC* on pp. 77–80.

23 Ansorge, *op. cit.*, n. 22, p. 39.

24 Gill had had discussions with Williams about the project but uncertainty existed since the Royal Shakespeare Company had earlier commissioned Williams to dramatize the book, written in 1963. The book was eventually used as the basis for a production by Joint Stock Theatre Company, founded by Gaskill and Max Stafford-Clark, and opened 28 January 1974.

25 Lewenstein has said that the (then) three Artistic Directors 'didn't work well together. The meetings were a constant battle, and quarrel. I was the chairman of the Artistic committee at the time and tried to referee the battles. I don't think any of the minutes can indicate how stormy they were' (Lewenstein, *op. cit.*, n. 10).

26 Gaskill's view in 1965 had been one of dissuading Council from attending first nights (see chapter 1, note 56). This was a small but significant reversal.

27 Gill gives an account of the evolution of his Webster production in *Plays and Players*, March 1971.

28 The translator, Steve Gooch, gives a very interesting account of Gaskill in rehearsal in *Plays and Players*, April 1971. See also the actor Bob Hoskins's account in *Plays and Players*, July 1971.

29 *Guardian*, 5 April 1971.

30 *Amateur Stage*, vol. 26 no. 4, April 1971, p. 30. In the same article, Gaskill

suggests the possibility of a new development in the growth of arts centres
in the country.

31 *Findlater*, p. 196. Though the production was a success, it did not prevent
a critic like Mary Holland in *Plays and Players* for July 1971, referring to
it as perhaps 'star-laden, crude and patently aimed at the West End'.

32 Brighton, *op. cit.*, n. 13.

33 Mary Holland, *Plays and Players*, October 1971. Beginning with the
programme for *West of Suez*, Anderson initiated a news feature called
'Court in Action', which provided items, photographs and production details
of current and future plays. By September 1972, he was complaining to
Lewenstein that the feature had disappeared 'presumably because no one
has the energy or the interest to keep it going. . . . It is deeply discouraging
to see how every creative effort in this direction is buried under a huge
weight of inertia . . .' (Letter to Lewenstein, 6 September 1972).

34 *Findlater*, p. 141. Christopher Hampton described the occasion of a rehearsal
of *Lay By*, when ' "I suppose you're responsible for this", Lindsay
Anderson said to me in a thunderous aside audible to the actors . . . and to
the authors' (*ibid.*, p. 117).

35 The original intention for *Lear* had been to take it first to the Belgrade
theatre festival, to which they had been invited on 9 June. The British
Council, however, refused a request for financial assistance.

36 David Hare, *Findlater*, p. 142.

37 *Guardian*, 1 April 1981.

38 Interview with the writer, 18 September 1984. John Osborne, when he saw
the petition, lashed out in a more abusive way at the signatories and was
of the opinion that 'you should all get the boot for crassness and treachery'
(letter to Gillian Diamond [the Court's Casting Director, who organized the
petition], 31 January 1972). Gillian Diamond subsequently wrote to
Anderson on 3 February to defend the signatories and to insist that their
action was 'not treachery or disloyalty – rather I think, the opposite'.
Accounts of the meeting were leaked to the press to the great annoyance
of the Management committee.

39 Gaskill, *op. cit.*, n. 5. There is no record of the pre-Council discussions
about the contracts in any minutes of the period.

40 Poke, *op. cit.*, n. 38.

41 Brighton, *op. cit.*, n. 13.

42 The most sympathetic account of the pressures at the Court during this
period is by Keith Dewhurst, *Guardian*, 22 February 1972, where the case
for subsidy for the Court as a special kind of theatre is coherently argued.

43 Rachel Roberts analyses her part in the play in *Plays and Players*, March
1972; Whitehead discusses the evolution of the script and its rehearsals in
Plays and Players, October 1972.

44 The prime mover in the Old Vic scheme was Lewenstein, with the support
of Greville Poke. Lewenstein proposed that Anderson should become
Artistic Director of the Court, Albert Finney to direct the Old Vic, with
himself as overall Director. Council approved the development of the scheme

but at a meeting of the Artistic committee of 3 December 1973, after a long and acrimonious debate, the committee voted against the proposal by six votes to one. The Artistic committee then circulated to Council members their objections. The document was signed by Page, Anderson, Wright, Storey, Jocelyn Herbert and Ann Jellicoe (who had returned as Literary Manager). In 1974, as the delay grew in the National Theatre's vacating the Old Vic, the Council finally vetoed the plan.

45 Letter to the writer, 28 December 1983.
46 Brighton, *op. cit.*, n. 13.

Chapter 8   Howard Brenton's *Magnificence*

1 Interview with the writer, 28 February 1985.
2 Of the plays up to 1973, *Gum and Goo* and *Gargantua* (1969) were for Brighton Combination; *Heads, The Education of Skinny Spew* (1969), *Wesley* (1970), *Scott of the Antarctic* (1971) were for Bradford; *A Sky Blue Life* (1971) and *How Beautiful With Badges* (1972) were staged at the Open Space; *Hitler Dances* (1972) first appeared at the Traverse Theatre; and his version of *Measure for Measure* (1972) opened at the Northcott, Exeter. For the Court, Brenton produced *Revenge* (1969), *Christie in Love* (1970), *Fruit* (1970), *Hitler Dances* (1972) and *A Fart for Europe* (1973, with David Edgar). Of these five plays, two (*Christie in Love* and *Fruit*) were Portable Theatre productions, and one (*Hitler Dances*) came from Edinburgh. A further Sunday night production was given in September 1971 of the multi-authored *Lay By*, again by Portable in association with the Traverse.
3 Brenton interviewed in *Theatre Quarterly*, vol. 5 no. 17 (March–May, 1975), p. 6.
4 Brenton, *op. cit.*, n. 1.
5 *Ibid.*
6 *Ibid.*
7 Interview with the writer, 5 December 1984.
8 Brenton, *op. cit.*, n. 1.
9 Interview with the writer, 21 February 1985.
10 Brenton, *op. cit.*, n. 1.
11 *Ibid.*
12 There were supporters of the play. Edward Bond, notably, 'let it be known to whoever I could that I thought it was a very good play, and that it was absolutely essential that it went on if that theatre was to continue in the role that it had created for itself' (Interview with the writer, 27 October 1984).
13 Brenton, *op. cit.*, n. 1.
14 Stafford-Clark, interviewed by Malcolm Hay, 20 December 1979.
15 There is a good account of the political background to the plays of this period in John Bull, *New British Political Dramatists*, London, Macmillan, 1984, chapters 1 and 2. See also, 'Messages First: An Interview with Howard Brenton', *Gambit*, vol. 6 no. 23 (1973), pp. 24–32.

16 Quotations from the play are from the edition published by Methuen, 1973.

17 Brenton, *op. cit.*, n. 1.

18 *Ibid.*

19 *Ibid.*

20 *Plays and Players*, July 1973.

21 Brenton, *op. cit.*, n. 3.

22 *Ibid.*, n. 1.

23 Stafford-Clark, *op. cit.*, n. 9. Babs was played by Robert Eddison and Alice by Geoffrey Chater. Apart from the last scene which involves Alice, the two older actors appeared only in scene four. Brenton remembers Geoffrey Chater's audition: 'The different generations of actors – he came to read, dressed as the character, a gentleman's suit like a businessman, bowler hat, black shoes. That care was incredible.' With the rest of the cast, 'You lay around, you did improvisations, you threw lines around a bit, but with Robert and Geoffrey you didn't touch a line in their presence. You behaved as if it was written absolutely on steel. Robert had this wonderful thing which Max had never met before. Max said, "I think if you could get off the punt here and walk down there?", and Robert said, "Yes, that's excellent", and didn't move. Max went up on the stage again and said, "I do think . . .", and Robert said, "Yes, it's excellent", and Max said "Well, shall we?", and Robert said, "Oh, no, no, I don't want to bother you with it now. I'll bring it in tomorrow." The old, formal way of rehearsing, some of which Robert still had . . . It was courtesy on his part, not to waste people's time. A different world' (Brenton, *op. cit.*, n. 1).

24 Lenin, as well as the tramp in scenes one and three, was played by a Russian. Nikolaj Ryjtkov worked with Stanislavsky at the Moscow Art Theatre and, because he bore a striking resemblance to Lenin, toured the Soviet Union reciting Lenin's speeches to huge audiences. He was arrested in 1936 and sent to Siberia for eighteen years. On his release in 1954, he escaped to the British Embassy in Austria. In England, he had done a little work for the BBC Foreign Service, but actually spoke very little English. He put his Siberian experience to use for the beginning of the play. Having developed the habit of being able to sleep at will, 'at least half an hour before the play began, Nikolaj would conceal himself under the newspapers on the set. As there was no curtain . . . he had to remain undetected and still . . . when suddenly he would rise to the amazement of the characters and the audience.' As Lenin, he incorporated a trick which he had used in Russian tours: 'He would cut out a maroon coloured piece of tinsel in the shape of a tiny triangle and glue it to the eyelid of his right eye. As he walked on to the stage, he would pose in a classic Lenin style and slowly turn his head towards the audience – he would then blink – the lights would catch the tinsel and his eye would flash red – to an astonishing effect' (Letter from James Aubrey to the writer, 5 June 1984).

25 Brenton, *op. cit.*, n. 1.

26 *Ibid.*, n. 20.

27 *Ibid.*, n. 1.

28 Stafford-Clark, *op. cit.*, n. 9.
29 Brenton, *op. cit.*, n. 20.
30 *Gambit, op. cit.*, n. 15.
31 Interview with Ronald Hayman, *The New Review*, vol. 3 no. 29 (August 1976), pp. 56–8.
32 Brenton, *op. cit.*, n. 1.
33 Interview with the writer and Malcolm Hay, 15 July 1977.
34 Interview with the writer and Malcolm Hay, 14 January 1978.
35 *Ibid.*
36 Brenton, *op. cit.*, n. 1.
37 *Ibid.*, n. 3, p. 13.
38 Stafford-Clark, *op. cit.*, n. 9.
39 *Peter Hall's Diaries* (ed. John Goodwin), London, Hamish Hamilton, 1983, pp. 49, 103–4.

Select bibliography

1 Primary Sources

(a) English Stage Company

Minutes of the meetings of the Artistic committee, January 1965–July 1972.
Minutes of the meetings of the Management committee, January 1960–July 1972.
Minutes of the meetings of the Council, January 1960–July 1972.
Duncan, Ronald, 'Notes on the Artistic Policy of the English Stage Company', 1 March 1960.
Devine, George, 'Memorandum on Artistic Policy – Aims and Objects', 13 May 1960.
Devine, George, 'Open Letter to the Brazilian Theatre', 1963.
'Memorandum on the Royal Court Theatre Studio', February, 1963–August 1964.
'Memorandum on the Royal Court Theatre Studio', August 1964–September 1965.
Devine, George, 'Memorandum on *Saved*', 28 April 1965.
Ten Years at the Royal Court, 1956/66, The English Stage Company, 1966.
Royal Court 1970, The English Stage Company, 1970.

(b) Taped interviews with the writer

Linday Anderson, 5 December 1984; Lindsay Anderson and David Storey, 29 April 1985; Edward Bond, 27 October 1984; Howard Brenton, 28 February 1985; Pam Brighton, 13 December 1983; Richard Butler, 7 January 1984; Anne Dyson, 10 October 1979; William Gaskill, 13 December 1983; Peter Gill, 3 April 1985; John Gunter, 29 March 1977; Lord Harewood, 11 September 1984; Nerys Hughes, 12 December 1983; Oscar Lewenstein, 14 December 1983; Greville Poke, 18 September 1984; Max Stafford-Clark, 21 February 1985.

(c) Other taped interviews

Edward Bond (Malcolm Hay and Philip Roberts), 15 September 1978; Howard Brenton (Malcolm Hay and Philip Roberts), 14 January 1978; William Dudley (Malcolm Hay), 19 July 1977; William Gaskill (Malcolm Hay and Philip Roberts), 22 March and 15 July 1977; Jane Howell (Malcolm Hay and Philip Roberts), 26 July 1977; Jane Howell (Malcolm Hay), 18 November 1977; Jack Shepherd (Malcolm Hay), 31 August 1977; Max Stafford-Clark (Malcolm Hay), 20 December 1979; Nicholas Wright (Malcolm Hay), 18 December 1979.

(d) Letters to the writer

Lindsay Anderson, 11 May and 13 December 1984; James Aubrey, 5 June 1984; J. E. Blacksell, 3 November 1984; Constance Chapman, 1 September 1984; Peter Childs, 5 March 1985; David Cregan, 6 December 1983; Bernard Gallagher, 17 January 1984; Donald Howarth, November 1983; Gordon Jackson, 28 November and 28 December 1983; Brian Lawson, 5 February 1985; Rosemary McHale, 26 April 1984; Don McKillop, 6 February 1985; Edward Peel, 1 May 1984; Maurice Roëves, 6 December 1983; Peter Schofield, 20 February 1985; N. F. Simpson, 6 December 1983; Frank Williams, 23 November 1983; Heathcote Williams, December 1983.

(e) Other Letters

Linday Anderson to: Nigel Lawson, 29 October 1969; Lord Goodman, 4 November 1969; Oscar Lewenstein, 6 September 1972; Hugh Cudlipp, 27 March 1975.

J. E. Blacksell to: Ronald Duncan, 18 January 1965; Lord Harewood, 10 and 18 December 1964; Greville Poke, 18 January 1965 and 2 January 1970.

Neville Blond to: J. E. Blacksell, 13 March 1968; Greville Poke, 3 November 1969.

Edward Bond to: Toby Cole, 8 April 1968; Tony Coult, 28 July 1977; Max Stafford-Clark and Danny Boyle, 5 November 1984.

Norman Collins to Neville Blond, 22 December 1969.

Gillian Diamond to Lindsay Anderson, 3 February 1972.

Doreen Dixon to Edward Bond, 5 and 22 April 1965.

Ronald Duncan to J. E. Blacksell, 12 November 1965.

Robin Fox to Lindsay Anderson, 16 July 1969.

William Gaskill to: Lord Harewood, 20 May 1966; J. E. Blacksell, 3 January 1967 and 29 January 1968; Neville Blond, 6 January 1967; Richard Scharine, 19 March 1971.

Lord Harewood to: J. E. Blacksell, 7 December 1964; Lindsay Anderson, 21 February 1974.

Joe Hodgkinson to J. E. Blacksell, 12 August 1970.

Keith Johnstone to Richard Scharine, March 1971.

John Osborne to Gillian Diamond, 31 January 1972.

Greville Poke to: J. E. Blacksell, 7 November 1958, 4 December 1969, 30 December 1969; William Gaskill, 27 October 1966; Neville Blond, 25 January 1968.

Heathcote Williams to Nicholas Wright, n.d.

2 Secondary Sources

Ansorge, Peter, *Disrupting the Spectacle*, London, Pitman, 1975.

Arden, John, Letter to *The Times*, 8 April 1968.

Arts Council of Great Britain, 17th Report, 1961–2.

Blond, Neville, Letter to *The Times*, 6 December 1969.

Bond, Edward, 'Drama and the Dialectics of Violence', *Theatre Quarterly*, vol. 2 no. 5, 1972.

Bond, Edward, *Plays: One*, London, Methuen, 1977.

Boulton, James T. (ed.), *The Letters of D. H. Lawrence*, vol. 1, Cambridge, Cambridge University Press, 1979.

Brenton, Howard, 'Messages First', *Gambit*, vol. 6 no. 23, 1973.

Brenton, Howard, 'Disrupting the Spectacle', *Plays and Players*, July 1973.

Brenton, Howard, *Magnificence*, London, Methuen, 1973.

Brenton, Howard, 'Petrol Bombs through the Proscenium Arch', *Theatre Quarterly*, vol. 5 no. 17, 1975.

Browne, Terry, *Playwrights' Theatre. The English Stage Company at the Royal Court*, London, Pitman, 1975.

Bull, John, *New British Political Dramatists*, London, Macmillan, 1984.

Daubeny, Peter, *My World of Theatre*, London, Cape, 1971.

Devine, George, 'The Royal Court Theatre: Phase One', in Harold Hobson (ed.), *International Theatre Annual*, vol. 2, 1957.

Devine, George, 'Vital Theatre', *Encore*, vol. 6 no. 2, March–April 1959.

Devine, George, 'The Right to Fail', *The Twentieth Century*, vol. 169, February 1961.

Devine, George, 'Court Account', *Guardian*, 2 April 1962.

Duncan, Ronald, *How to Make Enemies*, London, Hart-Davis, 1968.

Elsom, John and Tomalin, Nicholas, *The History of the National Theatre*, London, Cape, 1978.

Esslin, Martin, 'Brecht and the English Theatre', *Tulane Drama Review*, vol. 11 no. 2, Winter 1966.

Evidence submitted by the English Stage Company to the Estimates Committee (Sub-Committee B), House of Commons, 1968.

Findlater, Richard, 'No Time for Tragedy?', *The Twentieth Century*, vol. 161, January 1957.

Findlater, Richard (ed.), *At the Royal Court, 25 Years of the English Stage Company*, Ambergate, Amber Lane Press, 1981.

Gaskill, William, 'Man for the Future', *Plays and Players*, March 1966.

Goodwin, John (ed.), *Peter Hall's Diaries*, London, Hamish Hamilton, 1983.

Gourlay, Logan, *Olivier*, London, Weidenfeld & Nicolson, 1973.

Gunter, John, 'Desert Island Discs', BBC Radio 4, 29 July 1983.

Hanson, Barry, 'Royal Court Diary', *Plays and Players*, April 1968.

Hay, Malcolm and Roberts, Philip, *Edward Bond: A Companion to the Plays*, London, Theatre Quarterly Publications, 1978.

Hay, Malcolm and Roberts, Philip, *Bond: A Study of his Plays*, London, Methuen, 1980.

Hayman, Ronald, *Playback 1* and *Playback 2*, London, Davis-Poynter, 1973.

Hayman, Ronald, 'Interview with Howard Brenton', *The New Review*, vol. 3 no. 29, 1976.

Jellicoe, Ann, *Some Unconscious Influences in the Theatre*, Cambridge, Cambridge University Press, 1967.

Jellicoe, Ann, 'Covering the Ground', in Susan Todd (ed.), *Women and Theatre. Calling the Shots*, London, Faber, 1984.

Johnstone, Keith, *Impro. Improvisation and the Theatre*, London, Faber, 1979.

Lawrence, D. H., *Selected Essays*, Harmondsworth, Penguin Books, 1950.

Lawrence, D. H., *England, My England*, Harmondsworth, Penguin Books, 1960.

Lawrence, D. H., *Complete Plays*, London, Heinemann, 1965.

Lawrence, D. H., *Three Plays*, Harmondsworth, Penguin Books, 1969.

McCrindle, J. F. (ed.), *Behind the Scenes: Theatre and Film Interviews from the Transatlantic Review*, London, Pitman, 1971.

Marowitz, Charles, 'State of Play', *Tulane Drama Review*, vol. 11 no. 2, Winter 1966.

Milne, Tom, 'And the time of the great taking over: an interview with William Gaskill', *Encore*, vol. 9 no. 4, July–August, 1962.

Milne, Tom, 'Taking Stock at the Court', in Charles Marowitz, Tom Milne and Owen Hale (eds.), *New Theatre Voices of the Fifties and Sixties: Selections from Encore Magazine 1956–1963*, London, Methuen, 1965.

Mindlin, Murray, *Forum World Features*, week of 27 November 1965.

Norman, Frank, *Why Fings Went West*, London, Lemon Tree Press, 1975.

Ripley, John, *Julius Caesar on Stage in England and America, 1599–1973*, Cambridge, Cambridge University Press, 1980.

Roberts, Philip, *Bond on File*, London, Methuen, 1985.

Rogoff, Gordon, 'Richard's Himself Again: Journey to an Actors' Theatre', *Tulane Drama Review*, vol. 11 no. 2, Winter 1966.

Sagar, Keith, 'D. H. Lawrence: Dramatist', *The D. H. Lawrence Review*, vol. 4 no. 1, 1971.

Sagar, Keith, 'The Strange History of *The Daughter-in-Law*', *The D. H. Lawrence Review*, vol. 11 no. 2, 1978.

Sagar, Keith, *D. H. Lawrence: A Calendar of his Works*, Manchester, Manchester University Press, 1979.

Signoret, Simone, *Nostalgia Isn't What It Used To Be*, London, Panther Books, 1979.

Sklar, Sylvia, *The Plays of D. H. Lawrence*, London, Vision Press, 1975.

Sklar, Sylvia, 'The Daughter-in-Law and My Son's My Son', The D. H. Lawrence Review, vol. 9, no. 2, 1976.

Storey, David, 'Journey through a Tunnel', The Listener, 1 August 1963.

Storey, David, The Changing Room, Harmondsworth, Penguin Books, 1973.

Taylor, John Russell, 'Ten Years of the English Stage Company', Tulane Drama Review, vol. 11 no. 2, Winter 1966.

The Theatre Today in England and Wales: The Arts Council of Great Britain, 1970.

Thomson, Peter, Shakespeare's Theatre, London, Routledge & Kegan Paul, 1983.

Todd, Susan (ed.), Women and Theatre, Calling the Shots, London, Faber, 1984.

Trial Run. The Royal Court Magazine for Schools, Spring 1963.

Tschudin, Marcus, A Writer's Theatre: George Devine and the English Stage Company at the Royal Court, 1956–1965, Berne, European University Papers, 1973.

Tynan, Kenneth, Tynan Right and Left, London, Longman, 1967.

Tynan, Kenneth, The Sound of Two Hands Clapping, London, Cape, 1975.

Wardle, Irving, 'Interview with William Gaskill', Gambit, vol 5, no. 17, 1970.

Wardle, Irving, The Theatres of George Devine, London, Cape, 1978.

Williams, Raymond, 'Drama and the Left', Encore, vol. 6 no. 2, March–April 1959.

Worth, Katharine, Revolutions in Modern English Drama, London, Bell, 1973.

Index